MUNICIPAL FINANCE IN INDIA
(Based on Orissa)

Gokulananda Dash

Foreword by
Prof. S.R. Maheshwari

CONCEPT PUBLISHING COMPANY, NEW DELHI-110059

ISBN 81-7022-208-7

First Published 1988

Gokulananda Dash (*b*. 1929-1986)

Published by
Ashok Kumar Mittal
Concept Publishing Company
A/15-16, Commercial Block
Mohan Garden
New Delhi-110059 (India)

Photocomposing by
Microtech Advance Printing Systems Pvt. Ltd.
New Delhi-110015

Printed by
Taj Press
A-35/4 Mayapuri
New Delhi

FOREWORD

Local government has always been an important level of the system of governance man has evolved over the centuries; and in years to come its role will expand in all directions. Urbanisation is today a global phenomenon, and India is witnessing a recklessly rapid expansion of its cities and other urban centres.

The demand made on urban government is of an unprecedented scale and most city governments are finding it extremely difficult to manager their affairs. Doctor Gokulanand Dash deserves praise for discussing in a most competent manner the problems which urban local governments in India encounter. This he has done by taking up a case study of urban local bodies in Orissa. The findings of his research hold valid not only for India but also for the Third World countries generally. Doctor Dash concentrates on financial administration of urban local bodies. Fulfilment of local governmental tasks requires efficient administration including financial administration. Doctor Dash comes to the conclusion that the real problem of the urban local bodies is not poor finances but weak financial administration. The question which has become important is how the available resources be effectively utilised to perform the functions assigned to them with the help of an effective financial administration. Financial consideration is present in almost all the activities of the urban local body, yet its administration is treated with neglect and indifference.

The mainstay of municipal finance has been its income from

taxation and fees including income from municipal property. There are several cases of non-utilisation of these sources. The rate of assessment of property tax and fees has been kept low and many urban local bodies have not explored lucrative sources of revenue like levying education cess and profession tax. In the case of property taxation neither all holdings have been brought under taxation nor has the assessment been revised periodically.

The existing Municipal Act does not provide for minimum rate for property taxes. The local authorities are not willing to levy taxes at maximum prescribed rates. The central valuation organisation prepares the rental value of buildings at old schedule of rates. Whatever tax is assessed is not collected and all collections are not brought to accounts due to several mal-practices. The lacuna in the tax administration creates distrust in the minds of tax payers resulting in poor collection.

It has, therefore, been suggested by the author that a minimum rate of each tax be prescribed for each category of urban local body. The rental value of buildings is to be fixed on the latest schedule of rates and the revision of assessment should be done at the end of every five years. Loop-holes in the tax collection have to be bridged by strict supervision and taking resort to coercieve measures like distress-warrant and suing the tax defaulters in the court of law. The Government should ensure payment of taxes in respect of Government buildings which are heavily in arrears. Above all, the tax machinery should be independent, and impartial.

Inspite of all the evils associated with the imposition of Octroi Tax, it can not be abolished without finding an alternative source of income. The viable alternative can be to levy a surcharge on the existing sales tax. The surcharge can be collected by the State Government through its existing agency and apportioned to the urban local authorities on the volume of collection from the area after deducting a certain percentage towards collection charges.

The findings show that the income from municipal property and some of the municipal enterprises is quite encourging but the source would earn better revenue if properly administered by increasing the rate of rent of market buildings and slum quarters. The scheme of providing guest houses should be undertaken by different Municipalities/Notified Area Councils from their own income and if necessary by resorting to borrowing. Similarly bigger municipalities may take to plying of autorickshaws and minibuses. Several enterprises like milk supply scheme, pisciculature and composting may also be improved as municipal enterprises basing on the local requirements. The managerial skill and business-like alertness will improve matters

Grants-in-aid from the State Government constitutes one of the important sources of income for the urban local bodies, but most of the grants paid are not based on any established principles. The flow of grants is uncertain. This not only creates imbalance in the finances of the urban local authorities but also leads to irresponsible spending and budgeting. The existing system neither reduces imbalances nor provides incentive for tax efforts. Grants remain unutilised for years together.

There must be a grants-in-aid code to regulate the sanction of grants. Grants must be correlated to tax efforts of the local authorities in the shape of imposition and collection. The sanction of grants should be made taking the ability of the local authority into consideration. The grants-in-aid payable should be foretold by the Government so that the expenditure could be planned ahead. The need for establishing a High Power Committee for administration in grants-in-aid and loans has been emphasised in the discussion. The sanction of grant and review of performances on account of such grants as to whether they promote efficiency and ensure standard services should be entrusted to this Committee.

Similarly the grant of loans should rest with this Committee which would examine the financial, technical and other abilities of local bodies before sanctioning loans for any purpose. Most of the urban local bodies have been burdened with loans and do not utilise the loans properly and timely. They do not derive any benefit but pay interest at a high rate meeting the same from their tax revenues. Most of the urban local bodies have defaulted in the repayment of loans and interest thereon. The administration of loan funds suffers from many lapses. No sinking funds are maintained to discharge the loan liabilities. The Government on whose authorities the borrowings are made does not take adequate measures to ensure proper administration of borrowed funds. It has been suggested that no loans should be incurred for unproductive purposes and even in case of productive purposes no loans should be incurred unless there is a prospect of their immediate utilisation.

Inspite of the increase in volume of expenditure in all the urban local bodies, most of them have failed to provide the desirable standard of services mostly due to misutilisation and misapplication of municipal funds. There is not proper planning of the expenditure nor has the desired financial control been exercised. Unless the public expenditure policy in the municipal level is planned, the proper utilisation of available resources can not be ensured. Moreover, the suitable technical machinery at the municipal level is not available to either plan or administer the expenditure.

The municipal fund could be properly utilised by avoiding wastage by proper planning, and improved method of budgeting, accounting and audit, and with the techniques of materials management. Most of the opposition to local taxes could be averted if the people are convinced that the resources raised are spent for their welfare with maximum economy and efficiency.

Lack of cost-conciousness on the part of the authorities in charge of spending municipal funds results in heavy expenditure as estimates of projects are often revised due to rise in prices and delay in execution causing loss to the local Governments. Cost conciousness can make the expenditure productive.

It is necessary to reorganise the urban local bodies both internally and externally. Externally it should reduce the Government control. The existing system of State supervision and financial control have not achieved the desired result in improving the financial administration. Even the creation of Directorate for municipal administration has not improved the working of local Governments due to bureaucratic attitude and unawareness of peculiar problems of the urban Government. It is necessary to delegate the power of sanction of estimates and the approval of budgets to Regional Deputy Directors for smooth working of the institution, review and evaluation of performance. For this purpose, Government should lay norms, prescribe standards and devote its time for overall supervision by prescribing reports and returns to ensure if the norms and standards have been observed instead of interfering in the daily routine of the urban local authorities.

Budget serves as an instrument of financial control. But it has failed to serve any effective purpose as most of the urban local bodies do not confine their financial activities within the budgetary limits. It has therefore been suggested, in conformity with the recommendation of other Authorities, to introduce performance budgeting which will be a major step towards making the budget a realistic document. The initial cost in training the municipal staff meeting other formalities on the way of its implementation will ultimately outweigh the benefits derived from it. Periodic reporting, advance planning and information system are the pre-requisites of the new system which should be ensured. The system will bring in change in the existing accounting systems which will exhibit both cost and returns.

It has been discussed at length that the existing audit practices under the Examiner of Local Fund Audit have failed to ensure financial discipline. It is therefore argued that audit should reorient its outlook and instead of being a tool of state control, should serve as management aid. It should change its pattern from proprietory audit to performance audit to evaluate performances on the basis of performance standards fixed for the purpose. The findings of audit should be laid before the State legislature in the from of consolidated Finance Accounts and Audit Review for the purpose of review of the financial working of the urban local Government which will raise the image and effectiveness of audit.

Municipal Governments function both as Government and business organisation which necessitate taking speady decisions in many matters of importance effecting the financial affairs of the urban local bodies. A review of some of the municipal decisions in Orissa concerning financial affairs disclosed several lapses and constraints. Municipal Councils are influenced by pressure groups, parties and associations in their decision making process. The quality of decision is largely dependent on the quality of information available, cooperation of municipal officials, knowledge of rules and laws on the

part of permanent officials and elected representatives which are wanting in many situations. The author argues that municipal activities should be subjected to legislative review. This will not only make the municipal councils accountable to the state legislature without affecting their autonomy in decision-making but will make them responsible and make their decisions meaningful.

Personnel System

Several measures have been suggested to improve the financial administration of urban local bodies but the performance of these institutions largely depends upon the abilities and quality of performance of the personnel. However good a system might be, its performance can not excel the quality of men who administer it. Under one administrative roof, activities concerning several aspects like engineering, education, health, trading and a host of other regulating activities thrive. The local governments frame bye-laws and other regulations take several decisions and execute them, receive claims and effect payments, assess taxes and enforce collection, maintain accounts of all activities and compile them. Thus a municipal Government administers so many activities under one roof which are uncommon in State/Central Government. With a view to discharging such enormous responsibility there is a greater need to employ efficient and well-qualified personnel.

The system of personnel in the urban local bodies of the state who handle the financial affairs has been examined in the study. It has been pointed out that the lone Executive Officer in the Municipal Government assisted mostly by a single Accountant with a few clerks is made responsible for almost all the activities concerning finance and its administration. There is no established policy or practices for recruitment, promotion and regulation of services of these personnel. It was therefore observed by the State Municipal Finance Commission Orissa (1975) that "Notwithstanding the qualification prescribed and procedure to be followed in selecting the candidate, the commission observed that under-qualified persons have been appointed in municipal services who are eventually found to be largely responsible for municipal mal-administration".[1]

----

1. *Report of the State Municipal Finance Committee,* Orissa - 1975,

The Executive Officer who is the head of the permanent executive is drawn from the cadre of different services of the State Government and is appointed on deputation on foreign service terms. In Municipality like Cuttack, Puri, Berhampur, Sambalpur & Bhubaneswar, Class-I Officers of Orissa Administrative Service are appointed as Executive Officers and for other urban local bodies, Class-II Officers from Orissa Administrative Service, Public Health Engineers, Assistants, Auditors and even Revenue Inspectors and Sanitary Inspectors are posted as head of the permanent Executive. Even one Superintending Engineer was appointed as Executive. Officer of Berhampur Municipality for years together. Similarly Health Officers and Engineers appointed to bigger Municipalities are drawn from the respective cadre of the State Government who are appointed on deputation. Officers coming on deputation from State Government are not only paid their pay and allowances from the Municipal fund but the municipalities bear the leave and pensionary contribution for the period of deputation. This system of bringing officers on deputation involves heavy payments.

Other municipal employees like clerks, overseers, accountants, tax collectors, etc. are appointed by the municipal council by recruitment and promotions from open market and their services belong to the individual municipal council and their service conditions are regulated under the existing municipal rules.

The need for having a State Municipal service was examined by different committees and commissions. It was pointed out that one of the essential conditions for management of urban local Government is "the development of a professionally competent cadre to build up expartise and accumulate experience specialising in urban management with all its growing complexties".[2] The State of Madras was the first to have organised a State Municipal service. Its example

----

p.132.

2. *Report of the Task Force on Planning And Development of Small Towns and Cities.* 1977 p. 94.

has been followed by the neighbouring States of Kerala, Mysore (now Karnataka) and Andhra Pradesh.[3] States like Maharastra, Punjab and Rajasthan have also introduced State Municipal services.

The State Municipal Finance Commission, Orissa also recommended for the creation of State Municipal Service consisting of two cadres namely:- (1) Orissa Municipal Administration Services (Junior) and (2) Orissa Municipal Services (Senior) to provide Executive Officers/Assistant Executive Officers in different categories of municipalities/Notified Area Councils and another service i.e. the Orissa Municipal sub-ordinate Administration/ Ministerial Service to provide personnel for field services, collection of tax, office work, typing, correspondences, accounts and others activities. The racommandationcovered an elaborate system of recruitment, training, promotion and disciplinary action for these personnel.[4]

It is needless to emphasise that due to conglomoration of heterogenous elements who have neither the training nor the education to administer varieties of activities of Municipal Government, chaos characterises most aspects of the administration including its administration in the financial field. The existing system of bringing officers on deputation from the State Government not only costs heavily but the officers on deputation do not develop the right attitude for running a local institution due to their short tenure. The subordinate officials are recruited locally without due weightage to merit. There is hardly any adequate system of training for these officials.

It is therefore suggested that the recommendation of the State Municipal Finance Commission for creation of the State Cadre of Municipal services to man the post of Executive Officers/Assistant Executive Officers in urban local bodies should be implemented fully. But there should be a separate department of accounts in Class-I & Class-II Municipalities which should be kept in full charge

----

3. *Report of the Rural Urban Relationship Committee-1966* p.75.

4. Report of the State Municipal Finance Commission, Orissa 1975, p. 138 - 36.

of an officer designated as either Assistant Executive Officer or Accounts Officer. This Department should keep accounts of all activities including tax administration. For some time past the tax administration of Berhampur Municipality was kept under the charge of a Finance Officer drawn from the cadre of Orissa Finance services.

It is further suggested by the author that tax administration, being of technical nature, should be kept under one officer with experience in tax administration especially in Class-I and Class-II Municipalities. In smaller municipalities/Notified Area Councils this work can be entrusted to a subordinate officer having experience in tax management.

Since the Executive Officer is saddled with several responsibilities under the statute, he should be relieved of the responsibility of drawing and disbursing power and in Class-I & Class-II municipalities: such responsibilities should be entrusted to the Accounts Officer in addition to keeping of accounts as in vogue in the urban local bodies of England. In smaller Municipalities this task can be managed by Executive Officer or by the Assistant Executive Officer. The Accounts Officer would be entrusted with precheck of all accounts and would work as Financial Adviser being responsible to the Municipal Council. This will, no doubt, improve the process of decision making in financial administration and improve the standard of working of the urban local Government.

Above all, the State Government should develop the facilities for providing training to the permanent officials and elected representative of the urban local bodies. For this purpose, the existing training facilities available under the Municipal Councils should be strengthened. There should be an Institute of Municipal Administration to provide training and research facilities with a view to improving the working of urban local Governments of the State.

Some of the burning and important problems of financial administration of urban local bodies have been touched in the present study. As indicated earlier, most of the the thinking on improvement of urban local Government has remained on paper only, even though sporadic and piecemeal action has been taken. If the State Government appreciates the difficulties of the Local Government and the latter understands its responsibility, both can work as partners and make an earnest effort to solve some of the pressing problems of citizens.

The present work by Doctor Gokulanand Dash is a most competent study in the field of local finance in India. It is based on extensive research and each finding is supported by empirical data. It is written in a lucid style. It is a standard work on the subject and Doctor Dash deserves all congratulations. It is a pity that he is no more with us. But this work will keep his memory alive.

Dr. S.R. Maheshwari
Professor of Political Science &
Public Administration
Indian Institute of Public Administration,
New Delhi.

PREFACE

The present study owes its inspiration to my long association with the working of Local Government and more particularly with the Urban Local Government. I gradually evinced academic interest in the subject. I could not have ventured to take up this subject as a topic for research but for the ungrudging guidance and able supervision of Dr. Baidyanath Misra, Professor & Head of the Department of Analytical and Applied Economics of Utkal University. I owe him many debts of gratitude.

In the process of my work I have taken the help of many persons associated with the Urban Local Bodies in various ways. It is, indeed, not possible to mention all of them but I owe a sense of gratefulness to many officers and staff including some elected representatives of Urban Local Bodies in Orissa, to Shri D. Nayak, of Bhubaneswar Municipality, and the Executive Officers of Baripada Municipality, and Nayagarh Notified Area Council. I acknowledge with gratitude the help I received from officers and staff of Urban Development Department and Bureau of Statistics of Government of Orissa in obtaining data and other information for my use. I am grateful to the officers and staff of Local Fund Audit Organisation of Finance Department, Government of Orissa for their cooperation in the collection of data and the supply of information from the relevant audit reports on the subject.

I wish to record my appreciation for the authorities of Indian Institute of Public Administration, New Delhi, Planning Commission, New Delhi, National Library, Calcutta, Parija Library of Utkal University and many other libraries in different colleges of the state for providing me the required literature for the study. Late Professor Dev Raj, Director, National Institute of Urban Affairs, New Delhi provided me with some of his unpublished works containing valuable data on the working of Urban Local Governments in different states and suggested some improvements in analysing the data collected by me. I regret his untimely death and wish that he would have been alive today to see the work done. My thanks are due to Professor Abhijit Dutta of Indian Institute of Public Administration for his valuable suggestions.

I am thankful to the authorities of Indian Council of Social Science Research, New Delhi for providing me with a contingent grant to undertake the research work.

I am really indebted to many great thinkers on the subject who have inspired me with ideas and plan of research. I must admit that I have been considerably influenced by their ideas in formulating my views and findings. Among them are Professor Gyan Chand, Mrs. K.U. Hicks, Professor S.R. Maheshwari, Professor G. Mukherjee, and Dr. R.N. Tripathy.

I am happy to record my thanks to my friend Shri Jatindra Mohan Mohanty, Reader, Department of English, Utkal University for his suggestions in improving the composition. I am also thankful to Dr. A.K.P.S. Swain, Reader, Department of Statistics, Utkal University for his suggestions regarding statistical aspect of the work.

I am grateful to the authorities of Finance Department, Government of Orissa for according me permission to undertake the research work. I owe my gratitude to Shri S. Kanungo, Secretary, Shri S.D. Sen, Additional Secretary and Shri K.P. Mishra, Deputy Secretary of the Department for the encouragement I received from them.

Finally I express my appreciation to my wife and children who have not only taken keen interest in my work, but spared me from the responsibilities of household, without which it would not have been possible for me to complete the work.

Gokulananda Dash

CONTENTS

LIST OF TABLES

LIST OF ANNEXTURES

ONE

INTRODUCTION

What is Local Government

Local Government is an integral part of the three-tier system of Government in India. It deals mainly with such matters as concern the inhabitants of a particular place or area and is subordinate to the State Government. It is manned by the elected representatives of the local area. A local Government administers the affairs of a village, a town or a city. Thus the system of local Government has the following five characteristics - "these are a local body, local inhabitants electing and ultimately controlling that body, autonomy of that body in the sense of freedom from the control of higher authorities within atleast a limited sphere, a recognition of the distinction between local and non-local services and local taxation".[1] The Urban Local Bodies are known as Municipality, Notified Area Councils, Forporations and contonment Boards to administer the affairs of town and cities and contonments. Rural Local Bodies comprise of Village-Panchayats, Panchayat Samities and Zilla Parishads. Their jurisdiction is limited to a specific area. Their functions are limited to provision of civic amenities and social welfare activities. For the purpose of carrying out these functions, power is given to the local Governments to raise money by taxation and by imposing fees and rates. The local Governments are also financed by the State Government in shape of grants-in-aid and loans.

Importance of Urban Local Government

The Urban Local Government in our country has assumed considerable importance after India achieved its independence. Due to partition of the country on the eve of Independence there was large influx of refugees from Pakistan. The resettlement of refugees gave rise to new towns like Faridabad and Kalyani etc., as well as some other towns in different parts of the country. Secondly as a result of the implementation of Five Year Plans, the country's economic activities developed in different dimensions giving rise to many new establishments related to commerce, industry, agriculture as well as to irrigation and power projects and administrative units etc., which ultimately grew up as new townships, such as Bhakra, Hirakud, Rourkela, Bhilai, Durgapur, Bhubaneswar, Chandigarh, etc. Besides, there has been regular flow of rural population to the towns and cities in search of employment opportunities and for availing of amenities of town life. This has resulted in increase of urban population creating new towns and developing satellite townships near metropolitan areas.

According to Census report of 1961, the urban population of India was 17.97 percent (78.94 Million) of the total population which increased to 19.90 percent (109.11 Million) in 1971. During the decade the total population of the country grew by 24.7 percent, whereas the proportionate growth of urban population was 37.9 percent. This urban population is administered by 3119 Local Governments throughout the country.

Even though the number of Urban Local Governments and the urban population compared to rural is not very high, yet their significance cannot be ignored. In this connection it would be appropriate to refer to the observation of the Royal Commission on East Africa which states: "The towns are the centres of social and intellectual life of economic enterprises and political activity. The efficient functioning of country's vital nerve centres, the urban areas depend very largely upon the efficiency and effectiveness with which their municipal Governments function and perform their multifarious obligatory and optional duties. A good or bad municipal Government does count in contributing to a country's economic development or in hampering it.[2]. The local Governments in urban areas undertake most of the essential functions for the citizens of the local body. These functions include provision of water supply, health and sanitation, primary education, roads and conservancy, provision of parks, playgrounds etc. Some Local Governments undertake the provision of transport and electricity too. They run maternity centres, dispensaries, burial grounds and many more services depending upon their financial ability and co-operation of the citizens.

In countries like U.S.A. the local Government undertakes many more functions like provision of gas, electricity, transport etc. Munro writing on American Local Government, states, "They want the cities to trim the trees in front of their houses, cut the weeds in vacant plots, provide band concerts in the parks, maintain public golf course, organise community dances and to do hundred other things which the people of last generations were supposed to do for themselves".[3] Throughout the world the functions of local Governments are more or less the same. They take care of the citizens from the cradle to the grave. They build human resources in providing essential amenities like water, electricity, education, transport and many other social services. Thus in a way the success of planning and ultimately the sustenance of democratic socialism largely depend upon the successful working of these institutions. Their failure to function effectively may result in paralysing the human civilisation and may frustrate the very purpose of State and National Governments.

Problem of Finance

Rapid urbanisation in its trail brings a host of problems such as housing for living, provision of water supply, health services and other social amenities. People want services, better amenities and at the same time to keep the tax at a low level. They are reluctant to pay the taxes and local rates. These amenities require huge funds. The Urban Local Governments' powers of taxation are limited. Most of the lucrative and productive sources of revenue are at the command of the State and Central Government. They are unwilling to part with them. All the activities of urban local bodies need proper planning and adequate finance. But the National Five Year Plans did not include the programme of Urban Development in the First and Second Five Year Plans. This was admitted in the Third Five Year Plan which said, "At the local level, municipal administration alone can undertake satisfactorily the task of providing the services needed for development in urban areas, expansion of housing and improvement of living conditions. Most municipal administrations are not strong enough to carry out these functions. They should be sufficiently strengthened by increasing their resources and personnel and by enlarging their jurisdiction and function... they should have separate plans of their own and these will be integrated with the plans of States".[4]. From the Third Five Year Plan, there has been provision for financing the urban development in shape of housing facilities, water supply and sanitation including urban regional development. Government of India have undertaken to provide assistance to the urban local bodies through the State Governments by arranging loans from the L.I.C. and H.U.D.C.O. The provision made in regard to financing of urban development in different Five Year Plans is given below.

National Plan Outlay

Millions of Rupees

Head of Department	Plan outlays in Public Sector		
	Third Plan	Fourth Plan	Fifth Plan
Urban & Regional Development	1276*	5290	5055
Housing	--	2510	6009
Water Supply & Sanitation	1057		9307

Source: The Report of the Task Force on Planning and Development of Small and Medium Towns and Cities, Government of India, p. 34.

* including housing.

To consider the question of improving the financial position of the urban local bodies, many Committees and Commissions have been set up by the Central and State Governments. A study of the reports of the Local Finance Enquiry Committee, 1951, Taxation Enquiry Commission of 1954, Report of the Committee on Augmentation of Financial Resources of urban local bodies and the Report of Urban-Rural Relationship Committee discloses that all these reports recommended to assign more sources of revenues to the local bodies for narrowing the gap between the resources and needs.

The reports also recommended certain administrative measures to ensure better financial management to improve the position of receipts in shape of taxes, fees and also to undertake certain profitable enterprises to make the local Governments self-supporting. Their recommendations covered various aspects of financial administration of these local Governments related to budgeting, accounting, expenditure planning, tax administration including replacement of Octroi etc. It is unfortunate that these recommendations have not been implemented by the State Governments but some stray attempts have been made by them to appoint Municipal Finance Commission to examine the condition of finances of the Urban Local Governments of their States.

Not much improvement is visible in the finance of urban local bodies nor in their financial administration. It is worthwhile to point out the observation of the Committee on Augmentation of Financial Resources of Urban Local Bodies in this regard. The Committee points out: "Our Local Government system has not been very effective mainly because of weak financial administration of our local authorities, particularly the manner in which they have often failed to meet their obligation and not having taken care to maintain soundness which is so essential to any financial structure. Discrimination in the assessment of taxes and inefficiency in their collections, complete disregard for their budgetary principles, diversion of government grants for specific purposes, corruption and embezzlement, are unfortunately common features of several of our local bodies. Any attempt to augment their financial resources will, therefore, be criticised unless they show definite improvement in their functioning and are freed from the evils of corruption, laxity and mismanagement".[5].

Financial Administration

The problem of financing the Local Governments has been heightened by the increase in prices, heavy cost of meeting the expenditure on establishment and on development activities. Added to this, the inefficiency in financial management has increased the magnitude of the problem. It is observed by K.Venkataram : "An ill organized financial administration can be as much a hardship to local bodies as paucity of finances".[6]. It is thus not possible to reduce the expenditure by curtailing its function as it will negate the very purpose of Local Government nor is it possible to substantially augment its resources. It is imperative that a well regulated financial system should be devised to properly harness the sources of revenue, regulate proper assessment and collection of such revenue, exercise adequate financial control, both internal and external, in regulating the expenditure by suitable budgeting method, and control and enforce a system of regular and effective audit and ensure accountability of those local bodies. Marshall observes that" public funds being taken from the citizens compulsorily by taxation, accountability is of supreme importance.... In Government, whether Central or Local, because the monies and goods are held in trust for the public, the precautions must be more elaborate. They must not only be sound but their soundness must be capable of easy demonstration, if only because of the shocks brought to public opinion by the misuse of goods and misapplication of funds".[7]. In such a context a study of the financial administration of urban local bodies will go a long way in revealing the weakness and strength in their working which, if considered, may shape the future of the local institutions known as grass roots of democracy.

The purpose of this study

Orissa has 91 urban local bodies. A list of the urban local bodies with the year of constitution, population as per census reports of 1961 and 1971 are given in Annexure-I. Some of the Municipalities/Notified Area Councils shown in the list have accelerated growth of population which may be due largely to the reasons discussed in para -2. The total urban population of the State comes to 16,85,948 as per 1971 Census which constitutes 8% of the total population. This is an increase of 400.69 percent over the urban population of 4,12,528 in 1941. The number of local bodies has also increased from 64 in 1961 to 76 in 1971 and further to 91 by the end of March 1976. The financial activities of these Local Governments also indicate significant improvement between 1961 and 1976 as shown below :

The Urban Local Bodies in Orissa comprise Municipalities and Notified Area Councils. They derive their powers and functions from the Orissa Municipal Act, 1950 and Municipal Rules, 1953 framed thereunder. The Government of Orissa appointed a Committee in 1961 to enquire and make exhaustive study of the problems relating to their financial condition.The Committee submitted its report in 1962 and recommended among other things to set up one Central Valuation Organisation for independent and impartial assessment and imposition of property taxes. It also recommended to appoint a separate Director for the smooth administration of urban local bodies. These recommendations have been implemented but many other recommendations of the Committee have been left unattended.

Year.	Total amount of receipts (In Rs.)	Total amount of expenditure (In Rs.)
1960-61	84,70,248	79,62,938
1971-72	3,31,55,105	3,39,93,551
1975-76	6,51,50,118	6,80,03,997

* Source: Local Fund Audit Organisation, Finance Department, Government of Orissa.

The State Government also appointed a State Municipal Finance Commission in 1974 to explore possible sources of finance for the urban local bodies and to suggest suitable measures to be taken to put the urban local bodies in a sound financial footing. The Commission gave its report in 1975. The Commission probed into the financial working of all the local bodies in the State and suggested many remedies to recover these local institutions from financial sickness with a view to ensuring proper financial discipline. Speaking of the unsatisfactory financial state of affairs it said: "The amount of expenditure on establishment on the average is 50%, the expenditure on developmental work is 15 to 18 percent. The local income in real sense has not increased at all. The public expenditure pattern lacks sense of priorities and directions as there is complete lack of planning".[8]. The Commission has also made drastic comments on poor provision of services and the poor rate of collection of taxes and fees. The Commission recommended that an additional amount of Rs. 6.03 crores would be necessary for the 84 Urban Local Bodies (then existing) to provide minimum standard of essential service to the people. The Commission suggested ways and means to obtain the required sum. But, it has to be examined if this gap between need and resources can be bridged by ensuring proper financial administration in arresting leakage of revenue and regulating expenditure without imposing an intolerable burden on the tax payers.

Financial administration embraces every branch of the administration. Financial arrangements do not operate in divesting the management of any responsibility. "Every member and every employee must feel financially accountable for his use of the authority's time and goods, or his responsibility-whether exalted or humble - for ordering materials, controlling labour or directing operation".[9]. A study of financial administration of urban local bodies would necessitate a probe into the working of different aspects of these institutions. In India, no study so far seems to have been made specifically on the financial administration of urban local bodies. Many writers have examined the local finances as a part of Public Finance and have discussed the financial administration of local bodies. These books and other reports have been used as references for the purpose of this study, a list of which is given in the Bibliography. No report or reference is available to show if any study on the financial administration of urban local bodies of this State has been made before. It is considered highly essential to make such a study to find out the shortcomings of the local administration of the State in its financial management with a view to exploring ways and means to regulate the financial administration of the urban Local Governments. This may enable the authorities in charge of their administration to bring about financial and administrative discipline.

In the present study it is proposed to examine:

1. Whether the existing tax structure and other sources of receipt of taxes and fees are adequate to yield the maximum receipts for the urban local bodies.
2. Whether the method of assessment and collection is effective to raise adequate resources as per the provision of tax laws.
3. Whether the pattern of expenditure conforms to the needs of the urban local bodies.
4. Whether the existing financial control (both internal and external), accounting procedure and audit practices are properly exercised to ensure financial discipline.

5. Whether accountability of urban local bodies to the legislature would amount to curbing its autonomy in decision making.

Methodology

As indicated earlier there are 91 Municipalities and Notified Area Councils in the State. Information relating to their financial position is based on data obtained from Local Fund Audit Organisation of Finance Department. Broadly the information relates to their receipts and expenditure for the year 1975-76 (the latest available published figures in the Annul Report of the Organisation for 1976-77). Of course the position of receipts is not indicative of the real finances of the local bodies as the receipts include grants and loans received from Government and other financing institutions and out of the receipts during the year unspent balances are carried forward to the next year. Rather the figures relating to expenditure are largely indicative of the spending capabilities of the urban local bodies. With a view to determining the financial position of the urban local bodies we have based our selection on the expenditure figures. On the basis of these figures the urban local bodies have been classified under the following categories:

Category - I	- having expenditure above Rs. 100 lakhs.				
Category - II	-	-do-	-do-	50	"
Category - III	-	-do-	-do-	25	"
Category - IV	-	-do-	-do-	10	"
Category - V	-	-do-	-do-	5	"
Category - VI	-	-do-	below	5	"

According to the above classification there is one institution under category-I,3 institutions under category-II, 2 institutions under category-III, 10 institutions under category-IV, 19 institutions under category-V and 56 institutions under category-VI. A list of such institutions with receipt and expenditure for the year 1975-76 is given in Annexure-II.

To make the study broad based the working of 31 institutions i.e., about one third of the total number of institutions in the State has been undertaken for study including Bhubaneswar Municipality which happens to be in the capital town of the State. All the institutions under categories -I, II and III numbering 6 have been selected.

Out of the remaining 25 institutions 3 institutions from category-IV, 6 from category-V and 16 from category-VI have been selected. Preliminary survey disclosed that these are towns of pilgrimage interest, tourist interest and some are industry based. We have also taken care to select some towns of the above category in the present study. Phulbani N.A.C., a town with highest population of Scheduled Tribes has been included in the study. Equal importance has been given to select towns from different districts and regions of the State. A list of urban local bodies thus selected for the study (under all categories) is given in Annexure-III.

Since out of 56 urban local bodies under category VI, 51 came into existence after 1960, it is therefore decided to confine the study to the years 1961-62 to 1975-76. However general survey relating to finances of the urban local bodies of the State has been made for the earlier period.

As no consolidated picture pertaining to these local bodies is available in the Administrative Department or any other organisation excepting the Audit Reports in the Local Fund Audit Organisation of Finance Department, it was considered expedient to collect information from the urban local bodies directly and to take figures from the Aaudit Reports in cases where no such information was available. Data relating to finances have been collected from the source and have been compiled and analysed. Since it will be too cumbersome and lengthy to analyse the data of every year, the figures for 1961-62, 1965-66, 1971-72 and 1975-76 have been analysed in the study. It is expected that these data will give a representative picture of the financial position of these institutions.

In preparing the study, all relevant literature available in the field including the reports of the Committees and Commissions appointed by the Government have been taken into consideration for the purpose of analysis and comparison. Audit Reports which throw a flood of light on the finances of these local bodies for the years have been examined. Case studies have been made by visiting some of the institutions and discussing with different executive authorities and elected representatives. Their vast experiences in the field have been taken into account while making our observation on different aspects of our study. Periodic discussions have been made with authorities on the subject and their suggestions and guidance have been taken care of while formulating our findings. Informations on different items were obtained from the urban local bodies on a proforma prescribed for the purpose.

ANNEXURE -I.

List of urban local bodies showing year of constitution and population according to census of 1961 and 1971.

	Name of the Municipality/ N.A.C.	Year of Constitution	Population as per census 1961	1971
	1	2	3	4
I.	**KORAPUT DISTRICT**			
1.	Rayagada Municipality	1955	14537	25064
2.	Koraput N.A.C.	1953	7461	21505
3.	Bunabada N.A.C.	1965	-	27980
4.	Umerkote N.A.C.	1962	-	9826
5.	Gudari N.A.C.	1972	-	4774
6.	Malkangiri N.A.C.	1974	-	7494
7.	Nowrangpur Municipality	1952	10380	13739
8.	Gunupur N.A.C.	1955	10180	12702
9.	Kotpad N.A.C.	1960	6368	9856
10.	Jeypore Municipality	1951	25291	34319
II.	**CUTTACK DISTRICT**			
11.	Cuttack Municipality	1876	146308	194068
12.	Kendrapara Municipality	1869	15830	20079
13.	Jagatsingpur N.A.C.	1972	-	15628
14.	Banki N.A.C.	1966	-	9296
15.	Jajpur Road N.A.C.	1961	5989	10805
16.	Choudwar Municipality	1961	13478	24300
17.	Jajpur Municipality	1869	13802	16707
18.	Athagarh N.A.C.	1973	-	8931
III.	**BALASORE DISTRICT**			
19.	Bhadrak N.A.C.	1960	25285	40487
20.	Balasore Municipality	1877	33931	46239
21.	Jaleswar N.A.C.	1964	-	6711
22.	Soro N.A.C.	1975	-	13605
23.	Basudevpur N.A.C.	1975	-	15395
IV.	**Keonjhar DISTRICT**			
24.	Keonjhar Municipality	-	12624	19340
25.	Joda N.A.C.	-	10567	17353
26.	Anandapur N.A.C.	1974	-	6312
27.	Barbil Municipality	-	19340	24342

V.	**DHENKANAL DISTRICT**			
28.	Angul N.A.C.	1955	5658	9053
29.	Bhuban N.A.C.	1972	9476	11350
30.	Dhenkanal Municipality	1951	13772	19615
31.	Talcher Municipality	1954	8147	11794
VI.	**KALAHANDI DISTRICT**			
32.	Junagarh N.A.C.	1969	5599	7876
33.	Khariar Road N.A.C.	1964	6400	9226
34.	Khariar N.A.C.	1972	-	7651
35.	Kesinga N.A.C.	1965	6000	8536
36.	Bhawanipatna Municipality	1951	14300	22908
VII.	**SUNDERGARH DISTRICT**			
37.	Rourkela N.A.C. (CI)	1963	35360	47076
38.	Siramitrapur Municipality	1960	20301	28063
39.	Sundergarh Municipality	1951	11329	17244
40.	Rourkela N.A.C.	1966	-	125426
41.	Rajgangpur Municipality	1957	13843	21876
VIII.	**BOLANGIR DISTRICT**			
42.	Bolangir Municipality	1950	18663	35748
43.	Kantabanji N.A.C.	1951	8863	10489
44.	Tarava N.A.C.	1967	5843	6417
45.	Sonepur Municipality	1951	7108	8084
46.	Patnagarh N.A.C.	1962	7592	10085
47.	Titilagarh N.A.C.	1951	7433	14504
48.	Binika N.A.C.	1976	-	7618
IX.	**PHULBANI DISTRICT**			
49.	Phulbani N.A.C.	1962	5650	10511
50.	Boudh N.A.C.	1961	6088	8891
X.	**SAMBALPUR DISTRICT**			
51.	Sambalpur Municipality	1883	38915	64675
52.	Hirakud N.A.C.	1962	-	15040
53.	Jharsuguda Municipality	1951	19227	24727
54.	Bargarh Municipality	1951	15375	22865
55.	Deogarh Municipality	1951	6839	8906
56.	Brajarajnagar N.A.C.	1968	-	31817
57.	Barapali N.A.C.	1962	-	9019
58.	Burla N.A.C.	1962	-	15587
59.	Kuchinda N.A.C.	1969	-	6838
60.	Padmapur N.A.C.	1965	-	7349

Contd.

XI.	**MAYURBHANJ DISTRICT**			
61.	Karanjia N.A.C.	1973	-	11311
62.	Rairangpur N.A.C.	1960	8119	11226
63.	Udala N.A.C.	1973	-	5116
64.	Baripada Municipality	1949	20301	28725
XII.	**PURI DISTRICT**			
65.	Puri Municipality	1881	60815	72674
66.	Bhubaneswar N.A.C.	1952	38211	105491
67.	Banpur N.A.C.	1973	-	8777
68.	Nayagarh N.A.C.	1953	3713	5209
69.	Nimapara N.A.C.	1973	-	8693
70.	Pipili N.A.C.	1972	-	6833
71.	Jatni N.A.C.	1972	-	25119
72.	Khurda N.A.C.	1960	12497	15879
XIII.	**GANJAM DISTRICT**			
73.	Barhampur Municipality	1885	76931	117662
74.	Kavisuryanagar N.A.C.	1960	7819	9500
75.	Purusottampur N.A.C.	1972	-	8898
76.	Belagunta N.A.C.	1973	-	7113
77.	Gopalpur N.A.C.	1961	3536	3583
78.	Surada N.A.C.	1962	8703	9833
79.	Polsora N.A.C.	1972	-	10579
80.	Buguda N.A.C.	1973	-	5148
81.	Parlakemundi Municipality	1855	22708	26917
82.	Bhanjanagar N.A.C.	1957	9952	12353
83.	Aska N.A.C.	1957	9024	12954
84.	Rambha N.A.C.	1964	5008	6771
85.	Khallikote N.A.C.	1972	-	6889
86.	Chatrapur N.A.C.	1955	7835	10835
87.	Hinjilikatu N.A.C.	1964	8028	10821
88.	Chikiti N.A.C.	1973	-	7087
89.	Kodala N.A.C.	1974	-	7344
90.	Digapahandi N.A.C.	1973	-	6386
91.	Kasinagar N.A.C.	1974	-	8200

ANNEXURE-II.

The position of Receipts and Expenditure of all the Urban Local Bodies in 1975-76

	Name of the Municipality/N.A.C.	Year of Constitution.	Receipts TRS.	Expenditure TRS.	Category
	1	2	3	4	5
I.	**KORAPUT DISTRICT**				
1.	Rayagada Municipality	1955	686	1089	IV
2.	Koraput N.A.C.	1953	511	744	V
3.	Sunabeda N.A.C.	1965	313	315	VI
4.	Umerkote N.A.C.	1962	181	344	VI
5.	Gudari N.A.C.	1972	97	130	VI
6.	Malkangiri N.A.C.	1974	102	60	VI
7.	Nowrangpur Municipality	1962	649	692	V
8.	Gunpur N.A.C.	1955	602	640	V
9.	Kotpad N.A.C.	1960	515	480	VI
10.	Jeypore Municipality	1951	2456	2375	IV
II.	**CUTTACK DISTRICT**				
11.	Cuttack Municipality	1876	11832	11588	I
12.	Kendrapara Municipality	1869	610	621	V
13.	Jagatsingpur N.A.C.	1972	78	107	VI
14.	Banki N.A.C.	1966	124	148	VI
15.	Jajpur Road N.A.C.	1961	374	363	VI
16.	Choudwar Municipality	1961	651	780	V
17.	Jajpur Municipality	1869	673	596	V
18.	Athgarh N.A.C.	1973	90	75	VI
III.	**BALASORE DISTRICT**				
19.	Bhadrak N.A.C.	1960	1273	1336	IV
20.	Balasore Municipality	1877	2469	2737	III
21.	Jaleswar N.A.C.	1954	85	122	VI
22.	Soro N.A.C.	1975	60	44	VI
23.	Basudevpur N.A.C.	1975	55	45	VI
IV.	**KEONJHAR DISTRICT**				
24.	Keonjhar Municipality	-	960	754	V
25.	Joda N.A.C.	-	475	641	V
26.	Anandapur N.A.C.	1974	151	124	VI
27.	Barbil Municipality	-	1124	1219	IV
V.	**DHENKANAL DISTRICT**				
28.	Angul N.A.C.	1955	746	651	V
29.	Bhuban N.A.C.	1972	279	257	VI

30.	Dhenkanal Municipality	1951	2010	1478	IV
31.	Talcher Municipality	1954	399	313	VI
VI.	**KALAHANDI DISTRICT**				
32.	Junagarh N.A.C.	1969	253	210	VI
33.	Khariar Road N.A.C.	1964	399	385	VI
34.	Khariar N.A.C.	1972	129	144	VI
35.	Kesinga N.A.C.	1965	320	273	VI
36.	Bhawanipatna Municipality	1951	753	764	V
VII.	**SUNDERGARH DISTRICT**				
37.	Rourkela N.A.C. (CT)	1963	1111	1326	IV
38.	Biramitrapur Municipality	1960	768	694	V
39.	Sundargarh Municipality	1951	592	597	V
40.	Rourkela N.A.C. (ST)	1966	1002	941	V
41.	Rajgangpur Municipality	1957	665	703	V
VIII.	**BOLANGIR DISTRICT**				
42.	Bolangir Municipality	1950	1244	1254	IV
43.	Kantabanji N.A.C.	1951	342	362	VI
44.	Tarava N.A.C.	1967	134	161	VI
45.	Sonepur Municipality	1951	262	298	VI
46.	Patnagarh N.A.C.	1962	285	295	VI
47.	Titilagarh N.A.C.	1951	571	464	VI
48.	Binika N.A.C.	1976	-	-	VI
IX.	**PHULBANI DISTRICT**				
49.	Phulbani N.A.C.	1962	233	263	VI
50.	Boudh N.A.C.	1961	211	176	VI
X.	**SAMBALPUR DISTRICT**				
51.	Sambalpur Municipality	1883	5823	5897	II
52.	Hirakud N.A.C.	1962	327	381	VI
53.	Jharsuguda Municipality	1951	1106	1053	IV
54.	Baragarh Municipality	1951	1477	1712	IV
55.	Deogarh Municipality	1951	479	623	V
56.	Brajarajnagar N.A.C.	1968	929	834	V
57.	Barpali N.A.C.	1962	241	289	VI
58.	Burla N.A.C.	1962	564	509	V
59.	Kuchinda N.A.C.	1969	118	123	VI
60.	Padmapur N.A.C.	1965	189	222	VI
XI.	**MAYURBHANJ DISTRICT**				
61.	Karnajia N.A.C.	1973	107	98	VI
62.	Rairangpur N.A.C.	1960	285	374	VI

63.	Udala N.A.C.	1973	98	107	VI
64.	Baripada Municipality	1949	863	1339	IV
XII.	**PURI DISTRICT**				
65.	Puri Municipality	1881	4926	5305	II
66.	Bhubaneswar N.A.C.	1952	3085	3847	III
67.	Banpur N.A.C.	1973	99	115	VI
68.	Nayagarh N.A.C.	1953	331	366	VI
69.	Nimapara N.A.C.	1973	98	91	VI
70.	Pipili N.A.C.	1972	153	205	VI
71.	Jatni N.A.C.	1972	295	311	VI
72.	Khurda N.A.C.	1960	340	350	VI
XIII.	**GANJAM DISTRICT**				
73.	Berhampur Municipality	1885	7542	7649	II
74.	Kavisuryanagar N.A.C.	1960	254	382	VI
75.	Purusottampur N.A.C.	1972	102	107	VI
76.	Belagunta N.A.C.	1973	132	116	VI
77.	Gopalpur N.A.C.	1961	200	225	VI
78.	Surada N.A.C.	1962	211	257	VI
79.	Polosora N.A.C.	1972	77	74	VI
80.	Buguda N.A.C.	1973	83	157	VI
81.	Paralakemundi Municipality	1855	1144	1376	IV
82.	Bhanjanagar N.A.C.	1957	803	895	V
83.	Aska N.A.C.	1957	594	521	V
84.	Rambha N.A.C.	1964	128	138	VI
85.	Khallikote N.A.C.	1972	115	137	VI
86.	Chatrapur N.A.C.	1955	283	339	VI
87.	Hinjilikatu N.A.C.	1964	361	347	VI
88.	Chikiti N.A.C.	1973	95	117	VI
89.	Kodalam N.A.C.	1974	88	114	VI
90.	Digpahandi N.A.C.	1973	230	164	VI
91.	Kasinagar N.A.C.	1974	-	-	VI

I	Expenditure above	Rs. 100 Lakhs =	1
II	Expenditure above	Rs. 50 Lakhs =	3
III	Expenditure above	Rs. 25 Lakhs =	2
IV	Expenditure above	Rs. 10 Lakhs =	10
V	Expenditure above	Rs. 5 Lakhs =	19
VI	Expenditure below	Rs. 5 Lakhs =	56
		Total =	91

1 **State Capital**
Bhubaneswar N.A.C.

2. **Industrial Township**
1. Rourkela (ST) N.A.C.
2. Brajarajnagar N.A.C.
3. Biramitrapur Municipality
4. Sunabeda N.A.C.

5. Chowdwar N.A.C.
6. Rajgangpur Municipality
7. Hirakud N.A.C.
8. Barbil (Mining Area) N.A.C.
9. Joda N.A.C.
10. Talcher Municipality

3. **Representing Urban-Advasis**
   1. Phulbani N.A.C.
   2. Koraput N.A.C.

4. **Places of Pilgrimage**
   1. Puri Municipality
   2. Jajpur Municipality

5. **Tourist Interest**
   1. Deogarh Municipality
   2. Rambha N.A.C.

ANNEXURE-III

Receipts and Expenditure of Urban Local Bodies for the year 1975-76: Selected for study.

Name of the Municipality/N.A.C.	Year of constitution.	Receipt TRS.	Expenditure. TRS.	Category
1	2	3	4	5
KORAPUT DISTRICT				
1.Koraput N.A.C.	1953	714	744	V
2.Sunabeda N.A.C.	1965	401	315	VI
3.Jeypore Municipality	1951	2457	2376	IV
CUTTACK DISTRICT				
4.Cuttack Municipality	1876	11833	10817	I
5.Jajpur Municipality	1869	745	783	V
6.Athgarh N.A.C.	1973	90	75	VI
BALASORE DISTRICT				
7.Balasore Municipality	1877	2469	2778	III
8.Jaleswar N.A.C.	1964	85	123	VI
KEONJHAR DISTRICT				
9.Joda N.A.C.	-	475	641	V
DHENKANAL DISTRICT				
10.Angul N.A.C.	1955	746	651	V
11.Talcher Municipality	1954	563	487	VI
KALAHANDI DISTRICT				
12.Khariar Road N.A.C.	1964	399	385	VI
SUNDERGARH DISTRICT				
13.Rourkela N.A.C (CI).	1963	1373	1326	IV
BOLANGIR DISTRICT				
14.Sonepur Municipality	1951	262	298	VI
15.Titilagarh N.A.C.	1951	571	464	VI
PHULBANI DISTRICT				
16.Phulbani N.A.C.	1962	233	264	VI
SAMBALPUR DISTRICT				
17.Sambalpur Municipality	1883	5824	5897	II
18.Deogarh Municipality	1951	479	623	V
19.Brajarajnagar N.A.C.	1968	929	834	V
20.Padmapur N.A.C.	1965	189	222	VI
MAYURBHANJ DISTRICT				
21.Rairangpur N.A.C.	1960	285	374	VI

22.Baripada Municipality	1949	863	1393	IV
PURI DISTRICT				
23.Bhubaneswar N.A.C.	1952	3085	3847	III
24.Puri Municipality	1881	4926	5305	II
25.Nayagarh N.A.C.	1963	331	366	VI
26.Khurda N.A.C.	1960	340	350	VI
GANJAM DISTRICT				
27.Berhampur Municipality	1885	8519	8566	II
28.Gopalpur N.A.C.	1961	200	226	VI
29.Surada N.A.C.	1962	211	258	VI
30.Rambha N.A.C.	1964	128	138	VI
31.Hinjilikatu N.A.C.	1964	361	347	VI

NOTES AND REFERENCES

1. Venkatarangaiya M & M.Pattabhiram : *Local Government in India*, p.1.
2. *Journal of the National Academy of Administration* : April-June '71. Vol. XVI NO.2 - p.35.
3. Munro W.B.: *Municipal Government and Administration*, p.120.
4. Third Plan Report - Government of India, p.693.
5. Report of the Committee on Augmentation of Financial Resources of Urban Local Government - 1963. p.19.
6. K. Venkataraman : *Local Finance in Prospective*, p.45.
7. Marshall A.H. : *Financial Administration in Local Govt..*, p.32.
8. Report of the State Municipal Finance Commission, Orissa, 1975, p.23.
9. Marshall A.H. : *Financial Administration in Local Government*, p.30.

TWO

GROWTH AND DEVELOPMENT OF URBAN LOCAL BODIES

The institution of local Government flourished in India from the Vedic period. The villagers themselves managed the simple affairs of the villages. They were said to be small republics. Central Government had very little control over them. There were also a number of urban local Governments in ancient and medieval India. The capital city of the States, pilgrim and market centres had Urban Local Government. In the Rig Ved, we find mention of *purapati* or lord of the city. Manu says: "And in each town let him appoint one Superintendent of all affairs (Sarbartha Chintaka) elevated in rank, formidable, resembling a planet among the stars". [1].Magasthenes also gives a description of town administration in the third century before Christ. His description shows that town Governments were administered by a Municipal Board of thirty members consisting of Six Committees. Each committee was assigned specific responsibility in the local administration. "The sixth committee was in charge of collecting the tenth of the prices of the articles sold. Fraud in the payment of this tax is punished with death".[2] Chanakya makes no mention of municipal Government but describes the chief official of the city as 'Nagaraka' under whom there were Divisional Officers to look after the administration of different parts of the city.

The town in Orissa flourished during the ancient period. Towns developed in places of pilgrimage and learning. Dantapura once the capital of Kalinga was a famous town known after the ivory palace of the king of Kalinga. During the period of Ashok, towns like Tosali and Somapa grew as seats of political interest. Kalinga Nagari was one of the famous towns during the reign of Kharavela. In medieval period some towns like Jajpur, Khiching, Boudh were also in existence under different names. These towns were centres of political and cultural activities. These towns had Municipal Government having its heads known as Puravasi (head of the town), Dandanaik (Magistrate), Dandapati (Police Inspector) and other officials. They were under the control of the Nagarpalaka (Chairman of the City Council).

Not much is known of the urban local Government during the Marhatta and Muhammedan periods. The city administrations were perhaps under the rigorous control of the Central Government. " A good deal of indigenous taxation has been retained in modern local finance; the 'chungi'of Muslim rules, the Sikh 'dharat,' the 'muhtarafa' of Maratha town have a descondant in today's Octroi".[3] India in the eighteenth century was predominantly rural in character. Most of the towns in existence were small market places with a population ranging from 5000 to 20,000 people. The headquarters of Governments, places of rulers, places of pilgrimage and trading centres grew in size and developed into urban centres. Such urban centres were Delhi, Murshidabad, Lucknow, Madurai, Kashi, Prayag, Amritsar, Surat, Patna and Ahmedabad. According to Sir Jadunath Sarkar, "the Moghuls were essentially an urban people in India and their most distinctive achievements were in developing urban administration".[4]. The Emperor used to appoint an official known as kotwal who was incharge of every aspect of city life. He controlled the local markets, checked weights and measures, supervised local prices. He also levied the local taxes, market dues, tolls and transit duties.

The Local Government in its present structure owes its origin to British rule in India. A beginning of the urban Local Government was made in 1687,when for the first time a local Governing body was set up for the city of Madras by a Charter from James-II. Its powers related to the building of a town hall, a jail and a school house. It could improve roads and improve lighting and conservancy and similar services. It had power to raise funds by taxing the inhabitants of the city. In 1726, Mayor's courts were established in Calcutta and Bombay. The Act authorised the Governor General of India to appoint Justices of peace in these towns who were authorised to levy taxes on houses and lands to provide for scavenging, police and maintenance of roads.

Municipal Government outside the presidency towns developed due to the Regulation XVI of 1814 to make arrangements for watch and ward and to meet the cost of such services by collecting taxes levied on households and lands. The First Municipal Act in 1842 applicable for Bengal envisaged that a town can be established if two third of its inhabitants demand so. A rate of 5 percent levied on annual value of houses and lands was the financial provision made in it. Under the Act of 1850, the towns were given wide range of tax powers including tax on land and buildings. Indirect taxes like present Octroi also were imposed in Bombay, U.P., Punjab and Central provinces.

A series of Acts were passed after the report of the Royal Army Sanitary Commission in 1863 for the establishment of Municipal Government in different provinces with the responsibility for sanitation, lighting and water supply. As a result of Sepoy Mutiny in 1857, the Indian Government met with serious financial deficits. "The Indian debt stood at 98 million pounds".[5]. Therefore the question of financial decentralisation giving responsibility for roads and public works to local bodies was examined by James Wilson, the then Finance Member.

During the sixties, India entered into world market. Cotton and jute industries developed. Railways awakened many quiet towns into noisy life. For example Kanpur, which was a village, with the arrival of railways in 1863 gradually acquired commercial importance and trade and industry developed giving impetus to the growth of urban areas. Changes in education and outlook also brought changes in social justice and political right. New urban communities arose around centres of industrial and commercial activities. The educated Indian people challenged the policies of British rule and demanded more political rights and greater share in the administration and public services. In subsequent years the dissatisfaction against British rule spread among larger section of the people and the urban centres became the focal section from where the educated Indian began to agitate for political freedom.[6].

Lord Mayo's resolution in 1870 on financial decentralisation visualized local self Government and tapping local source of revenue to give relief to Imperial Finances. Lord Ripon, who succeeded Lord Mayo as Governor General of India, resolved in 1882 to make local Government Self Governing. To him, Local Government was predominantly 'an instrument of political and popular education'.[7].

Lord Ripon's resolution of 1882 opened a new phase in the history of Local Self Government in India. In his resolution he emphasised that two thirds of the members of a municipality should be non-official. System of election should be enforced. Government control should be exercised in raising loans and levying taxes by the Municipality. Above all, the resolution envisaged that the local bodies must be endowed with adequate financial resources to carry out their functions. To this end, certain sources of local revenues should be made available to the local bodies which should also receive suitable grants from the provincial budget. Consequent on Ripon's resolutions the revenue and expenditure of the local bodies considerably expanded.

The main items of income and expenditure of Municipalities during Ripon's time were :

1. Octroi which formed about 52% of the total tax income in Bombay to 93% in the Punjab.
2. House taxes which formed about 3% in N.W.P., 4% in the Punjab to about 47% in Madras and Asssam.
3. Tax on Trade and Profession in N. W. P. (4%) and in Madras (17%).
4. Tolls in Bombay, Madras, Bengal and Assam.
5. Rents and prices varying from 10% in Bengal to 18% in Madras.
6. Fees and fines.
7. Grants in aid varying from 10% in Bengal to 18% in Madras.

On an average 9% to 10% of the total expenditure of Municipalities were incurred on General Administration. A large proportion of annual expenditure varying from 35% to 50% was made on public health (including water supply) and public works accounted for from 17% in Madras to 21% in Assam.[8]

Even though Lord Ripon's enthusiastic resolution to extend local self Government has been regarded as 'Magnacarta' of Indian Local Government, "in financial sphere they were subject to large measure of official control and their local autonomy was more shadowy than real".[9] But for years to come, there was slow development in the affairs of Local Government. The social group living in towns did not develop an essential attachment with the civic activities, rather attachment was more for religious festivities and social conventions and the institution was more utilised to agitate for the national movement to free the country from the British Rule.

In 1907, a Royal Commission was set up to enquire into the administrative and financial relationship of the Government of India with the Provincial Governments which vis-a-vis examined the relation of Local Governments. In their recommendations published in 1909 the Commission while recommending administrative arrangements inter-alia recommended the following financial resources for the local Governments.

a. Municipalities should be constituted for urban areas.
b. Municipalities should be given the necessary authority to determine the taxes and to prepare their budgets after keeping a minimum reserve fund. The Government should give grants for public works like water supply, drainage schemes, etc.
c. Outside control over local bodies should be restricted to advice, suggestion and audit.
d. The Government control over the municipal powers of raising local loans should continue and the prior sanction of Government should be obtained for lease or sale of municipal properties.
e. The Municipality should have the responsibility of primary education and if funds so permit should spend some amount on secondary schools.

Municipal services did not attract the Indians of ability. The Municipal Councils did not have much independence in passsing their budgets and there was much resistance to fresh taxation. There was not much progress on the Commission's recommendations till the Government of India Act of 1919 was passed.

National movement for independence gained grounds and stirred the British Government. The world war(1914-18) led the country's economy to financial crisis. Prices rose sky-high. The Britishers felt that more Indians should be associated with the administration of their country in all levels. Thus came the historic Government of India Act of 1919 which opened a new era in the history of Local Self Government in India. Local Self Government became a transferred subject where a clear cut demarcation of tax powers of local bodies were laid down. The following taxes were included in the local list under this Act.

1. Toll.
2. A tax on land and land values.
3. A tax on buildings.
4. A tax on vehicles and boats.
5. A tax on menial and domestic servants.
6. A tax on animal.
7. An Octroi.
8. A terminal tax.
9. A tax on trade, professions and callings.
10. A tax on private markets.
11. A tax imposed in return of service rendered such as (a) water rate; (b) lighting rate; (c) drainage rate; (d) fees for the use of markets and (e) other public conveniences.

These elaborate tax sources assigned to the local bodies created a lot of enthusiasm in different provinces and Municipal Acts were amended giving more power to the local bodies. The local bodies due to their ambitious programmes incurred expenditure faster than they could earn and because of their inexperience in managing the affairs, resources were put to great strain. As H. Tinker put it: "In many Municipalities, financial problems were only aggravated by their new liberty. The wide public dislike of increased taxation was now unbridled; even the collection of existing taxes was conducted with less vigour, and the amount outstanding at the close of the financial year began to grow and grow. In some cases, members of Municipal Boards were themselves examples to the rest of the community in the non-payment of taxes".[10]

The Taxation Enquiry Committee set up in 1925 considered the problems of finances of Local Governments and observed that finances of local bodies are inadequate to match the services assigned to them. They recommended replacement of Octroi by property tax and taxes on sales. The Simon Commission appointed in 1930 to review the progress made under 1919 Act also observed the 'inadequacy of financial resources of local bodies', paucity of trained personnel and pointed out the reluctance of the elected members to impose local taxes. Giving unconditional grants to local bodies led to financial irresponsibility in not imposing and collecting taxes. It observed that "the management of the finances of local authority has deteriorated since the reforms and this laxity is not 'adequately corrected by such powers of audit as the provincial Government possess".[11]

Government of India Act of 1935

Under the provision of the Act of 1935 the powers of taxation given to the local bodies under the 1919 Act were withdrawn. The local bodies derived their powers from the Provincial Legislature. The functions of the local bodies were expanded but the financial powers were curtailed. Since there were three lists of power of taxation under the Act of 1935 viz; Federal list, Provincial list and Concurrent list, the local bodies depended upon the provincial legislatures for assignment of sources of revenue. Provincial Governments were reluctant to part with their lucrative sources of revenue to the local bodies. Provincial Governments also exercised control over the local bodies in respect of proposals for new taxation and for reduction or abolition of an existing tax. Thus the Municipalities depended on the State Governments for grant-in-aid which resulted in wider control of the State Governments over the local bodies.

Independence and After

The Constitution of India came into force in 1950. The local Government was included within the meaning of 'the State' under Article 12 of the Constitution of India. The subject of Local Government was allotted to the State Government which figures under entry 5 of the List-II of the 7th Schedule of the Constitution which reads as follows : "Local Government, that is to say, the constitution and powers of Municipal Corporation, Improvement Trust, District

Boards, Mining Settlement Authorities and other local authorities for the purpose of Local Self Government or village Administration".

Thus all local Governments became subordinate to the State Government. They exercised such powers and discharged such functions as were assigned to them by the State Legislature. The State Governments had authority to exercise supervision and control over the local bodies. The relationship of the State Government vis-a-vis the local bodies has been defined by the respective Acts of the Legislatures.

"The Constitution divides the public revenues of the country into two parts only; one for the Union and the other for the State and permits the state authorities to allot any resources at their discretion to local bodies out of the state share of the public revenue".[12] Naturally a local body's power of taxation is limited to the extent of powers given to them by the State Government. The powers of taxation given by the Government of India Act of 1919 to local bodies were assigned to the Provincial Government under the Government of India Act of 1935. In the Constitution of India, two items of taxes which belonged to local bodies earlier were included in the Union List. Under Article 276 of the Constitution, the amount payable in respect of any person by way of taxes on profession, trades and callings and employment to any of the local authority shall not exceed Rs. 250.00 per annum unless a rate higher than that was charged by a local authority before the commencement of the Constitution. Similarly under Article 285 of the Constitution the property of the Union shall be exempt from all taxes imposed by State or by any authority within the State unless such properties of the Union were taxed prior to commencement of the Constitution.

Though the Local Governments became self governing institutions under the Constitution of India, they lost their financial autonomy granted to them in the Act of 1919 and became dependant on the mercy of the State Legislature for their subsistence.

Position in Orissa

Orissa became a separate province in 1936 with areas carved out of Madhya Pradesh, Madras and Bihar. The new province consisted of six districts which had only 8 Municipalities. The urban population of Orissa according to 1941 Census was 4,12,528 which was 3% of the total population of the province. Among the 8 Municipalities existing in 1936, Berhampur Municipality was the oldest which had been constituted in 1855. Jajpur and Kendrapara Municipalities were established in 1869 and Cuttack in 1867, Balasore in 1877, Puri in 1881, Sambalpur in 1883 and Paralakemidi in 1886. Other urban local bodies were constituted after 1949 excepting those which were in existence in the princely states. With the merger of the princely states in Orissa in 1948 and Mayurbhanj State in 1949 Orissa was divided into 13 districts. Thus the urban local bodies in the province increased to 29.

The Table II-1 shows that the present urban population of the State is hardly 8% of the total population but the rate of growth from 1941 to 1971 is 400.69 in comparison to All India growth rate of 242.22 and the number of urban local bodies has gone upto 91 in 1975-76.

TABLE-II-1.

Year	Total Population (in lakhs)		Urban population as percentage to total population				Growth Rate	
	Orissa	India	Orissa		India		Orissa	India
			Urban population	Percent to total population	Urban population in millions	Percent to total population		
1	2	3	4	5	6	7	8	9
1901	103	2363	254684	2.47	26	11.02		
1911	114	2521	275159	2.42	26	10.32		
1921	112	2514	281498	2.52	28	11.16		
1931	125	2790	317524	2.54	34	12.19		
1941	138	3187	412528	3.00	45	14.11	100	100
1951	146	3611	594070	4.06	62	17.17	144.01	137.78
1961	175	4392	1109650	6.32	79	17.98	268.99	175.56
1971	219	5470	1685948	7.68	109	19.91	400.69	242.22

Source : Report of the State Municipal Finance Commission - Orissa, 1975. p. 11 & 13).

In some of the princely states of Orissa, there existed municipalities prior to their merger in the province of Orissa in 1948 and 1949. The powers and functions of these local bodies were regulated by the Acts/Rules framed by the respective states. There were two Municipalities in the Sonepur State namely Sonepur and Binika in 1901. The revenue of the municipalities was collected from Octroi which was annually leased out by the Municipal Council. The Municipalities maintained local dispensaries, expenditure on roads and primary education was met from the Municipal funds.

Baripada Municipality under the Mayurbhanj State came into existence in 1905 under Regulation-I of 1905 of the Mayurbhanj Municipal Regulation. The regulation was framed primarily for Baripada Municipality but it was indicated in the Statement of 'Objects and Reasons' that the same may be extended to the Sub Divisional Headquarters at Bahalda and Karanjia or to any suitable locality. But till today Bahalda has not been declared a town and Karanjia was declared a Notified Area Council only in 1973. "The Regulation of 1905 was drafted on the model of the Bengal Municipal Act".[13] The regulation prescribed elaborate rules and procedure regarding the working of the Municipal Council. Some of the salient features are indicated below :

1. The members of the municipal council were known as Commissioners and they were appointed by the Chief (Ruler of the Mayurbhanj State) and he had powers to remove them if they were found guilty of misconduct. Similarly, the Chairman of the Municipality was appointed by the Chief (Sec. 7 & 8).
2. The Chairman had the authority to make appointments and remove persons of the Municipal Council (Sec.39).
3. The State contributed to the 'Municipal Fund' annually a sum equal to the amount that shall be spent for the purpose mentioned in the Regulation (Sec.46).
4. Account Books of the Municipality were open to inspection by any tax payer (Sec. 46).
5. There was provision for imposition of the following taxes and fees :

a. a tax upon persons occupying holdings within the Municipality
b. a rate on the annual value of the holdings situated in the Municipality (Sec. 60)

c. a tax on carriage, horse and other animals
d. a fee on the registration of carts
e. a fee for the cleansing of privies and cesspools.

The holding tax was to be assessed on the annual rental value of the holdings not exceeding six percent of the total. The detailed procedures for assessment, collection and exemption of such taxes and fees were prescribed. The accounting procedure and forms of accounts of the municipality were prescribed. The rules and procedure relating to taxation and finance are more or less analogous to the provisions in the present Municipal Act of 1950 and Rules framed thereunder in 1953.

The Nayagarh Town (under Nayagarh State) was declared a Municipality in 1945 under the Nayagarh Town Municipal Rules, 1945. In these rules there was provision for election of Municipal Councillors(Commissioners)who were to be approved by the Ruling Chief, and the Chief Minister was to be the Chairman of the Municipal Board. The Rule prescribed the powers of the Board. "The Board had powers regarding imposition of taxes, method of assessment, realisation of taxes, allotment of expenditure of these taxes".[14]

As indicated earlier, Orissa became a separate province in 1936 with portions of Madras, Madhya Pradesh and Bihar. There were two sets of Municipal Laws prevailing in different districts of the province. The Madras District Municipal Act, 1920 was in vogue in the districts of Ganjam and Koraput. The Bihar and Orissa Municipal Act, 1922 regulated the activities of Municipalities in the districts of Cuttack, Puri, Balasore and Sambalpur.

It is desirable that the salient features of the above 2 kinds of Municipal Acts may be discussed in order to know the functioning of these local bodies in different districts. As regards their primary objective to provide civic amenities to the citizens, there was hardly any difference but in respect of other provisions, the broader aspects are discussed below.

1. As per Madras Act, 1920 and Bihar & Orissa Act, 1922 the councillors and Chairman held office for a term of 3 years. The Chairman

was elected by the councillors. In Madras 3/4th of the councillors were elected members, whereas in Bihar and Orissa 4/5th of Councillors were elected. To be eligible to vote, one must be of 21 years of age in both the Acts, but Madras prescribed a residential qualification of 120 days or more, but Bihar and Orissa Act was more rigid and made it one year. The fiscal qualification of voter in Madras was payment of property tax, a tax on companies or property tax or surcharge on income tax, but in Bihar and Orissa Act any male person paying a maximum of Rs.1.8 towards municipal tax, or paying or being assessed for income tax, or being a resident of any holding or part of a holding which had been assessed to or had paid Municipal taxes or fees of Rs.1.8 (Rs.1.50 p) was entitled to be a voter. In Madras only male voters were eligible to be member of the Council, whereas in Bihar and Orissa any person enrolled as a voter could stand for election.

2. In both the Acts, there was provision for appointment of different committees for transacting the business of the council.

3. The Provincial Government had power of supervision, inspection, approval of the budget, approval of introduction of new taxes or abolition of any existing taxes.

4. In Bihar and Orissa Act the elaborate list of purposes for which municipal fund is applicable was given, whereas the function of the municipality was specified in Madras Act.

5. In Bihar and Orissa, the Council was competent to determine the appointment in different grades including their salary and leave etc., whereas in Madras the Chairman had power to make appointment to posts carrying a salary of Rs. 50.00 or less.

6. As regards Municipal revenues, the kinds of taxes imposed in both Madras, Bihar and Orissa were the same.[15]

i. A tax on property which included holding tax, lighting tax, latrine tax, scavenging tax, drainage tax etc. was imposed. This tax was assessed on the basis of annual rental value of the land and buildings (10% per annum, both the Acts). There were certain limitations regarding imposition of service taxes i.e. lighting, water, drainage, etc.

ii. Tax on income, profession, calling and trade.

iii. Pilgrim tax (in Madras only).

iv. A tax on dogs, fee for regulation of dogs and carts.

v. A fee on vessels.

A tax on income was a surcharge on the income tax. Taxes on trade were 'Octroi' and terminal taxes. In Madras there was neither Octroi nor terminal tax, but in Bihar and Orissa such taxes provided a major source of income. Both the Acts provided elaborate principles and procedure regarding financial management of the local bodies which included different administrative enactments and accounting procedures and forms of accounts.

Both the Acts vested the power of direction, control and supervision over the Municipality on the provincial Governments. The District Magistrates and Divisional Commissioners had powers of inspection. The District Magistrate had powers to direct execution of any work as an emergency measure. The provincial Governments had power to create, abolish or modify the territorial jurisdiction of a Municipality. They had power to supersede and decide the percentage of nominated councillors. They had power to sanction posts, their salaries and allowances. No tax could be imposed, abolished or reduced without sanction of Government. No loans could be incurred by the local authority without prior approval of the Government. All resolutions of the Council required confirmation by the Government. The provincial Government enjoyed the powers to alter the provision in the budget if it considered that adequate provisions were not made to discharge the liabilities and to maintain a minimum closing balance. A close scrutiny of both the Acts reveals that supreme authority over the urban local bodies was vested in the provincial Governments even though the Municipal Councils enjoyed a representative status.

The Madras District Municipality Act, 1920 was amended in 1933. This amendment separated the deliberative functions from those of the executive, and appointed Municipal Commissioners to Municipalities for the execution of the resolutions of the Council. This radical change was due to maladministration by some Chairmen during 1920-33. The Bihar and Orissa Municipal Act of 1922 was also amended in 1930, 1931, 1932 and 1935. The Bihar and Orissa Local Fund Audit Act of 1925 was replaced by the Orissa Local Fund Audit Act, 1948. The provision of this Act will be discussed later. The municipalities under the respective jurisdiction of different Acts, i.e., Madras Municipality Act, 1920, Bihar and Orissa Municipal Act, 1922 and Regulation of Princily states were regulated till the Orissa Municipal Act, 1950 came into operation in 1951. As such now all the Municipalities and Notified Area Councils of the State are administered under the Orissa Municipal Act, 1950 and rules framed thereunder. The relevant provisions of the Act and Rules have been discussed in the concerned chapters.

NOTES AND REFERENCES

1. *Report of the Orissa Local Body (Urban) Administration Enquiry Committee*, Government of Orissa, p.3.
2. Venkentarangeya M. & Pattabhiram M. : *Local Government in India*, p.71.
3. Tinker, H. : *The Foundation of Local Self Government in India*, Pakistan and Burma, p.15.
4. Tinker, H. : *The Foundation of Local Self Government in India, Pakistan and Burma*, p.17.
5. Tinker, H. : *Foundation of Local Self Government in India*, Pakistan and Burma, p.35.
6. *Report of the Rural-Urban Relationship Committee* - Volume-I. p.8.
7. Maheshwari S.R. : *Local Government in India*, p.17.
8. *Report of the Committee on Augmentation of Financial Resources of Urban Local Bodies*, p. 6-7.
9. Gyanchand : *Local Finance in India*, p.28.
10. Tinker, H. : *Foundation of Local Self Government in India*, Pakistan and Burma, p.120.
11. As quoted in the *Report of the Committee on Augmentation of Financial Resources of Urban Local Bodies*, p.8.
12. *Report of the Committee on Augmentation of Financial Resources of Urban Local Bodies*, p.17.
13. *The Mayurbhanj Municipal Regulation* - Statement of Objects and Reasons - Regulation-I of 1905.
14. *Nayagarh Town Municipal Rules*, 1945 - Rule-14.
15. *Bihar and Orissa Municipal Act*, 1922. *Madras District Municipal Act*, 1920.

THREE

INCOME PATTERN OF URBAN LOCAL BODIES: TAX REVENUE

I

Scope and Importance of Revenue

It is necessary to discuss the finances of the urban local bodies, with a view to examining their financial administration. "On its practical side, financial administration is that part of the Government Organisation which deals with the collections, preservation and distribution of public funds, with the co-ordination of public revenues and expenditure, with the management of credit operation on behalf of the State and with general control of the financial affairs of the public household".[1] For properly assessing the effectiveness and efficiency of a system, we must know the objectives which the system aims at and the problems involved therein. A study of financial administration should, therefore, embrace the study of (a) assessment and collection of revenues including custody of such funds, (b) incurring of expenditure, and (c) the general management and control of financial affairs including the preparation and execution of the budget. The present chapter will deal with the sources of revenue, methods of assessment and collection of such revenues.

The functions of the urban local bodies mostly relate to providing essential services like health, sanitation, water supply, education and many other important amenities to the citizens which form a part of their total responsibility to improve the living conditions of the citizens. To tackle these the local bodies need adequate finances. Urshulak Hicks observed "If local bodies are to play any significant part in economic or social development, they must clearly have access to adequate finances".[2] The finances should match the functions assigned to them.

In the United States of America the powers and functions of the local authorities depend upon the terms of the charter of the individual cities. In England, the local authorities are supported by the Central Government. In India, their duties and functions are prescribed in the Acts/Rules framed by the State Governments and therefore, their powers of taxation and scope of income are dependent to that extent on the respective State Acts. The powers and functions of the local Governments are more or less similar throughout India with minor variations. Their functions can be broadly classified as obligatory and optional. These functions are performed depending upon their financial capacities.

In India, the main sources of income of the urban local bodies are as follows :

1. Income from taxation

i. Taxes on property including service taxes	a. Tax on Land & buildings b. Water Tax c. Lighting Tax d. Latrine Tax or Conservancy tax e. Drainage tax
ii. Octroi Tax	This tax is not levied in Andhra Pradesh, Assam, Bihar, Kerala and Madras.
iii. Taxes on animals and vehicles	
iv. Taxes on trade callings.	

Income from non-tax revenue

This comprises receipts from markets, slaughter houses, municipal buildings and municipal enterprises.

Grant-in-aid

There are two types of grant: general purpose grant and grants for specific purposes. Grants are also given by the State Governments in the way of sharing of certain taxes which are collected by the State Government. Of these taxes, a percentage of the tax is retained towards collection charges and the rest are distributed to local bodies. These are motor vehicle tax and entertainment tax.

Loans

Loans form a part of the income of the urban local bodies since loans are received from the State Governments and other financing institutions for different remunarative schemes and even for meeting expenditure on ordinary activities. (In Orissa loans are granted by the State Government for meeting the expenditure due to payment of additional dearness allowance to the municipal employees. Even loans are received for payment to owners of buildings for conversion of dry latrines to septic ones).

The tax revenue of the municipalities may be classified as direct and indirect taxes. Direct taxes include (a) Taxes on property, lands and buildings including Service Taxes, (b) Taxes on trades and callings, (c) Taxes on persons, (d) Fees or fines, (e) Taxes on animals, servants. Indirect taxes include 'Octroi,' terminal taxes and entertainment tax. These indirect taxes occupy an important place in the local revenues.

The Taxation Enquiry Commission (1953) recommended that the following taxes and duties should be reserved exclusively for the local bodies:

a Taxes on lands and buildings
b Octroi
c Taxes on vehicles other than those mechanically propelled
d Taxes on animals and boats
e Taxes on profession, trades, callings and employments and
f Taxes on advertisements other than those published in the newspapers.

The Commission also recommended that the local bodies should impose a Show or Theatre Tax and a duty on transfer of property to be collected with the stamp duty by the State Government. These recommendations were also supported by the Committees on Augmentation of Financial Resources of the Urban Local Bodies. Also the Committee on the Rural Urban Relationship (1966) generally agreed with the recommendations of the Commission. But the power of imposing such taxes belongs to the State Governments and they normally do not want to part with their powers. In fact, as observed by the Rural-Urban Relationship Committee, some of the State Governments levy taxes in urban areas which ought to be transferred to the local bodies. In Uttar Pradesh, urban property tax similar to holding taxes imposed by municipalities in Bihar and Orissa are imposed by the State Government in urban areas. In Madhya Pradesh, Punjab and Assam, the State Governments are levying profession taxes. Such encroachments by the State Government on local sources of revenue weaken the financial structure of Local Governments.

All the local bodies do not levy all the taxes as detailed above as they are generally averse to levying taxes mostly due to a fear of loss of popularity. A study undertaken by the Rural-Urban Relationship Committee disclosed that in 1962-63, 21% of the local bodies levied no property tax, 54% did not levy service taxes, while about 27% did not levy vehicle taxes. The Committee on Augmentation of Financial Resources of Urban Local Bodies also reported that in 1960-61, 35% of the municipalities in Gujrat, 18% in Madhya Pradesh, 38% in Punjab, 83% in Rajasthan and 40% in Uttar Pradesh were levying neither property taxes nor any of the service taxes.[3].

There has been no improvement in the position of levy of house tax as non-levy of such taxes by majority of municipalities in Uttar Pradesh, Punjab, Haryana, Himachal Pradesh and Madhya Pradesh has also been reported by the Task Force on Planning and Development of Small and Medium Towns and Cities.[4]. The rates of many such taxes levied were kept low. The proportion of non-tax revenue was lower in Orissa, Bihar, Assam and Kerala in comparison to other places. Grants-in-aid contributed an important source of income in Andhra Pradesh, Assam, Bihar and Orissa. The Rural Urban Relationship Committee further recommended that the State Governments must provide adequate source of revenue to local bodies through allocation and sharing of revenues and the local bodies on their part should effectively exploit the allocated resources and raise optimum non-tax revenue.[5].

Grants

The State Governments provide grants-in-aid to urban local bodies for financing both plan and non-plan schemes and to meet the deficit in general. Grants are given usually for the following purposes.

a. Grants for improvement of roads.
b. Grants for schemes like construction of town halls, parks and office buildings.
c. Grants for conversion of dry latrines to septic latrines.
d. Grants for meeting a part of the dearness allowance of the employees of the local bodies.
e. Grant for meeting the loss caused due to natural calamities.
f. Grant for environmental development.
g. Grant for the execution of remunerative schemes like market buildings, dwelling houses on rent, extension of street lighting, pisciculture.

Loans

It is not possible for the urban local bodies to provide funds for the execution of developmental activities when the resources at their disposal are even scarce to match the obligatory functions. Expenditure for investment in capital projects, like water supply, slum clearance, residential buildings, hospitals, markets are financed from borrowed funds. Such borrowings constitute a regular source of receipts to urban local bodies. Inspite of their limited borrowing power, they borrow from the State Government and other financing institutions like Life Insurance Corporation and HUDCO with the guarantee of the State Governments.

Sources of income of urban local bodies in Orissa

The functions and powers of the urban local bodies in Orissa are regulated under the provisions of the Orissa Municipal Act, 1950, and the Orissa Municipal Rules, 1953. Different Sections of the Act provide for levy of taxes and fees by the local bodies for different purposes. The rules framed under the Act also prescribe the procedure for imposition and collection of such taxes and fees. The nature of taxes and fees leviable by the urban local bodies are indicated below.

1.	Taxes (a) Direct:	Holding tax, Latrine tax, Lighting tax, Water tax, Drainage tax, Education tax.
	(b) Indirect:	Octroi, Terminal taxes.
2.	Rates (Service taxes):	Water, Light, Latrine & Drainage.
3.	Fees:	For market, slaughter, dog registration, vessels, industries and factories, offensive and dangerous trades, education, cart stand, taxi stand.
4.	Income from Municipal Enterprises & remunerative schemes:	Market buildings, shopping centres, residential houses, pisciculture, ferry ghat, guest house, petrol pump, milk supply.

In addition to the income derived from the above taxes and fees including receipts from remunerative schemes, the urban local bodies receive grants from the State Government and loans from the State Government and other financing institutions.

The position showing receipts of all the urban local bodies of the State from different sources during the years 1961-62 to 1975-76 is given in Table-III-1 which shows that receipts from Government grants during the year 1963-64 were the highest due to the creation of many new urban local bodies during 1962-63. These new institutions had minimal income from their own sources and they largely depended upon Government grants. As such receipts during the year from own sources were lower than in other years. Receipts on account of loan were the highest during 1971-72 and receipts from own sources were the lowest during the year.

The financial position of 31 urban local bodies has been studied for the years 1961-62 to 1975-76 and the position of receipts for the above period is given in Table-III-2. The position of the samples studied is well comparable with the position of receipts of all the urban local bodies shown in Table-III-1. Even though the position of receipts from Government grants declined during the year 1965-66 (Sample Study) compared to receipts on account of grants during

1963-64 (whole State), the receipt from Government grant was the highest during 1971-72 as per figures in both Table III and III-2. The position of receipts from own sources during all these years ranged from 55.31 percent to 68.47 percent as per samples studied whereas the position of receipts from own sources in respect of all the urban local bodies as in Table-III-1 varied from 56.30 percent to 68.39 percent. Receipts on account of loan during all these years as in Table-III-1 & III-2 depict more or less the same position as in 1971-72, when the receipts under this head were the highest and during 1975-76 the lowest.

As may be seen from Table-III-2, there has been a sharp rise in volume of total receipts from the year 1961-62 to 1975-76. In comparison to the receipts of 1961-62, the rise in receipts during 1965-66, 1971-72 and 1975-76 comes to 102.49, 353.19 and 586.06 percent respectively. The volume of receipts from own sources has risen from 45.53 lakhs in 1961-62 to about 91 lakhs in 1965-66, 183 lakhs in 1971-72 and 343 lakhs in 1975-76. Similarly, the receipts on account of Government grant during all these years have risen from 24.38 lakhs during 1961-62 to about 153 lakhs in 1975-76 but the percentage of receipts from grants compared to total receipts during 1975-76 being 30.46 was the lowest. Even though the volume of loan had risen from about 3.10 lakhs in 1961-62 to about 5.38 lakhs in 1975-76, the percentage of receipts on this account in comparison to other years was the lowest in 1975-76,being only 1.07 percent and was the highest in 1971-72, being 9.11 percent.

The general rise in volume of receipts is due to increase in urban population and area from the year 1961-62 to 1975-76 and due to an increase in the number of urban local bodies during the period. The rise in prices also resulted in an increase in cost of buildings which increased the rental value of buildings to afford for a higher amount of assessment towards property tax. Introduction of Octroi in many urban local bodies also brought larger amounts to their revenue.

Receipts from own sources

As indicated in Table-III-1 and III-2, the mainstay of municipal finance is the receipt from their own sources of revenue. Receipt from their own sources comprises taxes, rates, fees, fines and receipts from municipal property and enterprises. Of all such receipts, the taxes and rates account for major receipts. The taxes and rates are broadly known as property taxes in the nature of Holding Tax, Water Tax, Lighting Tax, Latrine Tax, Drainage tax and a tax on profession and calling. Octroi tax also occupies an important place in the revenue pattern of the urban local bodies as may be seen from the subsequent discussions.

The figures in Table-III-3 show that gradually the income of the urban local bodies from their own sources of revenue is on the increase. During the year 1961-62 the income of only 6 local bodies from their own sources exceeded 60 percent whereas during 1965-66,the income of 14 local bodies exceeded sixty percent. There was a decline during the year 1971-72 but ten urban local bodies secured revenue to the extent of 50 to 60 percent from their own sources, against 4 during 1965-66. The largest number of local bodies, being 22, earned income from their own sources of revenue exceeding 60 percent during 1975-76. There has been marked improvement in raising revenue from their own sources during all these years.

TABLE-III-1: Total Receipts of Urban Local Bodies in Orissa during the years 1961-62 to 1975-76.
(Figures in lakhs); (Brackets Indicate percentage to total receipts)

Source of Receipts	1961-62 *	1963-64 **	1971-72 ***	1975-76 ****
Own Source	58.83	77.07	238.98	522.79
	(68.39)	(58.33)	(56.30)	(67.91)
Government Grant	24.99	54.36	141.70	237.56
	(29.05)	(41.14)	(33.39)	(30.86)
Loans	2.20	0.69	43.77	9.48
	(2.56)	(0.53)	(10.31)	(1.23)
Total.	86.02	132.12	424.45	769.83
	(100)	(100)	(100)	(100)

Source: * Government of Orissa Publication - pp.34-35 (State Level Conference of Urban Local Bodies, 1966.)

** Ibid.

*** Government of Orissa - Report of the State Municipal Finance Commission - 1975,p.32

**** Government of Orissa - Annual Report of 1976-77. Local Fund Audit Organisation, Finance Department. p.103.

TABLE-III-2: Receipts of the Urban Local Bodies from 1961-62 to 1975-76 in respect of samples Studied.

(In Rs.)

Source of receipts	1961-62	1965-66	1971-72	1975-76
Own Source	45,53,219 (62.36)	90,94,381 (61.52)	1,83,00,201 (55.31)	3,42,93,106 (68.47)
Government Grant	24,38,045 (33.39)	52,01,302 (35.18)	1,17,73,181 (35.58)	1,52,59,017 (30.46)
Loans	3,09,850 (4.25)	4,88,004 (3.30)	30,14,175 (9.11)	5,37,879 (1.07)
Total	73,01,114 (100)	1,47,83,687 (100)	3,30,87,557 (100)	5,00,90,002 (100)
No. of urban local bodies	20	28	30	31

(Figures in brackets indicate percentage to total receipts)

Source: Collected from the records in Local Fund Audit, Finance Department and from the urban local bodies.

TABLE-III-3: Income from own sources as percentage of Total income from 1961-62 to 1975-76.

Income from own Sources as percentage to total income	Number of urban local bodies			
	1961-62	1965-66	1971-72	1975-76
0 - 10	x	x	x	x
10 - 25	x	2	3	1
25 - 40	3	5	3	1
40 - 50	4	3	4	1
50 - 60	6	4	10	6
Above 60	6	14	10	22
	19	28	30	31

II

Property tax

In the modern system of municipal finance, property tax has assumed unique place throughout the world. "The primary reason for its being so important is the fixity of the taxable object. As a fixed object property is more permanent than income and it is difficult to escape it by selling it in which case there is also somebody to pay the tax".[6]. In England, United States of America, Australia, Canada as well as in India, this tax has been the main source of income for the urban local Governments. In Orissa the property tax is levied as per provisions in Sections 131 and 132 of Orissa Municipal Act, 1950. The tax on land and holdings is known as 'holding tax' as per the Act. In West Bengal and Bihar this tax is also known as the holding tax though in other States it is called 'house tax'. According to Section 131 of Orissa Municipal Act 1950, a "tax is levied on holdings situated within the municipality assessed on their annual value". The Municipal Council is also empowered to impose within the municipality the following taxes :

a. a latrine tax on the annual value of holdings;
b. a water tax on the annual value of holdings;
c. a lighting tax on the annual value of holdings;
d. a drainage tax on the annual value of holdings;

It may be seen that the basis of all such taxes is rental value of the holdings. At the same time the basis of assessment, collection and other procedures for administration of such taxes are more or less similar. The holdings which are used as places of public worship, religious assemblage, dharamasala, sarai, monastery or registered as public burial and burning grounds are exempted from the levy of holding tax. Under Section 131 (B), of the Orissa Municipal Act, 1950 certain categories of Government holdings used as court, police station, fire station, educational, medical, public health and cultural institutions are also exempted from the levy of holding tax.

Section 132(4) of the said Act also exempts holdings from levy of holding tax if the annual value does not exceed sixty rupees. The system of exemption of such public institutions for payment of property taxes is also prevalent in the United States of America and such exemption is based on the following assumptions:

"The theory behind such exemption is that, such institutions perform functions, that would, in their absence, be performed at public expenses. The value of their services to the public, it is assumed, exceeds the amount the public loses from the remission of taxes.[7].

Rate of Levy

The holding tax is leviable at a rate not exceeding ten percent on the annual value of holdings.

Water tax and lighting tax are leviable at a rate not exceeding ten percent/five percent of the annual rental value of the holdings.

No municipal council can impose water tax where the council does not distributess water or where there is no water supply system. Similarly no lighting tax can be imposed if no street lights are provided. It is also provided in the Act that in fixing the rate, at which the water and lighting tax is to be imposed, regard shall be had to the principle that total net proceeds of the tax, together with the estimated income for payments for water or lighting as the case may be, supplied from the works for special contract or otherwise shall not exceed the amount required for making, extending or maintaining the water supply or lighting system as the case may be together with an amount sufficient to meet the proportionate amount of the cost of supervision and collection and the repayment of and payment of interest on any loan incurred in connection with any such supply or system".[8].

The latrine tax and drainage tax are leviable at a rate not exceeding ten percent of the annual value of the holding subject to the same conditions as are applicable to water and lighting tax.

Thus an urban local body which decides to impose all the above taxes at the maximum permissible rate may have to impose the taxes at 45% of the annual rental value of the holding (holding tax 10% + water tax 10% + lighting tax 5% + latrine tax 10% + drainage tax 10% = 45%) provided the local body fulfils all the conditions and restrictions prescribed for the imposition of all such taxes.

This study covering 31 urban local bodies revealed that holding tax was levied by 30 urban local bodies, water tax by 14 urban local bodies, lighting tax by 21 local bodies and latrine tax by 20 urban local bodies, whereas drainage tax was levied by 5 urban local bodies only. As such the local Governments which did not provide water supply system and drainage system did not impose the taxes, but there is no reason to justify the non-imposition of latrine taxes by the remaining 10 local bodies when they are spending huge amounts for cleaning the latrines. One Notified Area Council which was constituted in 1964 at Jaleswar has not levied any tax till now, even the holding tax has not been imposed by the Council. This obviously shows the unwillingness on the part of the local council to harness the given sources of revenue by imposing taxes.

Rate structure of different taxes

The rate of levy of different taxes by the urban local bodies shows that out of 30 urban local bodies only 3 have levied holding tax at the maximum rate of 10% of the annual rental value and two councils have imposed this tax at 2% of the annual rental value. Largest number of councils i.e., 7, have levied this tax at 5% of the annual rental value and the remaining local Governments have levied this tax at varying rates. Similarly out of 14 urban local bodies imposing water tax, 5 of them have imposed this tax at 2% and only one of them has imposed this tax at 8% of the annual rental value and, in case of others, the rate of levy varies from 1% to 7%. The position in respect of lighting tax is still discouraging. Out of 29 urban local bodies imposing this tax, 9 of them levy at 2% of the annual rental value against the maximum permissible limit of 5%, 7 of them at 3%, 5 of them at 4% and 3 of them at 5%. Even 5 urban local bodies levy this tax at the rate of 1% . Latrine tax has been imposed by 20 urban local bodies out of which only one institution levies the tax at the maximum permissible limit of 10%, 2 of them levy the tax at 1%, 6 of them at 2% and others between 3% to 9% . Drainage tax is levied by the lowest number of urban local bodies i.e. 5 who impose this tax at the rate of 1% to 5%. It cannot be said that the rate of service taxes has been kept low by the local bodies adhering to the condition imposed by the Act to restrict the levy of this tax to the required expenditure, because the examination of this aspect reveals that all the urban local bodies spend much more than what they receive from the imposition of these taxes.

The rate of property tax prescribed by the Act for urban local bodies in Orissa is not lower in comparison to the rate prescribed by the Acts of other States. For example the latest study conducted by the National Institute of Urban Affairs, New Delhi on the rate structure of different taxes in different States (unpublished work of the Institute) reveals that the maximum rate of property tax is 28% in Andhra Pradesh and 25% in Uttar Pradesh whereas the prescribed maximum limit in Maharastra is 17%. In Karnataka the rate is 17.5%. In Tamil Nadu the rate of property tax is perhaps the highest, being 32.5% and a separate rate is charged in case of water tax. The rate of property tax in Bihar is 40%. The Municipal Gazetteer Volume-I of West Bengal shows that the maximum prescribed limits of different taxes for urban local bodies of West Bengal are:- holding tax 10%, conservency tax 10%, lighting tax 3% and water tax 7.5%.

TABLE-III-4: Rate at which property tax is levied in different local bodies.

Rate at which each tax is levied	Number of local bodies				
	Nature of tax				
Percentage of the annual rental value	Holding tax	Water tax	Lighting tax	Latrine tax	Drainage tax
1	-	1	5	2	1
2	2	5	9	6	1
3	6	2	7	2	1
4	2	1	5	x	1
5	7	1	3	3	1
6	5	2	x	3	x
7	2	1	x	2	x
8	2	1	x	1	x
9	1	x	x	x	x
10	3	x	x	1	x
Total number of local bodies	30	14	29	20	5

Therefore the maximum rate prescribed for the urban local bodies in Orissa is the highest of all the States mentioned above. The actual working of the taxes as revealed from the analysis is more indicative of the intention to exploit these sources of revenue than the rate fixed by the Act. Most of the urban local bodies in Orissa levy these taxes at a very low rate which adversely affects the revenues of these institutions. The urban local bodies have obviously taken the advantage of the lacuna in the Act. Unlike Acts of other States the minimum rate of taxation has not been prescribed in the Orissa Municipal Act, 1950. The municipal councils in Orissa have intentionally levied taxes at low rates.

Such a statutory minimum rate of 10% of house tax, 2 percent of lighting tax and 5 percent each for water and sewerage tax was recommended by the Rural-Urban Relationship Committee (1966) in their report (p.96).

Basis of levy of taxes

The yield from any tax depends not only on the rate but on its assessment and efficient administration. The administration of property tax requires specialised training, skill and ability of high order on the part of the assessors. In India the tax on property is on the owner whereas in England it is on the occupier. In England the rate is calculated at an amount in the pound on the "rateable value of each 'hereditament". (This is a technical term used to describe each separate rate assessment, e.g., house, shop, office.) The system of rating is based on both the theories of taxation i.e. ability to pay and payments for benefits received. The valuation of properties for rating purposes takes three values into consideration, gross, net annual and rateable. " The best method of calculating gross value for commercial and domestic properties is to ascertain the rent which would be offered in a free market assuming that there were no legal restriction upon the rents which could be charged e.g. restriction under the Rents Acts".[9] In United States of America, the taxable value is the price which a property would bring in a free market whereas in England it is based on the argument that it is taxable because it can bring rent to the owner. "Hence the taxable value is the rent which property would fetch in a free market".[10] The Orissa Municipal Act prescribes that the levy of property taxes in the urban local bodies should be assessed on the annual value of holdings. "'Holdings' mean land held under one title or agreement and surrounded by one set of boundaries".[11] The annual value of a holding is determined on the gross annual rental, at which the holding may reasonably be expected to let, less a deduction, in case of buildings only, of fifteen percent of such annual rent and the said deduction shall be in lieu of all allowances for repairs or on any other account whatsoever.

Holdings with buildings which are not intended for letting or for residence of the owner himself, the annual value of such holding is deemed to be an amount which may be equal to but not exceeding 7.5% of such actual cost of construction of the building which can be ascertained or estimated in addition to a reasonable ground rent for the land comprised in the holding. The provision in the Orissa Municipal Act regarding assessment of taxes on annual rental value is analogous to the British system and similar system is prevalent throughout the country.

It will not be desirable to ignore the recommendation of Taxation Enquiry Committee, 1953 and Local Finance Enquiry Committee of 1951 in this regard. Both the committees favoured continuance of rental value method of assessment of property on the ground that "The fixation of rental value of residential and rented out buildings which form the bulk of the buildings in towns and cities, is simpler than the determination of their capital value. Further, capital values of properties fluctuate to a more significant extent than rental value. The levy of the tax on actual reasonable rent is levied on the actual or potential income from the property and to that extent is a more equitable method of taxation than one based on capital value".[12] The Committee of Ministers on Augmentation of Financial Resources of Urban Local Bodies also ultimately agreed that it is not necessary to make an outright departure from the present system. Thus the practice followed in India has the sanction of celebrated authorities behind it. Mrs. U.K.Hicks observes: "if renting is substantially prescribed, it is agreed that annual value is the basis, because really everything has a rent, while sales may be infrequent.".[13]

Machinery for assessment

The crux of the problem of assessment is the determination of the annual value of the holdings. In this connection it was pointed out by the State Municipal Finance Commission that "In determination of annual value, a lot of favouritism, nepotism, corruption and fraudulent methods are adopted. As a result people of position and means escape payment of their due share of the tax, whereas the poorer sections are forced to pay relatively more".[14]. With a view to avoiding all such malpractices and to ensure impartiality and independence in the matters of assessment, the Taxation Enquiry Commission, (1953), the Local Finances Enquiry Committee (1951) and the Rural-Urban Relationship Committee (1966) recommended the setting up of a central valuation organisation under a full time valuation officer. "Centralised assessment offers an uncomplicated and ef fective means of obtaining uniformly high standard assessment throughout the State, by the use of professional staff following standard methods of procedures under central direction".[15] These recommendations have been implemented by some State Governments and assessment of taxes has been conducted by Valuation Officers in Rajasthan, West Bengal, Assam, and Andhra Pradesh.

The Municipal Acts of different States assign the responsibility of assessment on the Executive Officers of the Municipal Councils. Similar provisions exist in the Orissa Municipal Act, 1950 regarding assessment of taxes by the Executive Officer. But Section 142 of the said Act provides for the establishment of a valuation organisation with a Valuation Officer for assessment of property taxes only. The provision was made in the Act in 1968 in the light of the recommendation of the Orissa Local Body (Urban) Administration Enquiry Committee of 1963. Government of Orissa have set up a valuation organisation in the State in 1970 under the administrative control of the Director, Municipal Administration. The duty of the organisation is to determine the annual value of all holdings within a municipality (after making enquiry in the prescribed manner) and prepare a valuation list in respect of each municipality and invite objection from the persons interested to file objection within sixty days from such publication. The valuation officer shall finalise the list of valuation of holdings after hearing the objection and views and send it to the council for their adoption. The Municipal Council is to decide the percentage at which a holding shall be assessed for holding tax and other service taxes.

Mode of assessment

As indicated earlier, the only basis for assessment of all such taxes (holding, latrine, light, water and drainage) is the determination of annual value of holdings. This task is entrusted to the Valuation Officer and the Valuation Organisation has adopted certain principles for determining the annual rental of holdings.

The local bodies of the State have been classified into four categories on the basis of growth potential. The area in each local body is again divided into three categories according to the location of the area based on the community facilities available to the area.

The holdings in each area are classified under two categories as major use or other use: major use implying use by the owner for domestic purposes. As such, each town irrespective of the category it belongs to has different types of areas according to its location and again each area has two categories of holdings. The Valuation Organisation has prepared a rate chart for determining the annual rental value of the holdings.

The rate arrived at in the chart is based on the schedule of rate of 1964 of State Public Works Department. A building has been divided into four parts - roof, wall, floor and amenities. Rates have been provided for pucca, pucca-kutcha and Kutcha holdings. This rate is arrived at by taking 7 1/2% of the rate provided in the schedule of rate of 1964. The rental value of the building is arrived at by first ascertaining the plinth area of the building and then multiplying the rates provided in the chart (the rate applicable to the building as per its location and then whether for major use or minor use - as different rates exist for such categories of buildings) with the plinth area. A deduction of 15% is allowed towards repair and maintenance of the building and 5% is added towards the cost of land. Thus the rental value of the building is arrived at. After final publication of the list of holdings with their rental value, the Municipal Council is to determine the rate at which the holding, light, latrine, water and drainage tax is to be assessed.

As a result of the establishment of a Valuation Organisation, the valuation of holdings in different urban local bodies of the State which were long due for revision of their assessment were taken up. But the Organisation took more than 5 years to prepare the valuation list of 71 urban local bodies. The fact remains that the final valuation of major urban local bodies like Cuttack, Puri and Berhampur is yet to be completed. The reasons attributed are mostly political. As the major sources of revenue for the urban local bodies i.e. the property tax, the assessment of which largely depends upon the determination of the rental value of the holdings the revenue suffers very badly due to the discretionary decision of the Municipal Council which ultimately fixes the rate at which the tax shall be assessed. The Orissa Municipal Act, 1950 also does not prescribe the minimum rate to be fixed for such taxes. On the other hand the Act prescribes the maximum limit. Therefore the efficiency of the Valuation Organisation in properly determining the rental value of holdings and bringing new holdings under assessment loses its effect due to the adoption of lower rates for the assessment of taxes. A typical example is found in the assessment of holdings of Sunabeda Notified Area Council which was done by the Valuation Organisation. The holdings brought under assessment rose from 1412 to 7418 and the new assessment was given affect to from 1.4.73. The rate of holding tax was fixed by the Council at 2 1/2% of the rental value of holdings. The rate prior to revision was 10 percent of the annual rental and the demand against holding tax was Rs. 2,27,336.00 per annum, and by fixing the rate at 2 1/2%, the amount of demand came to be the same. Had the local council continued to levy the tax at 10 percent of the annual rental value, the yield of holding tax would have been four times more than the current demand. It cannot be said that by lowering the rate of levy the position of collection improved as the percentage of collection of property tax in 1971-72 (at the old rate) was 72.88 percent and in 1975-76 (at the new rate) it came down to 58.10 percent.

The adoption of lower percentage of rates after valuation by the Valuation Organisation is numerous. A few instances are cited below.

These cases indicate that had the old rates continued after the revised valuation they would have fetched larger revenue to these local bodies to improve their financial stability. Again in some of the Municipalities which had higher potentialities and where the inhabitants could afford to pay higher rates of taxes, the rates were deliberately kept low to give benefit to the rich and influential house owners since they could mould the opinion of the Municipal Councils to adopt a low rate. It was observed by the State Municipal Finance Commission, Orissa, 1975 in their Report at page 38, that Sambalpur Municipality, inspite of Government's repeated instruction during the period from March 1964 to December 1974 to impose holding tax, refused to impose this tax. This tax was imposed from 1.4.75 only at a rate of 2 1/2 percent. The rate of tax was invariably kept low since the minimum rate was not prescribed by the Act. The Municipal Acts of other States have prescribed both the minimum and maximum rates for such taxes.

Name of the urban local body	Rate before revision	Amount of demand (Rs.)	Rate after revision	Amount of demand (Rs.)
1. Jeypore Municipality	6	85297	4	1,34,805
2. Khariar Road N.A.C.	7	46321	3	19,002
3. Titilagarh N.A.C.	10	56016	5	85,639
4. Phulbani N.A.C.	8	20835	5	24,555
5. Nayagarh N.A.C	10	22305	6	23,470
6. Bhubaneswar N.A.C.	7	886874	5	14,98,074
7. Suruda N.A.C.	8	17573	5	22,304

Revision of assessment

A frequent revision of the value of property is necessary in order to secure a larger volume of revenue consequent upon the rise in the value of property due to rise in prices and other factors. According to Section 146 of the Orissa Municipal Act, 1950, the valuation list should be revised in every five years. Such revisions were never done and some valuation lists dating from the year 1961-1962 are still current. As a result even a 40 percent rate on the basis of valuation of 1961-62 became as good as ten percent rate of 1975-76. Such non-revision of taxes usually puts the local bodies to a great loss. The details given below indicate that revisions were effected even after a lapse of twenty years and there are some local bodies where no assessment has been effected from the date of their constitution.

Therefore, due to non-revision of assessment the urban local bodies lose a substantial portion of their legitimate earnings. Towns like Cuttack, Puri and Berhampur have developed very fast due to growth of commerce and industry. Many new areas have been included in the municipal areas and some areas which were undeveloped have been developed due to growth of infrastructure (transport, communication, water supply, sanitation etc.). Development of new areas within the town and the development of existing areas have increased the number of buildings. Such constructions obviously escape assessment due to non-revision of the assessment and the local authorities lose quite a good deal of revenue. It was found in respect of Bhubaneswar Notified Area Council that vast areas were not covered by assessment even though the areas contained large holdings and were liable to pay Municipal Taxes. Vani Vihar (where Utkal University is located) was included in the municipal area from 1971. The area contains 315 residential holdings and about 50 non-residential holdings (office, library, class room, laboratory etc). But they were assessed for taxes only in 1977 by the Valuation Organisation.

	Name of the Municipality	Date of last assessment	Date of revision/ assessment
1.	Balasore Municipality	1954-55	1.7.75
2.	Sonepur Municipality	Not assessed	1.4.73
3.	Cuttack Municipality	1961-62	Not yet revised
4.	Jajpur Municipality	1951-52	1.4.76
5.	Talcher Municipality	1955-56	1.4.75
6.	Berhampur Municipality	1953-54	Not yet revised
7.	Jeypore Municipality	1961-62	1.4.76
8.	Baripada Municipality	1953-54	Not revised yet
9.	Puri Municipality	1953-54	Not yet revised
10.	Sambalpur Municipality	Not assessed	1.4.77
11.	Deogarh Municipality	1963-64	1.4.77
12.	Jaleswar N.A.C.	Not assessed	Not assessed yet
13.	Gopalpur N.A.C.	1961-62	1.10.75
14.	Suruda N.A.C.	Not assessed	1.4.77
15.	Khariar Road N.A.C.	1967-68	1.4.76
16.	Joda N.A.C.	1964-65	1.4.74
17.	Bhubaneswar N.A.C.	1953-54	1.4.77
18.	Nayagarh N.A.C.	1953-54	1.4.76
19.	Rairangpur N.A.C.	1962-63	1.4.76
20.	Rourkela (C.T.) N.A.C.	1965-66	1.7.76

The Central Government buildings are not liable for levy of holdings taxes, but are subject to levy of service taxes. Government of India in the Ministry of Finance in their letter No. 4(7)-65 dated 29.3.67 decided that levy of service taxes in respect of Central Government buildings should be enforced on the rental value of such properties and the rental value may be determined on the basis of 9 percent of the capital value. This decision was not given effect to by most of the urban local bodies in Orissa. There are a large number of Central Government buildings in the Bhubaneswar Municipal area. The Municipal authorities assessed these holdings for payment of service taxes amounting to Rs. 6,39,308.00 but no central authorities paid the service taxes excepting the Central Public Works

Department, Bhubaneswar.

In England, the work of assessment of property taxation rests on an independent and impartial body called 'Board of Inland Revenue'. Professor Gyanchand in his book 'Local Finances in India', (p.110), observed : "The creation of a Provincial Valuation Department is a measure of financial reform which will help and not hinder the growth of Local Self Government in India". The Government of Orissa rightly acted in appointing a Valuation Officer in the establishment of valuation organisation due to which there has been some increase in the revenues of almost all the local bodies where valuation of holdings has been undertaken by this organisation. With the removal of certain deficiencies as noted under, the organisation could successfully function as an instrument to augment the revenue of the urban local bodies.

i. The rate chart adopted by the organisation for valuation of properties are based on the Public Works Department Schedule of Rate of 1964. The Public Works Department has revised and re-revised the schedule of rate in 1972, in 1975 and in 1979. The cost of construction of a building as per Schedule of Rate of 1964 was around Rs. 18/- per sq.ft., which became almost Rs. 32/- as per the schedule of rate of 1972 and Rs. 40/- as per schedule of rate of 1975 and has become Rs.55/- in the Schedule of Rate of 1979. But the organisation continued till 1979 to work out the valuation at the rate of 1964 even though the rates have risen very sharply in the meantime. Thus the valuation based on the old rate is much less than what it would be at the current schedule of rates.

ii. There is a provision under the rules that the cost of valuation shall be borne proportionate to the expenditure of the organisation by the urban local bodies. We have observed that there is an abnormal delay in finalising the valuation of properties. The dilatory process does not only delay the receipt of more revenue to the urban authorities but it also increases the cost of local bodies. Thus in the process the burden of local authorities increases.

iii. The hearing of objections against the valuation resting on the Valuation Officer may not always meet the ends of justice. As such, appeals against such valuation should lie with some judicial authority and not on an administrative officer in the rank of Additional District Magistrate.

iv. Finally a few instances which are cited below show that the Valuation Organisation is not impartial. This tarnished the image of the organisation.

a. In the case of valuation of holdings in Jeypore Municipality on a public complaint, the Government in Urban Development Department ordered in 1975 asking the Executive Officer of the said Municipality to reassess the holdings under section 147 of the Orissa Municipal Act, 1950. On reassessment of holdings the tax rose to Rs. 1,903,712.00 from Rs. 85,300.00. Consequently the amount of other service taxes also increased in comparison to the amount arrived at on the basis of earlier valuation made by the valuation organisation. It may be noted that the rate of assessment was not changed.

b. In Bhubaneswar Municipality the valuation made by the Valuation Organisation reduced the annual rental of certain buildings. But this aspect was overlooked and consequently the taxes receivable by the Municipality were reduced. A few such instances are as follows.

c. As indicated earlier the area in each town is divided into 1st order, 2nd order and 3rd order locality according to its situation. This classification is done by the Valuation Organisation. Such classification is the basis of determining the rate of valuation of the property. There are of course certain criteria for such classification but the use of discretion and other considerations cannot be ruled out.

Name of the building	Amount of tax assessed by Municipality earlier	Amount assessed by the Valuation Organisation
1. State Museum	Rs. 19000.00	Rs. 9000.00
2. Rabindra Mandap	Rs. 6854.00	Rs. 2394.00
3. Tribal Research Bureau	Rs. 1316.00	Rs. 823.00
4. Sub-jail	Rs. 1499.00	Rs. 907.00

Other Taxes

In the foregoing paragraphs the potential sources of receipts have been discussed. Other sources of taxation of the urban local bodies as provided in the Act are discussed below.

i. **Profession tax**

Property tax imposes the tax burden on the owners of property in a municipal area which may leave out persons without property. But the imposition of profession tax along with property tax facilitates the municipality to tax almost all the residents of an urban local body. Profession tax is a levy on the income. To facilitate levy of this tax by the local bodies, the Constitution of India under Article 276 makes provision for the same. However the Article imposes a limit on the levy of such taxes. Levy of this tax should not exceed Rs. 250.00 per annum unless a higher rate was in force prior to the commencement of the Constitution.

The Orissa Municipal Act, 1950 (Sec 189) provides for the levy of a Profession Tax if the Council by resolution so decides. The tax is leviable on every company, firm, association or Hindu undivided family transacting business in the municipality area and every individual who exercises a profession, out of calling or transacts any business or holds any appointment whether within or outside the municipality area but resides in the Municipality. Rule 507 of Orissa Municipal Rules, 1953 prescribes rates for levy of such taxes on different slabs of income. No income below Rs. 3600 per annum is taxable. For annual income of Rs. 3600 to Rs. 4000, Rs.12 is fixed as Profession tax and additional Rs. 3 for any subsequent thousand up to Rs. 6000 and additional Rs. 6 more for every subsequent thousand up to Rs.14,000 and Rs.125 for more than Rs. 14,000. Inspite of all the importance attached to this tax, only one Notified Area Council i.e., Padmapur out of 31 Urban Local Bodies covered by our study imposed this tax. The receipt from this tax was Rs.2055, Rs.2477 and Rs.3358 during the year 1965-66, 1971-72 and 1975-76 respectively. The percentage of yield from this tax was negligible.

This source of taxation needs improvement in the light of the recommendations made by the Orissa Municipal Finance Commission in their Report of 1975 and the levy of this tax should be made compulsory for all the urban local bodies.

ii. Tax on carriage, carts and other animals

Section 176 of the Orissa Municipal Act, 1950 provides for the levy of such taxes by the Council at the maximum rate provided in the third schedule appended to the Act. The Schedule prescribes a maximum rate of Rs. 20 each per annum for 4 wheel carriages run by horses, Rs.10 each for 2 wheel vehicles including cart, Jhatka and Tangas excluding bicycle, Rs. 4 each for bicycle, Rs. 4 for each rickshaws, Rs.8 each per cycle rickshaws and horses and Rs.2 each for bulls or buffaloes and Rs.1 each for pigs, goats or sheep.

The Orissa State Municipal Finance Commission's Report of 1975 collected data for revenues received out of this tax and recorded at page 41 of their report that 79 urban local bodies of the State imposed this tax. Their receipt out of this source amounted to Rs.4,25,564 against 100481 numbers of carriages, carts and animals involved. As such the total income out of this tax is very negligible. The rate of tax is kept low and yet the evasion is rampant. To improve this source of revenue the rate schedule should be revised to keep pace with time and steps should be taken to check evasion. On the whole with the introduction of modern transport system, hand drawn rickshaws and carts, Jhatkas and Tangas are losing their importance in a town life and hence taxation on such carriages etc. is losing its importance.

iii. Poll Tax

No poll tax is imposed by any local body in Orissa even though there is provision in the Act for levy of such a tax at the rates prescribed therein. However the Orissa State Municipal Finance Commission has recommended to abolish this tax from the provision of the Act. Since poll tax is inequitable there is no harm in abolishing this tax.

iv. Terminal Tax

This tax is not levied by any Municipality/Notified Area Council in Orissa, but is levied by one Lodging House Fund, Puri which gives a portion of its collection to Puri Municipality for improving the arrangements for pilgrims who visit Puri town in thousands every year.

v. Education Tax

Education tax may be levied by any Council with the previous sanction of the State Government at a rate not exceeding 25 percent of the holding tax and profession tax under Section 364 of Orissa Municipal Act, 1950. Out of 31 urban local bodies examined in the study, only one Notified Area Council i.e., Khariar Road levied this tax @ 15% of the holding tax. The Notified Area Council received Rs. 8618-00 during the year 1975-76 from this source of revenue. Every urban local body maintains its own educational institutions and incurs huge expenditure every year from its own resources. It is, therefore, necessary that this tax should be levied and improved by all the urban local bodies.

Fees and Fines

The urban local bodies are empowered under the provisions of the Orissa Municipal Act, 1950 and Orissa Municipal Rules, 1953 to collect fees on markets, slaughter of animals, registration of dogs, vessels, industries and factories, offensive and dangerous trades, fees from the students of educational institutions run by the local authorities, taxi stand and cycle stand.

It has been observed by the Orissa State Municipal Commission in their Report of 1975 that the urban local bodies have not utilised their taxing powers fully and there is plenty of scope to raise resources substantially by making the best use of them. For this purpose they have to improve the machinery for assessment of taxes and fees. In case of fees, no effective demand is made nor any proper assessment list is prepared. No effective measures have been taken to assess the amount recoverable on this score. The rates of certain fees are quite old and need revision. If proper steps are taken in this direction, the fees will prove to be a substantial source of income for the urban local bodies of the State.

New Sources of Revenue

It has been observed by the Local Finances Enquiry Committee, 1953, Rural Urban Relationship Committee, 1966, Orissa State Municipal Finance Commission, 1975 that resources at the disposal of urban local bodies are not adequate to finance their growing requirements. The Orissa State Municipal Finance Commission have recommended for the imposition of the following taxes by the urban local bodies of Orissa to ensure their fiscal autonomy and safeguard against possible encroachment by the State Government.[16]

1. A show-tax on cinema and theatres.
2. Advertisement tax excepting on newspaper advertisements.
3. A surcharge on consumption of electricity.
4. Duty on transfer of property as surcharge on stamp duty.
5. Urban Land Tax (levy in increments of urban land value).
6. A general conservancy tax.

Discussion in the preceding paragraphs has shown that the urban local bodies are not willing to fully utilises the tax powers given to them. They have levied different taxes at low rates. No sincere efforts have been made for their proper assessment and collection. No suitable machinery for administration of such taxes exists in any Municipality/Notified Area Council. In such a context it will be futile if additional powers of taxation are given to them because they will rarely bring additional revenue to the local fund. It is therefore desirable to take steps to properly utilise the available tax sources instead of providing additional power of taxation.

Collection of Tax and fees

Low assessment of taxes and fees is the cause of weak finances of urban local bodies. Low percentage of collection of such taxes and fees aggravates the weakness. Poor standard of services by the urban local bodies is said to be the cause of reluctance on the part of people to pay taxes. On the other hand, poor collection of taxes is the cause of poor services. This is a vicious circle. The efficiency of tax collection depends largely on the character of the tax collectors, which is not always above reproach. Since corruption has become almost chronic in every walk of life, the Urban Local Governments are no exception to this. The audit reports of Local Fund Audit Organisation bear testimony of rampant corruption prevailing in different urban local bodies.[17] The reports describe several methods adopted by the persons in charge of collection of taxes and fees. The cashiers who are supposed to receive the taxes collected by the tax collectors also connive with the tax collectors and do not take proper account of such collections (they are supposed to check the collection from the receipt books) before receiving the amounts collected. The tax collectors do not deposit the amount in the municipal fund and retain the same for months together. Out of the total collection made, a portion of the amount is deposited and the balance is kept by the tax collectors. The Rural Urban-Relationship Committee in their report, 1966, sadly commented on the poor state of collection of taxes by the urban local bodies and suggested measures to improve the method of collection by giving adequate legal powers to the Executive Officer to collect the arrears and by introducing incentives in the form of rebates for prompt payments and disqualifying persons having arrears to contest in municipal elections. They even suggested to dissolve the municipal councils in case of habitual defaults in collecting higher percentage of taxes.[18]

The position in respect of 1961-62 shows that out of 16 urban local bodies, 4 collected between 21 to 30 percent of the demand,2 collected between 31-40 percent, 5 between 41-50 percent and the remaining 5 obtained collection between 51 to 60 percent. None of these local bodies collected taxes beyond 60 percent. During 1965-66 out of 26 urban local bodies, only 2 of them collected taxes and fees beyond 60 percent. In most of the cases, the collections were found to be very poor, below 10 percent in respect of 2 urban local bodies, between 11-20 percent in respect of 3 urban local bodies, between 21-30 percent in case of 4 local bodies and between 31-40 percent in case of 10 local bodies. The number of urban local bodies collecting between 51-60 percent was 4 against 5 during the previous year.

The collection made by Brajarajnagar Notified Area Council during the year 1975-76 was 98.67 percent being the highest amongst all urban local bodies whereas the percentage of collection of Sonepur Municipality being only 5.46 percent was the lowest. There was a remarkable improvement in the rate of collection of Angul Notified Area Council, it being 91.39% during the year 1975-76 against the previous rate of 45.05 percent in 1971-72 and 37.00 percent in 1965-66. Similar was the position in respect of Jeypore Municipality. The growth rate in the trend of collection in Sunabeda Notified Area Council is significant as 60.26 percent was collected during 1975-76 against the previous percentage of collection of 18.60 and 45.27 during the years 1965-66 and 1971-72 respectively. The Rairangpur Notified Area Council, Khurda Notified Area Council, Nayagarh Notified Area Council, Suruda Notified Area Council and Hinjilikatu Notified Area Council and Deogarh Municipality also showed better trend in collection during the year 1975-76 in comparision to their performance in previous years. It is significant that the rate of collection of the following institutions declined during the year 1975-76 in comparison to previous year. They are Cuttack Municipality, Balasore Municipality, Joda Notified Area Council, Talcher Municipality, Khariar Road Notified Area Council, Titilagarh Notified Area Council, Padmapur Notified Area Council, Berhampur Municipality.

A close analysis of the trend in collection disclosed that due to a special drive launched by the Executive Officer of Jeypore Municipality, the percentage of collection went up to 79.96 percent. The Municipality was divided into 3 zones keeping each zone under a special squad of tax-collector with one tax Daroga as the head of the squad. The team made door to door collection of arrears including current demands. In case of difficulties, the Executive Officer appeared on the spot. He has also introduced a system of issuing Pass Book to each tax payer for recording any payment of tax to avoid fraud and manipulation. The Tax collectors who achieve higher percentage of collection are rewarded with merit certificates and promotion in deserving cases. In Brajaraj Nagar Notified Area Council, most of the holdings belong to one Paper Mill. The high rate of collection is due to payment of arrear taxes by the Paper Mill. In other urban local bodies, personal approaches and initiatives on the part of collection staff including Executive Officers have obtained better results. Bigger Municipalities like Cuttack, Puri and Sambalpur have taken an indifferent attitude with the result that the tax-administration in those towns is chaotic for which the Municipal Council owes heavy responsibility.

According to rule 200 of Orissa Municipal Rules, 1953, the council is required to review the position of collection of different taxes and fees and suggest measures for the collection or remission of arrears. To facilitate such review by the Council, the Register of Demand and Collection as prescribed in rule 178 of the Municipal Rules is to be maintained in each Municipality and brought up-to-date before the close of the year. The Executive Officer is required to prepare an arrear list of taxes periodically and always at the end of the year from the Demand and Collection Register duly checked with Tax Collectors' ledger and the progress statement prepared as per rule 200 of the Municipal Rules. The rule makes the tax collector responsible for collection of taxes. The study discloses that this Register was rarely brought up-to-date by any urban local body in time. Thus the council had little opportunity to know the position of collection of taxes.

Due to inaction at all levels, huge amounts of taxes and fees remained uncovered and with the passage of time the dues became time barred. The position of total outstanding taxes and fees for all the urban local bodies of the State comes to Rs. 1,99,40,794 out of which Rs.54,21,965 have became time barred.[19] No legal action can lie for recovery of such a huge amount. Every year due to failure to effect timely recovery, heavy amounts of taxes and fees are getting time-barred and no coercive measures can be taken for recovery of these amounts. It is by persuasion, that the amounts, if not in full, atleast a part can be recovered. Thus the local bodies lose huge amounts due to lack of vigilance on the part of all concerned.

The earlier discussions reveal that the following factors are responsible for low rate of collection:

1. The Government does not pay timely service taxes in respect of holdings belonging to them leading to heavy arrears.

2. The staff for collection and supervision are inadequate to cope with the work.

3. The legal provisions in the Act are not sufficient to ensure prompt collection.

4. Appeals against improper assessment are not finalised

promptly.

5. Laxity on the part of the Municipal Council to enforce stringent measures like distress, warrant, sale by auction etc.

6. Unwillingness on the part of collecting agency to take prompt and timely action. The Collectors being local people are reluctant to enforce law against their neighbours. Their influence in the council precludes the council to take action against the officials who fail in their duty.

7. The period of limitation operates against collection (dues of the local body become time barred after 3 years due period).

8. Remission and writing off of taxes and fees by the Council due to accumulation of arrears.

The provision in the Orissa Municipal Act, 1950 regarding collection of taxes is quite progressive. It makes provision for payment of taxes quarterly (Sec 159(2)). There is provision for granting rebate not exceeding ten percent when the tax due is paid within 14 days. The Act also prescribes stringent measures in case of non-payment of taxes on issue of notice to levy warrant of distress and sale (Section 162) by the Executive Officer on the defaulting tax payer. The Executive Officer is empowered to apply to the Collector of the District for recovery of arrear tax dues when he fails to realise, as arrear of land revenue together with the cost (Section 169). In addition, the Municipal Council is empowered to sue a person for default in payment in a regular court of law. "The local bodies in Madhya Pradesh, Rajasthan and West Bengal lack the power to recover arrear of municipal taxes as arrear of land revenue. The Assam Municipal Act does not make tax on land and buildings as first charge on property. In the Municipal Act of Assam, Uttar Pradesh, Kerala, Rajasthan, West Bengal, the local bodies are not empowered to proceed against immovable property".[20]

Orissa Municipal Act, 1950 does not lack such provisions, but mere provision in the Act is not enough. The effectiveness of the provision depends largely on the alertness of the persons in the tax-administration to enforce these provisions. Going to court of law in volves expenditure and the procedure is lengthy and vexatious. What is more effective is door to door approach for collection. Throughout the country the rate of collection of taxes by the local bodies is poor due to various reasons discussed. Only in the Southern States of Kerala, Tamilnadu and Andhra Pradesh which have had a long tradition of State Municipal Commissioners as executive with full responsibility for collection have the revenues been collected to the extent of 90 percent.

It is necessary to eliminate the interference of elected members, who instead of pleading for relaxation, should, as a body, fix responsibility on the Executive Officer to ensure collection. Since the efficiency of tax collector depends upon the degree of civic consciousness of the people, apart from prescription of awards for high percent of collection, the punishment for delinquency in collection should be enforced. No body should escape the operation of law. The payment of grants-in-aid by the state should be linked with tax efforts. The council as a whole should be made responsible for the failure to achieve a high rate of collection. Provision should be made to collect taxes at the existing rates pending finalisation of appeals. The period of limitation should be changed from 3 years to 6 years. Each Tax Collector should be assigned a particular area of the municipality and the target for collection of taxes for each quarter should be fixed so that he would strive to achieve the target for a reward.

A system of pass book as in vogue in Jeypore Municipality (which was circulated by Government in their letter No. 27479 dated 25.9.76) may be adopted everywhere to create confidence in the tax payer that his taxes are taken to the books of accounts of the Municipality. A collection squad may make door to door collection. The people will be forced to pay the taxes for fear of loss of prestige. Besides, tax administration in bigger municipalities like Cuttack, Bhubaneswar, Puri and Berhampur should be kept under the control of a Revenue Officer having special training and skill in tax administration. In other urban local bodies, an officer of the Local Government subordinate to the Executive Officer should be kept in charge of tax administration instead of making the Executive Officer responsible for all acts of commission and omission. In some local Governments an officer is kept in charge of administration of Octroi.

In such municipality, the Officer in charge of Octroi should also look after the administration of other taxes and fees.

III
Octroi Tax

Octroi Tax - its growth

The word 'Octroi' is of French origin. Octroi is an indirect tax and is a levy on entry of goods into a local area for consumption, use or sale. It is now being levied by the urban local bodies of Gujarat, Maharashtra, Rajasthan, Karnataks, Punjab, Uttar Pradesh, Orissa, Jammu and Kashmir. No Octroi is levied in Andhra Pradesh, Tamil Nadu, Kerala and Bihar."The Government of Madhya Pradesh has recently abolished octroi by an ordinance issued on the 1st May, 1976". The revenue derived by the urban local bodies of different States from this source of tax are given below.

Name of State	Income through Octroi 1960*	At present
1. Karnataka	2.05 crores	9.12 crores (73-74)+
2. Uttar Pradesh	2.20 "	18.00 " +
3. West Bengal	-	20.60 " +
4. Maharashtra	5.65 "	54.00 " (74-75)+
5. Orissa	3.72 lakhs	2.35 " (76-77)**
6. Gujarat	4.53 crores	7.58 " (75-76)+ +

Source -
(*) Rural Urban Relationship Committee.
(+) Nagarlok October-December ' 77 Vol.IX (based on data collected by Ministry of Works and Housing, Government of India) p.39.
(+ +) Nagarlok (April-June '78) Vol.X, p.31.
(**) Memorandum submitted by Government of Orissa to 6th Finance Commission.

The above table shows that this tax as a source of revenue has gained in importance in different States. But the demand for its abolition has also gained ground rapidly. Almost all the Committees and Commissions who have examined the question of local finance have described the evils of Octroi and many have recommended its abolition. The Taxations Enquiry Commission while emphasising the evils of Octroi, however, recommended the local bodies to continue the levy of this tax. The Local Finance Enquiry Committee suggested that the 'terminal tax' be transferred to State-list from the Union-list in the Constitution of India to replace 'Octroi'. The Committee of Ministers on augmentation of financial resources of urban local bodies recommended gradual replacement of Octroi by a turnover tax or by a surcharge on sales tax or by a terminal tax which should be free from the evils of Octroi. While discussing on Octroi the Rural-Urban Relationship Committee observed that Octroi being an old tax people have got used to it. "It is a flexible source of revenue which the municipal bodies can exploit in case of need".[21] The Committee, however, recommended that there should be greater efforts to raise revenue for civic purposes from property and other taxes. They did not agree with the views of the Committee of Ministers for Augmentation of Resources of Urban Local Bodies to replace Octroi by terminal tax or a turnover tax. They recommended that loss of revenue due to abolition of Octroi may be compensated by allocation of the proceeds of vehicle tax and entertainment tax by the State Government and by the imposition of surcharge on sales tax and by increasing grants-in-aid. The Committee further recommended that the position arising from the abolition of Octroi may be examined by the Municipal Finance Commission to be set up by the State once in every five years.

The question of abolition of Octroi as recommended by several Committees and Commissions was examined by the Municipal Finance Commissions of some States. The Orissa State Municipal Finance Commission examined the position and observed: "It has the sanction of usage and has been in force for a long time with the necessary organisational staff to cope with the pattern of collection. As a matter of fact, neither rates of Octroi are high nor is it levied on through traffic. Rather the amount collected by this light duty is spent for providing marketing and trading facilities due to which trade prospers. Hence the question of abolishing octroi should be thought of in the long run after finding a suitable substitute".[22] The report of the Gujarat Octroi Enquiry Committee in its Report (1972) expressed that the "best alternative to Octroi is to levy a turnover tax at differential rates, which is collected at a single point or at two points in tune with the current sales tax system".[23] The Karnataka Municipal Finance Enquiry Committee in their Report (1975) favoured the Municipal turnover tax for replacing octroi. In spite of all the emphasis on the evils of Octroi and on its gradual replacement, it cannot be denied that the abolition of octroi will adversely affect the finance of urban local bodies.

Octroi as a source of revenue

The term 'octroi' as a tax does not find place in the Constitution of India, but the tax which is imposed as 'Octroi' is covered under entry 52 of the State list of the Seventh Schedule of the Constitution. Entry 52 provides for "Taxes on the entry of goods into a local area for consumption, use or sale therein". The tax is imposed by the Corporation, Municipalities and Notified Area Councils under the provisions of the Acts administering such local bodies. The Orissa Municipal Act, 1950, (Section 131 (1)(KK) provides for the levy of Octroi Tax on goods brought within the limits of Municipality for consumption, use or sale by the Municipalities and Notified Area Councils after obtaining approval of the State Government. The progress of levy of the tax in Orissa was however very slow till the year 1962-63. The Biswanath Das Committee in 1962 observed that only two municipalities out of 50 local bodies availed of this taxing power and recommended that other local bodies should make resort to levying this tax. The Sambalpur Municipality levied Octroi since 1905 under Central Provinces Municipal Act, 1903. Deogarh Municipality also levied this tax before 1936. Of the municipalities studied here only 3 urban local bodies out of 19, in 1961-62, imposed Octroi which increased to 6 in 1965-66 and to 12 in 1971-72 and reached 17 during 1975-76. The year-wise details given below show how the volume of receipts from this taxation has increased from year to year. The details showing the position in respect of income from Octroi in relation to receipts from own sources and in relation to total receipts of each urban local body during the years 1961-62, 1965-66, 1971-72 and 1975-76 are given in Annexure-VII.

Receipts of Octroi of the Sample Municipalities

Year	Amount received from Octroi	Percent of receipt to total receipt	No. of urban local bodies imposing Octroi
1961-62	3,65,281	5%	3
1965-66	17,01,712	11.51%	6
1971-72	48,30,485	14.60%	12
1975-76	1,28,42,828	25.61%	17

It is seen that the revenue from Octroi has increased considerably during the period 1961-62 to 1975-76. The volume of receipts increasing with the passage of time is mostly due to the growth of trade and commerce in and around the towns imposing such a tax. Of the local bodies imposing Octroi, it is found that receipts from Octroi during the year 1975-76 accounted for 30-40 percent of their revenues in respect of 7 urban local bodies and even 6 local bodies received between 40-50 percent of their revenues whereas during the year 1971-72 only 4 Urban Local Governments received 30-40 percent and only 2 between 40-50 percent. It is still encouraging to find that one local body received between 50-60 percent and another above 60 percent during the year 1975-76 whereas no local body received from 'Octroi' in the range of 60 percent during 1971-72 and 1965-66. Their receipts from Octroi during 1971-72 and 1965-66 were mostly within the range of 30-40 percent.

It has been invariably observed that the urban local bodies levying 'Octroi' did not make sincere efforts to improve the property-taxes as a major source of revenue. The reasons are obvious. 'Octroi' as an indirect form of taxation did not touch the tax payers directly whereas the enforcement of property tax involved unpopularity.

During the year 1961-62 only 3 Municipalities imposed Octroi Tax. They were Sambalpur Municipality, Sonepur Municipality and Deogarh Municipality. Sambalpur Municipality earned a sum of Rs.3.33 lakhs from Octroi which was 38.28% of the total receipts but received only a sum of Rs.71,988 from the property tax (latrine tax) which was only 8.38 percent of the total receipts. The Municipality did not impose any holding tax or even lighting tax etc. Sonepur Municipality did not impose any property tax during the year even though it received from Octroi Tax a sum of Rs. 21,992 which was 35.82 percent of the total receipts.

During the year 1965-66 the new urban local bodies which imposed this tax were Talcher Municipality, Jeypore Municipality and Berhampur Municipality. Of all these municipalities, Jeypore Municipality received a sum of Rs. 2 lakhs from Octroi which was 30.21 percent of the total receipts whereas receipts from property tax were only 15.19 percent, being one lakh of rupees. The receipts from Octroi in respect of Berhampur Municipality being Rs.8.01 lakhs were 33.07 percent and receipt from property tax being Rs. 6.02 lakhs was 24.85 percent of the total receipts.

Among all the urban local bodies which levied Octroi tax during 1971-72, the receipts of Khariar Road Notified Area Council from Octroi tax were 23.73 percent against the receipt of 10.07 from property tax. The remarkable increase in the percentage of receipts from Octroi tax in Brajaraj Nagar Notified Area Council which was 59.71 percent against 10.07 from property tax was mainly due to the industrial importance of the town having a large paper mill which had to pay a substantial amount by way of Octroi for the import of raw materials for the Paper Mill. The receipt from Octroi tax in Balasore Municipality during the year 1975-76 was 35.80 percent against 9.52 percent from property tax.

The position of receipts from Octroi in relation to property taxes discloses that receipt from property tax is invariably lower. The position in respect of all those institutions which have levied Octroi tax from 1961-62 onwards till 1975-76 shows that the rate of receipts from Octroi is much more than the rate of receipts from property taxes.

TABLE-III-5: Position of Octroi receipts during the years 1961-62, 1965-66, 1971-72 and 1975-76 in relation to total receipts and in relation to receipts from own sources.

	1961-62		1965-66		1971-72		1975-76	
Rate of percentage	Total receipts	Own sources	Total receipts	Own sources	Total receipts	Own sources	Total receipts	Own sources
1	2	3	4	5	6	7	8	9
0-5	-	-	1	-	2	-	-	-
6-10	-	-	-	-	2	2	-	-
10-20	1	-	-	-	3	1	4	1
20-30	-	1	1	1	3	2	6	1
30-40	2	-	4	1	1	4	6	7
40-50	-	1	-	2	-	2	-	6
50-60	-	-	-	1	1	-	1	1
Above 60	-	1	-	1	-	1	-	1
Total no. of urban local bodies levying Octroi	3	3	6	6	12	12	17	17

Octroi is levied at entry gates of a town fixed for the purpose and is manned by Octroi tax collectors and moharirs. Every vehicle carrying goods to the town for sale, consumption or use is detained at the gate for valuation of the goods for the purpose of taxation. The tax is imposed either on the value of goods or on their weight as per rate-chart prepared by the Council for the purpose and approved by the Government. These rates are not uniform throughout the State. But the system of Octroi administration in Orissa is not very much different from the system in vogue in other States.

It can yield adequate revenue to the local bodies if affective steps are taken to improve its administration. The Audit Reports of Local Fund Audit Organisation of the State cite numerous cases of maladministration, a few of which are cited below.

1. Transit passes are issued to trucks carrying goods outside the town and such passes are issued at the entry gate and are surrendered at the exit gate of the town. It was observed in Bhubaneswar Notified Area Council that transit passes which were granted to several trucks carrying different goods worth Rs.2,50,256 were not surrendered by them. It is suspected that goods carried by these trucks were sold, used or consumed inside the town by avoiding payment of Octroi Tax.

As per Council resolution of Bhubaneswar Notified Area Council a sum of Rs.2 was collected from each truck granted transit passes. In several cases money collected for granting transit passes was not deposited in the Council fund resulting in a misappropriation of Rs.368 (Audit Report No.7 of 1979-80).

2. Berhampur Municipality sustained a loss of Rs.78,280 due to non-realisation of Octroi tax in respect of goods covered by unsurrendered transit passes.

Octroi tax was collected at rates lower than the approved rate and thereby the municipality sustained a loss of Rs.7409.

Octroi tax collected was short credited by Rs.225 (Annual Report of 1970-71 - Local Fund Audit, Finance Department).

3. In Jajpur Municipality Octroi tax amounting to Rs.4893 was misappropriated by the collecting staff and the Octroi Superintendent. The amount was not accounted for in daily collection register and Cashier's Cash Book (Annual Report 1977-78).

4. By interpolating value of goods in assessing the Octroi tax, the Octroi staff of Bargarh Municipality misappropriated Octroi tax of Rs.2927 (Annual Report of 1977-78).

Objection against Octroi

Many Committees and Commissions have discussed the evils of Octroi and have recommended either its abolition or its substitution. The broad features of allegation against Octroi may be : summed up as follows

1. The form in which Octroi is levied in India offends all canons of taxation.
2. Levy of Octroi either on valorem basis or weight basis is not free from defect. Knowledge of price mechanism and experience and skill of assessment are not available with the staff entrusted with the responsibility. Consequently most of the items escape fair assessment.
3. Defective assessment gives rise to corruption and malpractices.
4. Indefinite detention of vehicles hampers free trade and commerce leading to un-necessary harassment.
5. The cost of collection is very high and refunds are cumbersome.
6. Low paid employees are given wide discretionary powers which are often misused and there is no effective supervision on their work.

The Indirect Taxation Enquiry Committee in their report - part-1 - October 1977 (24) examined the position of Octroi levied by urban local bodies and observed that the incidence of the tax is regressive, its administration is cumbersome and vexatious. The numerous barriers set up for collecting the tax at the points of entry affect the free trade. The cost of collection of the tax is disproportionately high in relation to revenue derived therefrom. Its economic impact encourages concentration of factories and industries in metropolitan areas to avoid Octroi for larger number of consumers.

The adverse comments against Octroi is common against all forms of indirect taxation. Most of the Committees and Commissions, however, agree to its continuance till suitable substitution is worked out as it is not possible to do away with such a major source of revenue for the local bodies. The L.K.Jha's Committee on Indirect Taxation observed:

"Some States argue that people have been accustomed to this and any new tax in its place may give rise to a good deal of resistance. Centre can be persuaded to make good the loss of revenue on account of abolition of Octroi".[25]

Replacement of Octroi

The Committees and Commissions suggesting alternatives to Octroi tax recommended the levy of (1), surcharge on sales tax or additional sales tax, (2) (a) Municipal Sales Tax (b) Municipal Surcharge on Sales Tax, (3) Municipal turnover tax, (4) other complementary levies. The Rural-urban Relationship Committee recommended the levy of surcharge not exceeding 25% of sales tax to replace Octroi, whereas the Committee on Augmentation of Financial Resources for Urban Local Bodies recommended the turnover tax. The B.P.Patel Committee on Municipal Finance in Maharashtra has recommended that Octroi should be replaced by a levy of turnover tax.[26] On the suggestion of the Road Transport Enquiry Committee (Keshkar Committee, 1967) to levy surcharge on sales tax, a separate municipal tax, a terminal tax, a turnover tax, the Orissa Municipal Finance Commission (1975) observed that the levy of sales tax would lead to variation of rates among urban local bodies which would result in disparities in price structure and increase the cost of collection. The Commission did not favour the idea of substitution of Octroi by a levy of other taxes.

As regards the suggestion of a surcharge on diesel, the L.K.Jha Committee on Indirect Taxation observed that 'it would have an adverse effect on cost and prices of goods'.[27] and suggested to State Government to improve the property taxation as a substitute to

Octroi. As the impact of Octroi falls on the people who come for shopping in towns, it affects the rural community. The Committee further observed that the 'cost of maintaining Municipalities should appropriately fall on the people who earn salaries, wages and profits in those areas, and not passed on to consumers outside.[28] The Committee's observation that resources for the upkeep of Municipal areas contingent on the abolition of Octroi should be found by the local authorities or by the State Government and not passed on to the Centre does not seem to be appropriate. The urban local bodies do undertake certain activities like water supply, education, slum clearance which are of national importance and as such the centre owes a responsibility to assist in financing such schemes. Thus the Central Government should share a part of the burden arising from the resultant financial imbalances of urban local bodies due to the abolition of Octroi.

In view of the facts discussed above it can be said that Octroi cannot be abolished without finding out an alternative for its substitution; because in a developing country like India, the collection of small amounts of direct taxes from the multitude of low income earners cannot replace an indirect tax like Octroi in which vast majority of people can be made to contribute something to the revenue without feeling the burden of it. Since there is a demand from all corners of the country in favour of its abolition, Orissa may have to abolish it, but its abolition would cripple the finances of the local Government and may consequently paralyse its activities. Therefore the recommendation of different Committees and Commissions including the recommendation of L.K. Jha Committee on Indirect Taxation to levy "a simple surcharge on sales tax or a turnover tax of one percent on commodities as recommended by Lakadawalla Committee for Uttar Pradesh"[29] seems to be more appropriate as an alternative to the abolition of Octroi. The other alternatives to the abolition of Octroi are the improvements in the system of property taxation, increase on the efficiency of municipal enterprises and augmentation of receipts from municipal properties.

NOTES AND REFERENCE

1. Lall, G.S. : *Financial Administration in India*,p.76.
2. Hicks, U.K. : *Development from Below*,p.276.

3. *Report on the Rural Urban Relationship Committee-* 1966,p.89.
4. *Report of the Task Force of planning and Development of Small and Medium Towns and Cities* - 1977,p.72.
5. *Report of the Rural-Urban Relationship Committee*,p.87.
6. Sinha, K.K. : *Local Finance in Developing Economy*,p.37.
7. Alderfer, Harold F. : *American Local Government & Administration*,p.383.
8. *The Orissa Municipal Act - 1950 - Sec. 133(1)(d).*
9. Hepworth, N.P. : *The Finance of Local Government*,p.59-60.
10. Sinha, K.K. : *Local Taxation in Developing Economy*,p.61.
11. *The Orissa Municipal Act - 1950 - Section 3(ii).*
12. *Report of the Committee on Augmentation of Financial Resources of Urban Local Bodies*, p.42-43.
13. Hicks, U.K. : *Development from Below*, p.360.
14. *Report of the State Municipal Finance Commission*, Orissa (1975), p.60.
15. *Report of the committee of Ministers Constituted by the Central Council of Local Self Government*, November,1963,p.39.
16. *Report of Orissa State Municipal Finance Commission*, 1975, p.56.
17. *Annual Report of Local Fund Audit Organisation of Government of Orissa*, 1976-77 & 1977-78.pp.16-17.
18. *Report of the Rural-Urban Relationship Committee*, 1966. p.99.
19. *Annual Report of Local Fund Audit Organisation of Finance Department*, Government of Orissa for the year 1976-77, pp. 15-16.
20. *Report of the Rural-Urban Relationship Committee*, 1966.p .99.
21. *Report of the Rural Urban Relationship Committee*, p.95.
22. *Report of Orissa State Municipal Finance Commission*, p.47.
23. Dutta, Abhijit : *Nagarlok* - October- December 1977,p.62.
24. *Report on Indirect Taxation Enquiry Committee*, 1977, Government of India, Ministry of Finance. p.1.
25. *Report of Indirect Taxation Enquiry Committee 1977*, Government of India, Ministry of Finance, p.58-59.
26. Satish Kumar : *Nagarlok* - October - December '77 Volume-IX Octroi - Can it be abolished. p.40.
27. *Report of the Indirect Taxation-Enquiry Committee*, Government of India, Ministry of Finance, 1977, p.59.
28. Report of the Indirect Taxation Enquiry Committee, Government of India, Ministry of Finance, 1977.
29. Report of the Indirect Taxation Enquiry Committee (Para 9-10) Government of India, Ministry of Finance, 1977, p.60.

FOUR

INCOME PATTERN OF MUNICIPAL BODIES: NON-TAX REVENUE

I

Income from Municipal Property and Enterprises

Non-tax sources

The non-tax source of revenue for municipal bodies in India can broadly be classified as (i)income from their own properties, viz, land and buildings, municipal markets, slaughter houses, ferries, parks, guest houses and dak bungalows (ii) income from municipal enterprises like gas, electricity, milk supply, transport services, tramways, water works, compost and such other trading activities and (iii) income from external sources such as sharing of tax receipts from the State Governments and grants from Governments and other authorities including loans.

Public utility services like electricity, water supply, gas,transport, milk supply have become indispensable for the citizens in an urban locality. In the words of N.P.Hepworth: "However,in regard to what are called the public utility undertakings- gas, electricity, water and transport - another reason for their acquisition by many local authorities was the need to control in the public interest a service with a monopolistic element".[1] In India, due to lack of resources and non-availability of technical personnel in the urban local bodies the prospect of taking up trading activities like gas, electricity and transport has become grim. In fact in our country the electricity is run by the Electricity Boards of different States. Transport services have become the monopoly of State Transport Organisation. Gas services are managed by private firms. Moreover running of trading activities like transport and water services depends largely on the size of the urban local body. But some municipal corporations in India i.e., Bombay, Poona, Delhi run bus transport service. But water supply is a very common undertaking taken up by most of the urban local bodies in India-mostly financed from borrowed funds. Apart from the financial difficulties, the proper accounting of such trading activities is of vital importance so as to know the actual cost of operation of such services with a clear distinction between the capital and revenue account.

Position in other countries

In the past local bodies in Madras, (now Tamil Nadu), Bengal and Bihar even maintained railways of their own from the operation of which they received income.[2] Similarly in England "Local authorities have, within about the last twenty years, lost two of their important (if not the most important) trading services namely gas and electricity.[3] It is also proposed to nationalise water services in England and it will no longer be a function of local authorities. The passenger transport service has also been taken away from local authorities. But in countries like the United States of America and Germany, the trading activities of local authorities have developed to a great extent bringing larger revenues to them. In the United States of America there is a decline in income from property taxation and the loss is compensated by income from "an increasing use of non-tax revenue of all types, special charges are levied for collection of refuse and garbage."[4] In Germany, the municipalities own and manage all industries concerning the necessaries, comforts and luxuries of the citizens. They render efficient services and derive large income out of such enterprises. The German Municipalities own estates outside the municipal limits and purchase fresh lands for providing recreation to the people and to earn revenue. "Berlin was an instance of great municipality owning agricultural estates of 45,000 acres in extent, manned almost wholly from the sewage of the city".[5] Municipalities in Japan earn a good deal of revenue from municipal enterprises such as street car, buses, trolly buses, water works and sewage.

Views and Suggestions

Municipal bodies in different States of our country derive their income from rent of municipal markets, lease of ferries, sale of composts, rent of guest houses, dak bungalows, and buildings and lands. The Rural Urban Relationship Committee considered the question of taking up trading activities by urban local bodies and recommended that "By and large municipal concerns should be run on commercial basis and be a source of revenue to the local body. The Committee would not like the municipal bodies to undertake enterprises involving risks or specialised knowledge."[6] The question was also raised by N.P. Hepwarth in his book 'The Finance of Local Government'. "The question of risk is most important. Should an organisation which is financed from the public purse put its funds at risk to profit".[7] Profits are legitimate springs of business enterprises and as such should not be objected to because the enterprises are managed by local bodies from local funds.

Income from the trading activities may reduce the tax burden on the localities. The local bodies can at least organise smaller trading activities like composing for the purpose of revenue from the human excreta, "which is fairly productive in some parts of India and not in others and can be made more productive every where".[8] Utilisation of soild waste and garbage collected in towns and cities as compost is a self paying proposition and the cost of production is highly economical. The Committee on Urban Wastes constituted by the Government of India (Ministry of Works and Housing), in their report (1975) estimated that with the urban population of over 109 million, it should be possible for the local authorities to prepare compost upto 18 million tonnes per year and the Committee recommended that the Central and State Governments and the local authorities should take steps to popularise compost through mass media, farmers' forums, co-operatives etc.[9]

The Municipalities in quest of additional non-tax revenues may invest funds in developing and acquiring sites and providing amenities like road, water supply, drain to sell at higher price. Another important paying proposition for the municipal authorities would be to take to marketing of milk with a view to improving the quantity and quality of milk in the local area and such schemes can be financed entirely from their own funds. The Orissa State Municipal Finance Commission in their Report, (1975), examined the question of remunerative schemes to be taken up by the urban local bodies and observed that "remunerative schemes which can be taken up by urban local bodies without much risk are shopping centres, market buildings, residential houses and petrol pumps".[10] The Commission suggested that separate accounts of such schemes should be kept and only profit should be reflected in the budget estimate. All the schemes should be run on business principles and should pay minimum dividend. The Fifth Five Year Plan also suggested that due to continuous and excessive rise in urban land values, the local authorities should allow land to be used as a resource for financing urban development.

Income from Municipal Property and Enterprises in Orissa

In the State of Orissa the urban local bodies received very insignificant proportion of their revenue from their own property and enterprises. A few Municipalities and Notified Area Councils took to Municipal enterprises like maintenance of guest houses, petrol pumps, milk trading and plying of auto rickshaws. No urban local body undertook the water supply scheme excepting Puri, Berhampur and Deogarh Municipalities. Other local bodies have water supply services but the schemes are managed by the Public Health Department of the State Government. The Local Governments levy water tax but the water rent is collected by the Public Health Department of the Government. The local bodies, however, bear the maintenance charges. Some urban local bodies undertake composting from garbage and human excreta. Pisciculture is also undertaken by the local authorities as a trading activity. The usual receipts from municipal property are on account of market rent, rent of land and buildings, lease of ferry ghats, receipts from pounds, town hall and slum quarters. Apart from the lack of managerial skill and improper accounting system, the greatest handicap to run such undertaking is finance. These schemes are mostly financed from loans from Government on payment of heavy interest. The revenues earned from such investments are hardly sufficient to meet the interest charges on borrowed funds.

Analysis of the income

The position of receipts from municipal property in respect of 31 urban local bodies of Orissa has been studied here. The amount received by each local body and the percentage of such receipts to total income of these institutions for the years 1961-62, 1965-66, 1971-72 and 1975-76 have been given in Annexure-VIII. Table IV-1 shows the total income of the sample urban local bodies in relation to receipts from municipal property. The table discloses that the volume of receipts during the years 1961-62 to 1975-76 on account of income from municipal property and enterprises has risen from 5.25 lakhs to 40.51 lakhs. The increase in volume of receipts during the years 1965-66, 1971-72 and 1975-76 in comparison to the base year 1961-62 is due to an increase of urban local bodies from 19 in 1961-62 to 27 in 1965-66 and to 30 and 31 respectively in 1971-72 and 1975-76.

The income from municipal property during all these years far exceeds the proportion of increase in number of institutions. The rise in volume of receipts is indication of the rise in percentage of receipts from this source to total income of the urban local bodies. During 1961-62, the receipts from Municipal property accounted for 7.18 percent of the total income of the urban local bodies whereas in 1965-66 they declined to 6.56 percent and there was a further decline of such receipts to 5.71 percent during 1971-72. However, the trend of decline was arrested during 1975-76 and the income was raised to 7.83 percent. 1975-76 was remarkable in all spheres of municipal activities because of the promulgation of emergency throughout the country. Conscientious efforts were made to collect the revenues of the municipalities with stringent measures which helped to increase the revenues. Moreover the source of revenue of municipal properties increased due to construction of many rental buildings and slum quarters during all these years.

Table IV-2 shows that most of the urban local bodies earned their non-tax revenue from municipal properties during the years 1961-62 to 1975-76 within the range of 5 -10 percent of the total revenue. During 1961-62, out of 19 urban local bodies, 10 institutions had their income between 10-20 percent. In 1965-66, out of a total of 27 institutions, 8 had income upto 5% and 7 between 10-20 percent and one each in the range of 20-30 and 30-40 percent. It was significant that the income of one urban Government exceeded 50 percent of its total income on account of receipts from its properties. During 1971-72, largest number of local bodies i.e. 12 received 5-10 percent of their income from their property. It was encouraging to note that 3 urban local bodies earned between 30-40 percent from this source of revenue in comparison to one in this range during 1965-66 and nine in 1961-62. But during the year 1975-76, 2 urban local bodies remained between 20-30 percent and three between 30-40 percent. The overall position during the year was encouraging. Efforts made during the year, if continued, would yield a good amount of revenue to the urban local bodies. The reason for low income in other years is attributable to the slackness of authorities in enforcing regular collection. Normally the rate of rent of land and buildings is kept low and properties are leased out. If the management of such properties is taken up by the local authorities, it would fetch high revenue. A few instances have been indicated later.

TABLE-IV-1: Income from Municipal property and enterprises during the years 1961-62, 1965-66, 1971-72 and 1975-76 of the sample urban local bodies.

Year of income	Total income of urban local bodies	Income from Municipal property	Percentage of income from municipal property to total income.
1961-62	7301114	525100	7.18
1965-66	14783687	969601	6.56
1971-72	33087577	1896581	5.71
1975-76	50090002	4050927	7.83

TABLE-IV-2: Percentage of income from municipal property and enterprises to total income.

Range of percentage	1961-62	1965-66	1971-72	1975-76
0-5	5	8	9	6
5-10	4	7	12	12
10-20	10	9	5	8
20-30	-	1	1	2
30-40	-	1	3	3
40-50	-	-	-	-
Above 50	-	1	-	-
Total	19	27	30	31

The percentage of receipts by Padmapur Notified Area Council in Sambalpur District and Hinjilcut Notified Area Council in Ganjam District was high. Their income from buildings and pisciculture was significant. Padmapur Notified Area Council earned Rs.25,065 towards rent of the market building during 1975-76 against an investment of Rs.13,500 in construction of the market building during 1973-74. Yield from lease of fishing tank was Rs.5125 per annum.Hinjilcut Notified Area Council also received Rs.48,375 towards the rent of market building against an investment of Rs.45,922. Old municipalities like Cuttack, Jajpur, Puri, Balasore whose percentage of receipt on this account is small have failed to earn proportionate increase in comparision to their investment in municipal properties due to slack administration. Another factor responsible for low income in Jajpur and Balasore municipalities is that trade and business do not prosper in these towns due to lack of development of infrastructure. Phulbani Notified Area Council and Sonepur Municipality come under this category of low income group. Bhubaneswar Notified Area Council has a low income from this source as the provision of market etc., is made by the Government and income from such sources goes to the Government fund.

Position in other States

The position of non-tax revenue of urban local bodies in other States is somewhat comparable to the position in Orissa. An analysis worked out by the National Institute of Urban Affairs on the basis of data collected by the then Ministry of works and Housing (now Urban Development) for about 400 urban local bodies in the country for the year 1975-76 indicates that the non-tax revenue accounted for 24.3 percent of the total income of these urban local bodies. The position of income from non-tax revenues of the urban local bodies in different States as given in the analysis is given below.[11]

1.	Maharashtra	1.57	percent
2.	Uttar Pradesh	6.83	-do-
3.	Karnataka	10.99	-do-
4.	Andhra Pradesh	8.30	-do-
5.	Madhya Pradesh	0.83	-do-
6.	Gujarat	6.51	-do-
7.	Rajasthan	9.26	-do-

However, the position in Orissa in comparison to other States is not bad, though there is plenty of scope to augment this source of revenue.

Position of income from municipal property

One should assess the prospect of municipal receipts from the source of non-tax revenue. These schemes are mostly financed from their own sources and in a few cases from the grants and loans obtained from the Government and other financing institutions. The investment in market buildings yields a good dividend and this scheme should be encouraged to augment the revenue receipts of urban local bodies. But slum quarters which are financed from loan funds do not fetch proportionate income due to fixation of low rent. Even though these quarters are meant for the occupation by the weaker sections of the society, they are mostly given on rent to businessmen, professional politicians and others. The scheme rarely serves the purpose for which it is designed under the patronage of the Central Government. In such a context the rent of such buildings should be fixed at market rent to yield higher revenue. For example, Gopalpur Notified Area Council constructed 4 numbers of slum quarters with a cost of Rs.61,200 from borrowed funds. Rent per quarter was fixed at Rs.40 per month. Thus four quarters fetched Rs.1920 per annum. The Notified Area Council repays the instalment of loans with interest @ $8\frac{1}{2}$%. The annual instalment of loan with interest repayable comes to Rs.10,600. This shows that the Notified Area Council bleeds through nose to repay the loan which is met from the tax revenue collected for meeting other expenses. The scheme has neither served its purpose nor has it yielded any revenue to the urban local body. On the other hand it has put the Notified Area Council to a loss. More or less the same condition prevails in almost all the urban local bodies and the position can be improved only by charging higher rent for occupation of these buildings.

Pisciculture has been taken up by 6 municipalities/Notified Area Councils out of 31 examined here. Pisciculture can be taken as remunerative. Manufacture of compost manure from waste and garbage has been taken up by some urban local bodies and is sold to public @ Rs.5 per ton, but the study reveals that in most cases, huge stock of compost is lying unsold for years due to want of demand. Unless efforts are made to popularise the use of compost as manure, this scheme should not be encouraged.

Municipal Enterprises

A few cases of trading activities and municipal enterprises undertaken by the urban local bodies in Orissa are discussed with a view to assessing the prospects of such undertakings in the State.

1. Berhampur Municipality constructed a Guest House in the heart of the town with an expenditure of Rs.4,87,380 and the building was completed in March 1966. The amount was spent from the loan obtained from the Life Insurance Corporation of India for which an interest of Rs.3,24,795 has been paid from the year 1963-64 to 1975-76. The local authorities leased out this building to a private party from 1.9.66 and received Rs.13,500 during the year. The local authorities undertook the management of the Guest House for two years during 1969-70 and 1970-71 and received Rs.35,975 during the first year and Rs.29,654 during the second year. It was again leased out from 1971-72 on an amount of Rs.26,400 and the lease amount was raised to Rs.35,520 during 1975-76 and again reduced to Rs.33,120-00 from 1976-77. The Central hall and dining hall of the Guest House were separately leased out on an annual rent of Rs.4520 in 1968-69 which was raised to Rs.7532 during the year 1977-78.Thus at present the Guest House brings a revenue of Rs.40,652 per annum to the municipal fund. Total income derived from the leasing out of the Guest House as well as from its own management during the period from 1966-67 to 1977-78 comes to Rs.4,06,119.

The Guest House has 11 single rooms and 12 double rooms with a central hall and dining room. The usual rent per double room is Rs.20 per day and for single room Rs.15 per day. Berhampur is a commercially important town and hardly any room in the guest house remains vacant. Thus excluding the renting out of the dining room and central hall, the room rent can bring an income of Rs.1,47,825 per annum. If the management of the guest house is taken over by the Municipality it would fetch an income of atleast rupees one lakh after meeting the establishment and other charges. Thus the municipal authorities lose around sixty thousand rupees every year by leasing it out.

2. Cuttack Municipality opened a petrol pump in January 1971 in the municipal area for sale of petrol and diesel to public. The Audit Report on the accounts of the municipality for 1975-76 discloses that the scheme earned a profit of Rs.1,48,570 during the years 1970-71 to 1974-75. The audit report however pointed out that the sale of diesel and petrol on credit resulted in a loss of Rs.3,74,210.[12]

3. Sunabeda Notified Area Council undertook the following enterprises :

a. A dairy farm was maintained since 1971 to supply milk among the inhabitants of the town and to earn a revenue to the local body. The total expenditure on the scheme from 1971-72 to the end of March 1976 was Rs.87,391 against which a sum of Rs.63,665 was received leading to a loss of Rs.23,726 due to mismanagement in production and sale of milk and supply of feed.

b. A fruit orchard was started and an expenditure of Rs.21,745 was incurrred till March 1976. The income from the orchard from the inception till March, 1976 was Rs.371, the resultant loss of income is attributable to sheer mismanagement.

c. Two auto-rickshaws were purchased with a view to providing transport facilities to the public and earning an additional revenue for the local body. A sum of Rs.43,997 was spent for the running and maintenance of these auto-rickshaws. The vehicles have been leased out from 1.11.74. The income from such vehicles till the scheme was abandoned was Rs.13,279 putting the Notified Area Council to a heavy loss of Rs.25,000.

d. It is, however, encouraging that the Notified Area Council opened a lodging house in its office campus for which a sum of Rs.21,286 was spent from 1972-73 to 1975-76 and an income of Rs.18,764 was derived. This scheme has a good prospect as there is hardly any private accommodation available in the town.

4. The Bhubaneswar municipality is located in the State capital. The municipality has constructed the largest number of slum build-

ings in the municipal area for providing housing facilities to the people belonging to weaker sections of the society. 148 quarters of different types were constructed during 1958-59 to 1961-62 with a loan amount of Rs.2,55,000. During 1974-75, another set of quarters of 37 numbers was constructed with an expenditure of Rs.2,98,163 from their own resources. In total 185 Quarters were constructed with a total expenditure of Rs.5,53,163. The rent of each quarter has been fixed at Rs.18 to Rs.23 depending upon the category of each building. The quarters are in occupation from the date of completion. There is an annual demand of house rent of Rs.45,924, but the recoveries are not regular and the house rent amounting to Rs.56,498 is outstanding at the end of March 1978 which includes an arrear demand of Rs.29,889.[13]

The quarters have been allotted to different categories of people who do not apparently belong to weaker sections of the society and cannot be categorised as slum dwellers. (The successive Five Year Plans of Government of India patronised these schemes for slum dwellers). The occupants of these quarters include 98 businessmen, 2 doctors, 1 pleader, 52 Government servants and 32 municipal employees. When the quarters are not available to people belonging to weaker sections of the society, there is no reason why the rent should be fixed at such low rates. The rent should be fixed at Public Works Department market rents so that the municipality should not meet the interest charges from the tax-revenue of the local body. The municipality has so far paid Rs.1,66,694 as interest towards the loan incurred during 1958-59 to 1961-62 amounting to Rs.2,55,000.

5. The Puri Municipality is one of the three urban local bodies in the State which manages its water works system for the town. The scheme of water supply was completed in 1935 with an estimated cost of Rs.10,30,000 and the management was entrusted to the Water Works Committee. The management was taken over by the Municipality in 1966. The Government have sanctioned a sum of Rs.38,02,000 out of which 2/3rd is grant and 1/3rd is loan for the improvement of the scheme to be borne by the Municipality. The work of improvement has been taken up by Public Health Department of State Government and is in progress since then.

The municipality levies water tax @ 7 percent of the annual

rental value of the holdings and receives water connection charges and collects consumers' bills towards water rent. It is interesting to find that against all annual demand of Rs.19,32,262, the municipality collected Rs.13,69,150-00 from the year 1964-65 to 1977-78 due to slackness on the part of municipal authorities in tax administration. (Even though the management was transferred to municipality from 1966, the water tax and water rent were collected from 1964-65.) A total expenditure of Rs.55,91,674 was incurred towards the maintenance of water works and the establishment cost during the same period. It is needless to comment on the economic viability of the scheme. The interest payable on borrowed funds has not been taken into account as the scheme for development is yet to be completed which may also yield an additional revenue by addition of new taps from the improved scheme. From the facts shown regarding the working of the scheme in Puri Municipality, it can be concluded that the scheme is not revenue earning and it adversely affects the finances of the urban local body. There is ample scope for increasing water rent and water tax.

Conclusion

The position as analysed above shows that it has become uneconomic for the urban local bodies to go in for any trading activities. Even the essential service like water supply is a losing concern. Other schemes like milk supply and transport services bring small revenues and run in loss. Compost scheme is economically viable provided sufficient awareness is created regarding its application as manure for agricultural purposes. The slum buildings as a welfare scheme for the weaker sections of the society have proved futile. They should be used as a general scheme for revenue purpose fixing rent at higher rate. The schemes that have attained some success are pisciculture and market buildings. The scheme for the provision of guest houses may also be suitably improved in areas having demand for the same. All such schemes should, as far as practicable, be financed from the sources of local bodies and not be subsidised by Government grants. Borrowing should be resorted to very sparingly to avoid payment of exorbitant rate of interest unless the scheme is economically viable to earn dividends. The non-tax source of revenue from municipal properties can be developed to yield higher revenue provided the systems of financing such schemes are properly regulated and Government assistance in rendering technical advice is assured. The urban local bodies should also improve measures to ensure proper assessment and collection of revenues from municipal properties.

II
Grants-in-aid

Need for grants-in-aid

The Local Government's functions are mostly local in character but some of their functions have also national importance. Such functions include provision of primary education, health services, water supply and communication etc. In the absence of local Governments performing such functions, the responsibility of providing such services would necessarily fall on the shoulder of the national or State Governments. This would cast a heavy burden on the State or national exchequer. When the local Governments discharge such responsibilities, they relieve the burden of the national and State Governments. Because of the very nature of functions assigned to the local Governments, their expenditure expands considerably with the process of economic development, but their revenues do not show an equivalant increase, as the sources of revenue assigned to them are usually inelastic. This situation calls for some financial adjustment between the higher level Governments and the local Governments either by sharing of tax revenues or by provision of grants-in-aid for both general and specific purposes. Thus, grants-in-aid is an instrument of fiscal adjustment and forms an important source of non-tax revenue for the urban local bodies.

All grants for whatever purpose they are made and in whatever way they are distributed result in transferring burdens from the local to the national tax payer and are likely to be redistributive in effect. The grants-in-aid system aims at one or more of the following objectives.[14]

1. to encourage the local authority to extend or improve their sources,
2. to distribute the burden of local Government more equitably,
3. to compensate local authorities for the loss of revenue,

4. to transfer the cost of particular service from the local tax payer to the national tax payers (provided the service has a national character).
5. to reduce the inequality among local bodies.

The grants-in-aid system in India is based on the old British model. "The Departmental Committee on Local Taxation of England specified three distinct functions of the grants-in-aid. They are the method by which the nation (a) contributes its own share towards the cost of semi-national services, (b) remedies inequalities in the incidence of local taxation, and (c) effectively supervises the administration of semi-national services".[15] This analysis equally applies to the system prevalent in India. In this connection the observations of U.K. Hicks are quite apt when she says: "All grants increase the resources of local bodies, but while some are intended to give them greater power of manoeuvre in general, others are intended to do this only for the smaller and poorer authorities which would otherwise have less than normal opportunities of putting their ideas into practice".[16] She further points out that some grants are designed to stimulate development of a particular service. They also enable the Government to exercise some control over administration. "Grant-in-aid serves as an instrument for the implementation of State policies by encouraging local bodies to undertake special programme".[17] Grants may also be used to stimulate local tax collection and assessment. Thus the system of grants-in-aid is a device not only to add to the volume of income of a local body but has the weapon with it of correcting the financial maladies of the local Governments.

Objection against grants-in-aid

The system of grants-in-aid has also certain evil effects. The arguments against this system are generally :

1. Regular State aid to local Governments may result in destruction of local spirit and initiative due to chronic dependance on State Government.
2. State Government gradually acquires control over the local authority which may affect the autonomy of such Governments.

3. This system leads to irresponsibilities in expenditure and lack of efforts for augmenting revenues from own sources.
4. General tax payers are made to pay for services in a local body which benefits only local people.

The arguments have, no doubt, some validity. Some of these aspects may also be seen from the analysis of trend of grants in this State as to how some of the local bodies have failed to increase their efforts and have remained contended with the State aid. The State Governments have also not achieved much success in regulating proper financial discipline in the urban local Governments inspite of such an instrument of grants-in-aid. However this does not mean that grants are unnecessary. If grants are made on a systematic basis and there is a proper co-ordinated national policy in sanctioning of grants, the evil effects of grants can be corrected. This point has been emphasised by all the Committees and Commissions and other authorities in discussing the rationale of grants-in-aid system and have recommended the adoption of a definite policy for grants-in-aid.

The Taxation Enquiry Commission in its Report (1953-54) observed : "No State has in this context a grants-in-aid code that embodies simple and defined principles".[18] The Commission recommended that there should be a basic 'general purpose' grant for each local body. The local bodies should be classified into certain divisions on the basis of population, area and resources etc. and grant should be related to these factors including the size of the normal budget. The basic grant should be sufficient to meet its obligatory and executive functions taking own resources into consideration. The grant should be assured for three to five years. There should be, in addition to general purpose grant, another grant for particular items of services on the condition that the particular service is maintained at particular level of efficiency and the local body exploits its own resources to the desired extent. The Commission also pointed out that grants of such payments are contingent upon State Government's own finance and vary from year to year and the promised grants do not materialise.

The Rural-Urban Relationship Committee in its Report (1966) recommended almost on the same line and observed[19] that any system of general grants should take into consideration the means and needs of the local body, and the pattern of assistance should be in direct proportion to the needs and in inverse proportion to means. In making grants it must be ensured that the local bodies exploit their own resources and provide a satisfactory minimum standard of service and amenities to the people. For providing proper inducement to the local bodies to tap their own resources of revenues to the maximum, the principle of matching grants should be fully exploited. The grants should be linked with level of taxation and revenue and expenditure performance. The above recommendation aims at prescribing a minimum standard of performance and making efforts to maximise tax income by the urban local bodies. But their recommendations by and large have not been implemented in any State excepting a few like Gujarat, Kerala and Madhya Pradesh. Other States have adopted some principles based on certain considerations.

Shared Taxes

The grants-in-aid as in vogue in different States also include the payments on account of shared taxes. The local bodies are deprived of levying certain taxes which fall legitimately under the ambit of local taxation. Such taxes are motor vehicle taxes and entertainment taxes. The entertainment tax is mostly paid by local resident and could easily be administered by the local authorities for their purposes. As regards motor vehicle tax, the Motor Vehicles Act, 1939 took away the powers of local bodies to levy taxes on the mechanically propelled vehicles. The local bodies spend heavy amounts on the construction and maintenance of municipal roads, which are frequently used by mechanically propelled vehicles inside a town. But the users of these roads do not pay any tax towards the cost of maintenance or construction of these roads. The motor vehicle tax and entertainment tax are levied and collected by the State Governments. As a matter of practice, the proceeds of both the taxes are shared between the State Governments and local bodies on certain principles. All authorities discussing on this issue agreed that the proceeds out of such taxes collected within a municipal area should be paid to the urban local body after deducting collection charges. But regarding Motor Vehicle Tax, it was agreed that since the municipal authorities do not provide all the roads in a State and major portion of the communication is managed by the State Public Works Authorities, atleast 25% of the proceeds of Motor Vehicle Tax may be paid to the local bodies. The amounts representing shared taxes are paid to the local bodies as grants-in-aid.

In Madras, Andhra Pradesh and Karnataka, the State Governments distribute the proceeds of entertainment tax to urban local bodies after deducting establishment charges. In Uttar Pradesh, 50% of the Motor Vehicle Tax collected is handed over to Municipalities. In Madras, Maharashtra, Andhra Pradesh and Gujrat, sharing of Motor Vehicle Tax with State Government is an important source of revenue to urban local bodies.

Basis of grants-in-aid

Grants-in-aid in India may be classified as recurring and non-recurring. Recurring grants may be subdivided into block grants or general purpose grants and specific grants. Non-recurring grants are given for a specific purpose to meet the initial expenditure - such as for the construction of office building, for water supply projects, for street lighting and such other similar services, whereas recurring grants are given annually. The block grants supplement the income of the urban local bodies. "They are designed to boost up poor local bodies to the minimum level of income that would be necessary to ensure that all of them are financially able to meet their essential liabilities".[20]

The basis on which such grants should be regulated has already been indicated by the recommendation of the Finance Enquiry Commission and the Committee on Rural-Urban Relationship. But the basis adopted by different States is at variance with each other. General purpose grants are given by various States mostly based on a rate per capita for each category of urban local body classified on population basis, whereas specific purpose grant is given for a specific purpose like water supply, drainage schemes to meet a percentage of the expenditure incurred on such schemes. In Madhya Pradesh such grants cover 30%, in case of Borrough municipalities in Maharashtra, it is $33\frac{1}{2}$% and in case of Karnataka, Kerala, Bihar, Madras and West Bengal it is 50% . In Orissa such grants are given at 1/3rd of the total estimate. Grants-in-aid are usually given for the developmental works of remunerative nature in Assam, Kerala, Maharashtra and Punjab. In Maharashtra and Gujarat, the State Governments give 75% of the Government land revenues on non-agricultural land and certain fixed percentage of land revenues realised within the municipal limits to the local Governments.

The Madhya Pradesh Government has adopted a detailed system of making grants for general purposes. The State Governments in Kerala and Gujarat appointed committees for evolving a grants-in-aid code for adoption by the Governments. The Gujarat Grants-in-aid Committee made an elaborate study on the problems covering grants-in-aid and recommended several measures for adoption by the State Government. The important features of the recommendation of the Committee are as follows.[21]

1. A basic per capita General Purpose Grant, based on population as enumerated at 1971 Census may be paid to all municipalities - @ 30% per capita per year to 'A' class municipality, @ 45% per capita to 'B' class and @ 60% per capita to 'C' class municipality.

2. An incentive grant @ 25%of all the grants paid during the preceding year may be paid to the municipality which fulfils all the conditions and attains the standard prescribed. The conditions include income from taxation, income from all other sources at the minimum prescribed per-capita for different municipalities; expenditure on establishment, income from municipal self-supporting items, recovery of municipal dues at 95 percent and expenditure on medical relief and public health activities.

3. Grants-in-aid for development works at the rate of 33 1/3% of gross cost for 'A' class municipalities and 50% for 'B' and 'C' class municipalities.

4. The rate of grants-in-aid for water supply and drainage schemes has been prescribed at suitable rates for different classes of municipality.

The rate of grants-in-aid for meeting the cost of dearness allowances and other activities of the municipalities has also been recommended. Compared with the above recommendations, the

Orissa Municipal Finance Commission, 1975, has shown more liberal attitude in recommending higher percentage of grants-in-aid for general purpose grants, more particularly for water supply and drainage schemes.

The rate of general purpose grant covers a rate of 50 paise to one rupee depending upon the class of the local body - i.e. 50 paise for Class-I, 60 paise for Class-II, 70 paise for Class-III and one rupee for Class-IV urban local bodies and the grant is based on population of the last census. The Commission also recommended an incentive grant similar to Gujarat based on certain prescribed standards. The quantum of grant for water supply and drainage scheme was recommended at higher rates. The Commission also recommended payment of grants in lieu of entertainment tax at a prescribed percentage on the collection of the tax within a town. The percentage prescribed was 50 for Class-I, 60 for Class-II, 70 for Class-III and 80 for class-IV (after deducting cost of collection at the rate of 4% of the gross amount). It was also recommended by the Commission to sanction at least 20 percent from the Motor Vehicle Tax to urban local bodies instead of limiting to Rs.15 lakhs per annum. "The Commission recommended that the grants-in-aid to urban local bodies should not be less than Rs.15 per capita of which at the rate of Rs.10 per capita should go as general purpose grant and Rs.5 should go as specific grant".[22] The recommendations of the Commission are under consideration of the Government. The effectiveness of the existing system of grants-in-aid in orissa has been discussed later.

Position in other countries

Grants-in-aid system has been developed in different countries as a device to finance the urban Governments. In United States of America, the urban Governments are not only financed by the respective State but by the Federal Government also for different purposes. Such grants are subjected to variety of conditions and standards prescribed by the State Government. In California the State grants are paid for financing expenditure on education to the extent of 50% and highways to the extent of 17% and public welfare by 26%.[23]

In France, the grants to local bodies are paid through the

"Equalisation Fund" maintained for the purpose. There is also a special 'Road Fund' and 'School Fund' financed by the national taxes. The grants are mostly specific and are subject to technical scrutiny, supervision and control.[24]

In United Kingdom the grant system is based on elaborate procedure and grants are sanctioned as specific grants to finance a particular service or scheme and general or block grants are in aid of local expenditure generally; they are not earmarked to a particular service. "Capital grants are grant-in-aid for capital expenditure on a particular scheme or type of schemes e.g. highways grants towards major works on principal roads, revenue grants-in-aid of revenue expenditure. Such grants constitute the vast bulk of Central Government Grants-in-aid".[25] The specific grants are given on percentage basis varying from 50 to 100 percent. Grants are given to finance the expenditure on police, approved schools and remand houses, probation and after care, civil defence, national park, urban development, housing improvement, sewerage, youth employment, rate rebate etc.

Position in Orissa and Other States

It has already been indicated that grants-in-aid constitutes an important source of income to the urban local bodies in Orissa. The receipts from grants have increased from Rs. 24.38 lakhs in 1961-62 to 52.01 lakhs in 1965-66 and from Rs. 117.73 lakhs in 1971-72 to 152.59 lakhs in 1975-76. The increase in volume is quite significant. The income out of grants-in-aid during 1961-62 was 33.39 percent of the total income of the local Government and it increased to 35.18 percent in 1965-66 and 35.58 percent in 1971-72, which however declined in 1975-76 giving way to higher percentage of receipts from its own sources. The position of income in Orissa from grants-in-aid as compared to the All India average of 13.2 percent (1975-76) is highly encouraging.[26] Similarly a survey conducted by collecting data from different municipal bodies in the country for the year 1975-76 by the Ministry of Works and Housing shows that grants received by Municipalities in Madhya Pradesh constituted 6.45 percent of their total receipts and in municipalities of Karnatak, Uttar Pradesh, Andhra Pradesh and Maharastra, they were 8.15, 16.84, 16.84 and 38.07 percent respectively. Except for Maharastra where the percentage of grants was higher than that of Orissa, in all the other

States the percentage of grants was lower in comparison to Orissa.

The study conducted by the Orissa Municipal Finance Commission taking all the urban local bodies in existence - (then 84) into consideration also indicated that the percentage of receipts out of grants-in-aid and shared taxes during 1971-72 was 33.39 percent of the total receipts. The present study (based on 31 urban local bodies) reveals a receipt of 35.58 percent during 1971-72 on account of grants-in-aid and shared taxes and 30.46 percent during 1975-76. The position of grants-in-aid in respect of sample studied here is well comparable with the total position of receipts of grants by 88 urban local bodies (out of total 91) during the year 1975-76. Out of the total receipts of all the urban local bodies during the year amounting to Rs.7,64,82,627, the receipts on account of grants-in-aid were Rs.2,37,55,682 which amounted to 30.86 percent of the total receipts (compared to 30.46 percent in case of 31 urban local bodies in the study).

In Orissa, the grants-in-aid given to urban local bodies constitute the following.

1. Shared taxes out of net proceeds of (a) entertainment tax and (b) motor vehicle tax. With a view to avoiding overlapping of jurisdiction and maintaining uniformity in tax rates and economy in tax administration, the State Government administers these two taxes and apportions a percentage of proceeds of such taxes to urban local bodies. The amount thus apportioned is given as grants-in-aid. Out of the total collected amount of entertainment tax, 50% is given to the urban local bodies realised in the area after deducting collection charges. A fixed sum of rupees fifteen lakhs is distributed among the urban local bodies towards Motor Vehicle Tax on the basis of the mileage of roads maintained by them.

2. Grants under plan and non-plan schemes are given for the following purposes.

a. Grants for improvement of roads under plan and non-plan schemes.
b. Grants for non-remunerative schemes like construction of office buildings, parks, town halls.

c. (i) Grants for meeting a part of the dearness allowance of the employees sanctioned for the local bodies (@ 50 percent from 1.1.1974 after introduction of revised pay scales).

(ii) Grants towards 62 percent of salary of the employees on sanctioned strength (This was introduced from 1.4.1974 after revised pay scales came into effect).

d. Grant for remunerative schemes - construction of market buildings, rental residential buildings, pisciculture, street lighting.

e. Grant for environmental improvement in slum areas.

f. Grant for flood restoration.

Grants given on account of dearness allowance of employees of local bodies cover 51.75 percent of the total grants. Entertainment tax grant covers 14.68 percent and Motor Vehicle Tax 8.92 percent and the remaining 24.65 percent covers grants for non-remunerative schemes, environmental improvement and improvement of roads. Per capita grants-in-aid comes to Rs.7.18.[27]

A study of the position of grants-in-aid received during the years 1961-62, 1965-66, 1971-72 and 1975-76 in respect of 31 urban local bodies studied, and the amount of grants-in-aid received during the years and the percentage of such receipts to total receipts would disclose the following features.

i. Grants sanctioned were not related to the tax efforts of the urban local bodies as a few examples cited in the Table-IV-3 prove that the percentages of receipts from property taxation were very low in comparison to grants received during the years. As the tax efforts are mostly related to property taxation, the percentage of grants received has been compared with the percentage of tax received from property taxes. The income of the following 13 urban local bodies from grants-in-aid during the years 1961-62, 1965-66, 1971-72 and 1975-76 exceeded 50 percent of their total income but their income from property tax was lower (less than 25 percent) in comparison to income from grants-in-aid as indicated against each. In case of other urban local bodies, even though they received less than 50% grants-in-aid, their income from property taxation was not encouraging.

TABLE-IV-3: Percentage of Receipts from Taxes.

Name of the urban local body	1961-62	1965-66	1971-72	1975-76
1.Jajpur Municipality	16.74	14.82	5.72	-
2.Sonepur Municipality	No tax levied	No tax levied	- -	- -
3.Rairangpur N.A.C.	5.55	5.09	-	-
4.Khurda N.A.C.	12.34	-	-	-
5.Gopalpur N.A.C.	27.37	-	-	-
6.Talcher Municipality	-	1.12	-	-
7.Khariar Road N.A.C.	-	4.03	-	-
8.Titilagarh N.A.C.	-	1.75	-	-
9.Rambha N.A.C.	-	1.50	-	9.77
10.Jaleswar N.A.C.	No tax levied	No tax levied	No tax levied	No tax levied
11.Angul N.A.C.	-	8.01	-	-
12.Suruda N.A.C.	-	11.38	-	-
13.Athagarh N.A.C.	-	-	-	No levy

ii. The basis of population does not seem to have been taken as a criterion for sanctioning grants as many urban local bodies with lower population have received higher percentage of grants-in-aid in comparison to urban local bodies with higher population. The 13 local bodies which received more than 50% grants were smaller in size and population compared to others which received less than 50% .

iii. It can be appreciated if higher percentage of grants are sanctioned to the urban local bodies which are constituted recently to make preliminary preparation to build the infrastructure to augment their tax base. But the details in the Table- IV-3 show that some of them were constituted as early as in 19th century (Jajpur Municipality) and yet received higher percentage of grants and their tax efforts were low or in cases of some (Jaleswar Municipality) no tax was levied.

iv. There was no regularity in flow of grants as the percentage of receipts from grants varied in high proportion from year to year as shown in the annexure in respect of Bhubaneswar Notified Area Council, Joda Notified Area Council, Talcher Municipality, titilagarh Notified Area Council, Nayagarh Notified Area Council and Gopalpur Notified Area Council.

v. Some urban Governments enjoyed the privilege of higher percentage of grants-in-aid and some continued to receive lower percentage of grants during all these years under study. Such urban Governments which received higher percentage of grants-in-aid are Jajpur, Jaleswar, Sonepur and Baripada and others which received continuously lower percentage of grants are Koraput, Sunabeda, Rourkela (C.T.).

vi. It was remarkable to find that some urban local bodies received grants-in-aid exceeding 75 percent of their total income during the year 1965-66 and such institutions are Talcher Municipality. Rairangpur Municipality and Nayagarh Notified Area Council.

vii. The trend of receipts of grants-in-aid by some individual municipalities declined during the year 1971-72 and 1975-76 as compared to the earlier years, because of the fact that their receipts from own sources increased during these years.

All such factors prove that grants were not released by the State Government on any approved principle or policy as most of the grants were released at the discretion of the Government except grants towards salary and Dearness allowance of the employees of local bodies which are sanctioned at the rate of 62 percent of the salary and 50 percent of the dearness allowance of the sanctioned strength of the concerned local bodies. Government is expected to take the following factors into consideration to regulate payment of grants-in-aid as suggested by the State Municipal Finance Commission(1975)[28]

a. The concerned urban local body must have levied service taxes and such taxes are administered on no loss and no profit basis.
b. The collection of tax should be atleast 80 percent.
c. The local body should not have reduced its resources by reducing or revising the taxes levied.
d. The loans due on account of principal and interest must have been paid.

e. In case of non-remunerative schemes, the local bodies must meet 50 percent of the expenditure as matching contribution.
f. There should be no encroachment on Government grants and grants should be utilised in time.

Instances have been given at different stages to the effect that collection of tax by the concerned urban local bodies is very low, yet the percentage of grants-in-aid paid is very high. The expenditure on different services like water supply, lighting and drainage etc. is much higher in relation to receipts from such taxes. Many of the local bodies have also reduced or revised their rates of taxes causing loss to their own income. It will be seen from subsequent discussion that heavy amount of loans and interest therefrom are outstanding against a number of local bodies. The audit reports of local fund audit organisation on the accounts of different urban local bodies disclose cases where no matching contributions have been paid by them. It has been indicated later that grants are lying un-utilised for years together. In spite of their failure to fulfil any of the conditions, the local bodies have continued to receive the patronage of the State Government in shape of grants-in-aid for all these years.

It, therefore, follows that grants are paid without any basis and completely at the discretion of the State Government. Obviously such discretion is used to favour the urban local bodies having sufficient strength to pull the wires at the higher level. The State Municipal Finance Commission (1975) has frankly admitted : "Due to various reasons it is difficult for the Government to deny or defer allotment to any urban local body even where it does not fulfil the conditions prescribed or furnished the information called for. In the result the amounts are distributed at the discretion of the Government".[29] Thus the system of grants-in-aid is a political weapon in the hands of the State Government to control the working of urban local bodies and to extend patronage to their kinsmen.

The allotment of grants-in-aid is the discretion of the State Government and is not based on any approved policy. As such, the very purpose of giving grants-in-aid with a view to reducing regional imbalances, to providing incentives to the local bodies, to ensuring better standard of service and to improving administrative efficiency has not been fulfilled. (Subsequent discussion will throw more light on this topic.) On the other hand it has led the urban local bodies to be lethargic (as no adequate efforts to improve their tax income has been made) and it has increased their dependence on State aid leading to irresponsible and extravagant expenditure.

Grants have been obtained by the urban local bodies without making arrangements for their utilisation. Excepting grants paid towards the salary of employees, all other grants have not been utilised during the year of sanction (stipulated in the sanction order for utilisation during the year). Even grants have been left unspent for years together. A review of the position of unspent balance at the end of 1961-62, 1965-66,1971-72 and 1975-76 in respect of samples studied shows that out of Rs.24.38 lakhs received during 1961-62, a sum of Rs.21.38 lakhs received during 1961-62, a sum of Rs.21.83 lakhs were left unspent and in the year 1965-66, out of the grants of Rs.52.01 lakhs received, Rs.36.02 lakhs could not be utilised. Against the receipt of Rs.117.73 lakhs during 1971-72, the amount unutilised comes to Rs.51.76 lakhs and during 1975-76, out of Rs.159.59 lakhs, a sum of Rs.31.49 lakhs was left unutilised. Thus the position of unspent grant at the end of 1961-62,1965-66,1971-72 and 1975-76 was 89.55, 69.25, 43.97 and 20.63 percent respectively.

The information compiled in the Table-IV-4 shows the balances remaining unspent in respect of some of these urban local bodies at the end of the year against the grants-in-aid received during the year. Such retention of heavy unspent grants was highest during 1965-66 and such cases persisted during the years 1971-72 and 1975-76. This clearly proves that grants of the previous years were left unutilised. The list furnished is only illustrative and not exhaustive, as in other cases the balances unutilised are also quite heavy but are less than the amount received during the year.

Due to non-utilisation of grants, the benefits which could be derived by their timely and proper utilisation were not only delayed but were also ultimately denied due to rise in cost of construction of projects. This situation creates a vicious cycle. Proper and timely investment of funds (received from grants-in-aid) in development work may create the infrastructure for the urban development which may attract the citizens to invest in creating urban properties. Such properties in shape of land and buildings may increase the revenue of the local body. On the other hand the municipal assets created out of grants-in-aid may increase non-tax revenue and tax revenues for the urban Governments. But such aspects were utterly neglected and yet Government grants were released which did not serve any effective purpose. Utilisation certificate in support of grants-in-aid of Rs.5,10,63,161 paid upto the end of March 1977 was not furnished by the urban local bodies, out of which Rs.2,80,09,227 pertain to the grants alotted up to 1975-76.[30] The position regarding heavy unutilised balance of Government grants at the end of each year and consequent non-submission of utilisation certificates by the local bodies was examined by the Public Accounts Committee of the State Legislature and in expressing their concern over such a situation, the Committee directed the Finance Department to investigate into the reasons of non-utilisation of grants and submit a report to them.[31]

Further, the uncertain and erratic allotment of grants-in-aid has put the urban local bodies to frame an unbalanced and unrealistic budget estimate for different years. In most cases, they do not receive funds through grants-in-aid for different purposes or receive a smaller amount against a heavy requirement which upsets their budgetary process. Instances of the above category are numerous and these have been discussed in Chapter-VI in analysing financial control. Release of grants-in-aid at the fag end of the financial year also puts the local bodies to difficulties as with their scanty and ill qualified personnel it is not possible for them to utilise the grants on time.

Though the principles which should regulate the allotment of grants-in-aid may not be discussed at this stage, it is worthwhile to suggest that the system of grants-in-aid should be linked more with the ability of the urban Government to utilise the grants in time rather than to fix a quota of receipt which would be lodged in the P.L.Accounts at the Treasury, forming a part of the Government fund. The matter of framing policy and allotment of grants-in-aid should be entrusted to a high power committee of the State. This Committee should be a sufficiently high powered body consisting of the Minister as its Chairman, Secretary of the Administrative Department, the Director of urban local bodies, a representative of Finance Department - preferably the Examiner of Local Fund Audit. The Committee should work like a Finance Commission to regularly review the financial working of the urban local bodies vis-a-vis their physical performance. The Committee should take note of the findings in the audit report on the accounts of these institutions and consider the question of sanctioning grants and loans for different schemes on the basis of financial capabilities of these institutions having regard to their past performance. They should ensure that forecast for grants and loans for coming 3-5 years is made ahead and such funds are provided in the State Budget for making available to urban local bodies.

TABLE-IV-4: Unspent balance out of Government Grants at the end of 1961-62, 1965-66, 1971-72 & 1975-76.

Sl. No.	Name of the Municipality/ Notified Area Council	Balance at the end of 1961-62 Rs.	1965-66 Rs.	1971-72 Rs.	1975-76 Rs.
1.	Jajpur Municipality	1,07,007	1,29,547	-	-
2.	Talcher Municipality	72,063	-	-	1,40,349
3.	Sonepur Municipality	43,350	48,669	1,13,386	1,59,110
4.	Deogarh Municipality	79,054	47,469	-	-
5.	Bhubaneswar N.A.C.	1,95,426	-	-	-
6.	Puri Municipality	3,76,539	-	-	-
7.	Koraput N.A.C.	-	1,21,313	96,224	-
8.	Jaleswar N.A.C.	-	29,468	63,791	75,235
9.	Joda N.A.C.	-	16,740	1,13,463	-
10.	Angul N.A.C.	-	13,754	-	-
11.	Rourkela (CT) N.A.C.	-	1,76,238	-	-
12.	Phulbani N.A.C.	-	22,681	-	-
13.	Rairangpur N.A.C.	-	2,68,974	-	-
14.	Khurda N.A.C.	-	79,950	85,446	1,59,862
15.	Gopalpur N.A.C.	-	45,505	48,214	1,44,638
16.	Suruda N.A.C.	-	27,680	-	59,974
17.	Rambha N.A.C.	-	10,740	39,381	1,77,999
18.	Hinjilicut N.A.C.	-	-	1,32,011	1,28,553
19.	Sunabeda N.A.C.	-	-	-	74,044
20.	Athagarh N.A.C.	-	-	-	67,916

While making such a suggestion, the limitation of the State

Governments in making future provisions in the State budget for their junior partner is not lost sight of. The State Governments themselves largely depend upon the Central Government to get their share and funds on the recommendation of the Finance Commission and Planning Commission. Under such uncertain conditions, it may not be possible on the part of the State Governments to extend a supporting hand to the urban local Government. In the alternative, the Committee should evolve ways and means to augment the income of the local bodies from their own sources so that gradually their dependence on the State exehequer even to meet their regular expenditure for general establishment (grants are made to meet 62 percent of the salary and 50 percent of the dearness allowance of the municipal employees) become less and less.

III

Local Borrowing

Need for Borrowing

It has already been indicated that the income of the local authorities constitutes receipts from their own sources in shape of taxes and municipal properties, the grants-in-aid received from the State Government and funds borrowed from State Government and other financing institutions. There was a time when the local authorities derived all the revenues they required from the proceeds of local taxes, but now local taxes are not the main source of municipal revenue. The Government assistance in the form of grant-in-aid is not adequate to bridge the gap between needs and resources. The local Governments have, therefore, to borrow to meet their growing expenditure.

Therefore, the question arises as to whether the local authorities should resort to borrowing from other agencies or finance the urban development from their own revenues. It is a baffling question. Financing from current revenue would save them from payment of heavy interest charges which borrowing entails. But financing of capital expenditure from ordinary revenues may not be considered prudent from the point of sound financial principle since such investments from current revenues would create assets of permanent nature, the benefit of which is extended to future generation. "When capital works are executed out of current income, the present generation is made to suffer for providing certain benefits for the future generation which is unfair and inequitable".[32] Thus the only way left is to resort to borrowing to meet the capital expenditure.

Borrowing by a local authority forms an important part of its financial administration. Every aspect of the borrowing has to be carefully regulated, otherwise it may lead to unremediable financial difficulties. Professor Gyanchand points out, "the financial history of the American local bodies is full of cases of reckless borrowing and consequent defaults and repudiations".[33] This was due to complete autonomy of Local Government. The political authorities of Local Government may be tempted to resort to borrowing to relieve the people from the tax burden as a vote-catching device. But such tendency is to be guarded against. There should be clear purpose for which loans are to be incurred. Loans should ordinarily be incurred for productive purposes. Borrowing for current expenditure, as a rule, should be avoided. There should be sufficient safeguards against the power of borrowing.

Purpose : Local Authorities Loans Act

The borrowing powers of the local authorities in India are regulated by the Local Authorities Loans Act, 1914. The procedure for sanction of loans, repayment of the same and the interest thereon have been prescribed in the Local Authorities Loans Rules, 1915 framed under the Act. The Act lays down that a local authority may borrow for the following purposes, namely [34]:

(i) the carrying out of any works which it is legally authorised to carry out;

(ii)the giving of relief and the establishment and maintenance of relief work in times of famines or scarcity;

(iii) the prevention of the outbreak of spread of any dangerous epidemic diseases;

(iv) any measures which may be connected with an ancillary purpose specified in clauses(i) & (ii);

(v) the repayment of money previously borrowed in accordance with law.

The rules framed under the Act prohibit such borrowing unless the work to be carried out is either (a) within the limits of the area subject to control of the local authority or (b) for the benefit of the inhabitants within these limits. No loan can be incurred by the local body unless sanctioned by the State Government. The period of loan ordinarily should not exceed thirty years. The normal method of repayment is on annual basis.

After the transfer of the subject of local self Government from the Centre to State Governments, the latter have framed their own Acts and Rules for regulating loans to local authorities and the provisions are similar to that of the Central Act of 1914 and rules framed thereunder. The urban local bodies usually borrow funds from the State Government even though there is no restriction for them to resort to public borrowing. Ordinarily State loans are available for capital expenditure like water-supply and drainage schemes. Loans are also sanctioned for schemes of remunerative nature to construct market buildings, shopping centres, guest houses, pisciculture etc. The terms of such loans are usually restricted to the life of the assets created. Loans are now advanced by the Central Government to the State Government for giving loans to urban local bodies for

i slum clearance and improvement schemes,

ii land acquisition and development schemes,

iii urban compost schemes.

With the introduction of five year plans, the Government of India have paid more attention for the development of urban areas since the Third Five Year Plan onwards and made provision of funds to flow in shape of grants and loans to State Governments for financing urban development. Now Central loans are available for housing and water supply projects. Other financing institutions have also taken up the scheme of advancing loans to the local authorities. The State Governments arrange loans from the Life Insurance Corporation of India for financing mostly water supply schemes and from the HUDCO for construction of houses for the urban areas.

Position of borrowing by Local Governments in Orissa.

The urban local bodies in Orissa have not lagged behind and have availed of borrowing facilities for the purpose of financing :

- i construction of slum clearance quarters;
- ii construction of market buildings, shopping centres;
- iii provision of street lighting;
- iv pisciculture;
- v purchase of trucks and tractors;
- vi payment of arrears of Dearness Allowance to employees;
- vii conversion of dry latrines to septic latrines.;
- viii provision of water supply;
- ix emergency situation arising from national calamities-famine, flood etc.

Loans for financing all the schemes have been advanced by the State Government and loans for water supply have been mostly financed by the State Governments and in some cases by the Life Insurance Corporation of India. The quantum of loans received by the urban local bodies during the plan periods in respect of all the urban local bodies of the State is as follows:

	Plan period	Total loan received.	Annual average loan.	Loan per capita.
1.	Third Five Year Plan	9,64,000	1,92,8000	0.94
2.	Fourth Five Year Plan	43,57,000	8,71,400	2.50
3.	Fifth Five Year Plan	44,00,000	8,80,000	2.00

(Source -Based on the figures compiled at P-79 of the Report of the State Municipal Finance Commission, Orissa - 1975).

The position datailed above indicates only the loans advanced by the State Government and excludes the loans received from other financing institutions. The quantum of loan assistance of the State

Government for capital financing is too meagre in considering the number of urban local bodies. Even though the total loan assistance in the 5th plan was higher than 4th plan, per capita assistance came down in the 5th plan due to increase in the number of urban local bodies from 64 to 84 during the 5th plan period.

In this study the position of loans received in respect of 31 urban local bodies has been studied for the years 1961-62, 1965-66,1971-72 and 1975-76 (covering receipt of loans from State Government and other agencies). The position of loan is reproduced below for ready reference.

Year of receipt.	Total loan received.	Percentage to total receipt.
1961-62	309850	4.25
1965-66	488004	3.30
1971-72	3014175	9.11
1975-76	537879	1.07

The details show that largest number of local bodies (21)incurred loans during the year 1971-72 and the amount of loan incurred was highest in comparison to all other years. This is comparable with the position relating to loan assistance by the State Government during the Fourth Plan period to all the urban local bodies. The sample study reveals that smallest number of urban local bodies i.e. 4 incurred loans during 1975-76 even though the amount of loan incurred was high compared to 1965-66 and 1961-62. The loan burden was more distributive in 1965-66 in comparision to the year 1961-62. The growth of indebtedness was highest in 1971-72 being 9.11 percent of the total receipts which is comparable to the All India average of 9.1 percent during the same year. [35]

A scrutiny of the pattern of loans incurred by the urban local bodies disclosed that loans incurred for different purposes varied from Rs.5000 to Rs.50 lakhs. Loans were received for financing both productive and unproductive activities. Unproductive schemes included construction of school buildings, town halls, office buildings and payment of arrear dearness allowance to office employees of local bodies. Apparently capital expenditure on such works are not productive, but they largely contribute to the human welfare which indirectly contributes to the economic growth of the country. The loans incurred for financing street lighting, pisciculture, construction of market buildings and shopping centres were mostly for a term of ten years with an interest of 5% to $6\frac{1}{2}$% whereas loans for water supply schemes, provision of guest houses and slum quarters were for a term of 20-30 years with the same rate of interest.

It has been discussed elsewhere that investment in construction of market buildings, guest houses and pisciculture was, though not profit earning but self-financing. The revenue received from these projects was capable of meeting the loan charges towards repayment of capital and interest, but investment in street lighting and pisciculture was uneconomic, due to low revenues received from lighting tax and from pisciculture. Moreover investment in street lighting and other services require smaller amounts which could be met from the ordinary revenues to avoid payment of heavy interest from the current revenues as the projects do not yield sufficient revenue to meet the debt charges. To make a general idea as to how the borrowing entails heavy payment of interest, a few examples are given below. A loan of Rs.1000 with 9% rate of interest will cost as follows if repaid by equal annual instalments of principal and interest combined.[36]

Period.	Annual instalment. Rs.	Total cost. Rs.
20 Years	110	2191
40 Years	93	3718
60 Years	91	5431

The figures given above show that a borrowing of Rs.1000/- would cost Rs.2197,Rs.3718 and Rs.5431 at the end of 20 years, 40 years and 60 years respectively. Similarly a loan of Rs.60,000 at 5% rate of interest when repayable within 5 years at an annual instalment of Rs.13,900 (principal+interest) would cost Rs.69,271 at the end of the term.[37] What a huge sum of money is needed to pay interest and repayment capital can be known from the rate schedule outlined above. The rate schedule indicates that the longer the period of loans, the more it costs to the local authority. Longer term loans spread the liability to the next generation whereas short term loans burden the present generation in discharging its liability. The ability of a local authority to discharge the debt liabilities largely depends upon the purpose for which the amount is borrowed and the assets created by investing such amounts and above all, the general management of the finances.

There is another important factor which determines the ability of the local body to discharge loan liability i.e. the ability to utilise the borrowed funds in proper investment to earn revenue without delay. In this context the ability of the local authority in Orissa may be analysed to clear its debt liabilities. It is not the volume of debt that really matters, but the ability to utilise the amount timely and to administer the borrowed fund to its desired goal that matters.

Apart from the smaller projects which are financed from borrowed funds and other projects involving investment of higher amounts which are capable of meeting loan liabilities, a few glaring instances are brought to light where due to want of proper management, the urban local bodies of the State are put to heavy loss in meeting the debt liabilities. Supply of piped water in an urban area is one of the essential functions of the local body and is based on the national policy. Of late Government of India have also shared the responsibility to finance such schemes by advancing loan to State Governments for extending loan facilities to urban local bodies. The State Government also provides grants-in-aid to local Government for financing a part of the expenditure on water-supply projects. In addition, loans are also arranged from the fife Insurance Corporation of India on the guarantee of the State Governments. Prior to April 1969, the State Government used to share the burden of financing the projects by paying 2/3rd of the estimate of individual project as grants-in-aid and one third of the estimate was borne by the local body. Towards the local body's share of one third, the State Government also advanced loans. The situation changed after April 1969 and the State Government sanctioned only 1/3rd of the estimate as grants-in-aid and 2/3rd was to be borne by the urban local bodies for which State Government arranged loans towards the share of the urban local body.

There are many examples to show that loan financing of such projects has impoverished the urban local bodies. According to the Report of the State Municipal Finance Commission, 1975, out of water-supply projects taken up during the Fourth Plan period in 60 urban local bodies, only 16 projects were completed by the end of

4th plan period. [38]This shows that huge sums were borrowed for which interest was paid but the projects remained incomplete depriving the local bodies of its legitimate share of revenue.

The list of institutions where the water supply projects have not been completed are given below.

The list shows the estimated cost of each project, year of commencement, share of the State Government, share of the urban local body and the amount borrowed and amount invested till March, 1979. Against every urban local body the quantum of its share and the source from which the funds have been borrowed to meet their share have been indicated which show that in most of the projects 2/3rd of the estimated cost is met from borrowed funds. Loans have been advanced by the Government in some cases and both by the Government and Life Insurance Corporation of India in some cases.

According to the existing arrangement, the urban local bodies do not execute the projects but only finance these projects out of loans and Government grants. The amount of the estimated cost of the project is placed by the local Government at the disposal of the Executive Engineer, Public Health Division of the area. He takes up the execution of the project through his agency and also maintains the project. Before completion of the projects in some cases, temporary arrangements are made to supply water in the urban areas. Temporary water-supply also yields some revenue. The urban local body takes the revenue assessed in the shape of water tax and the rent of water tap and connection charges are collected by the Public Health Department. In addition to revenue thus collected the Public Health Department also demands the payment from the local body towards maintenance charges of the water supply system which is much higher than the amount collected towards water tax.

The list shows that projects taken up during 1960-61 (in respect of Rourkela (C.T.) Notified Area Council, Puri Municipality and Berhampur Municipality, Bhubaneswar Notified Area Council) with large amounts of borrowed funds have not been completed till the end of March 1979. The rate of interest for these borrowed funds varies from 5 percent to 9 percent. The interest accrued to such debts needs no elucidation as indicated already that a sum of

Rs.60,000 makes a loan burden of Rs.69,271 at the end of the 5th year at the rate of 5 percent interest. The term of these loans extends to 30 years and the rate of interest in many cases is higher than 5 percent. According to the term of the loan, if the interest is not paid in time, the borrower is to pay compound interest . Most of the urban local bodies do not pay the instalments regularly and are liable to pay interest at compound rates. In some cases the annual instalment of loan plus the interest payable exceeds the total revenue of the urban local body. Sometimes Government have been pleased to adjust the grant payable to urban local body towards the overdue instalment of Government loan and interest thareon.[39]

The Public Health Department does not take the responsibility to complete the schemes on time. The local body stands a mute observer to such a situation and bleeds through nose to pay the debt liabilities. It does not get the additional revenue as the projects are not completed and it pays from the ordinary revenue earned otherwise towards the payment of instalment of loan and interest thereon. In addition, the grants due to the local bodies are adjusted by Government towards the payment of instalment of loans and interest thereon depriving the local bodies of any developmental work. It is curious again to find from the list that the water supply scheme of Berhampur Municipality has been decided to be abandoned after an investment of Rs. 52.86 lakhs (loan by local body 20.32 lakhs) as the project is considered not viable.

In our discussion with the Chairman of the affected local bodies, they have expressed that such schemes have been imposed upon them and the Chairman had expressed frankly that the Public Health Department continues its existence only on the payment made by them towards water supply project. Even they do not receive any accounts, progress report in respect of the amount is deposited by them with the Public Health authorities. Earlier completion of the projects might result in abolition of some Public Health Divisions and the delay enables them to exist. Each estimate includes an amount of $17\frac{1}{2}\%$ towards departmental charges for maintenance of the establishment for execution of the project and the amount is paid by the urban local body from borrowed funds. Neither the Government nor the Public Health Engineers seem to be very bothered by the precarious financial position of the local bodies.

The situation has come to such a stage that many urban local bodies have failed to discharge the loan liabilities in respect of loans received from the Life Insurance Corporation of India and other financing institutions. Since loans from the Life Insurance Corporation of India were released on Government guarantee, Government has sanctioned loans to these local authorities to clear the outstanding amounts of loan and interest thereon to the Life Insurance Corporation of India.[40] This further adds to the loan burden of the urban local bodies. Therefore, it is imperative that Government should take measures to assure timely completion of the projects to enable the urban local bodies to receive adequate revenues from such projects atleast to meet the loan charges. It was also suggested by the Committee on Augmentation of Financial Resources of Urban Local Bodies that it would be desirable to make provisions in the enactment regarding redemption of debt from the revenues of the scheme. But instances cited above show that it takes years and years to complete the projects to become revenue earning. Even if enactments are made, the possibility of redemption of debts from revenues of the scheme seems doubtful.

Another striking feature of the debt administration of the urban local bodies is the non-utilisation of loans for the purpose for which the loans are incurred. Either the loans are not utilised or are utilised for other purposes. The loans are not utilised properly and timely but the revenues earned from the tax payers are utilised to pay the interest charges even though they do not derive any benefit out of such borrowed funds. This aspect has been commented on repeatedly by the Examiner of Local Accounts in the Annual Reports.[41]

The position shows no improvement. Huge amounts of loans recieved for different purposes are lying unspent at the end of March 1976. There were unutilised amounts against 26 urban local bodies out of 30 local bodies. In case of Sonepur Municipality the loan of Rs. 21430 received during 1964-65 was kept unutilised upto March 1976. This is not an exception. Many others had also the same problem. Heavy unspent balances exceeding one lakh are shown against Cuttack Municipality, Bhubaneswar Notified Area Council, Rourkela Notified Area Council, Deogarh Municipality, Puri

Municipality, Berhampur and Balasore Municipality. It may, therefore, be desirable not to sanction loans unless the local bodies utilise the loans on time. In the alternative, the amount sanctioned may not be drawn unless the formalities for execution are finalised to avoid payment of heavy interest charge.

It is the Local Governments' weak finances and improper administration of loan funds that make them unable to clear the loan liabilities. The administration of loan rests more with the Government than with the urban local bodies. While sanctioning loans Government should not only see to the financial ability of the local Government to pay off such debts but to physical ability to utilise these amounts. The Local Authorities Loan Rules 1915, (Central Rules) and the Orissa Local Authorities Loan Rules, 1975 have laid down stricter condition for loan administration. According to rule 10(d), the local body should furnish certificates of utilisation within a period of one year from the date of drawal. This provision cannot be ensured when the Public Health Department of State Government fails to utilize the loan for water supply scheme.

The Orissa Municipal Act, 1950 (Sec 116-a) provides repayment of loan and interest as the first charge on the Municipal fund. Rule 150 of Orissa Municipal Rules, 1953 strictly prohibits that the balance of loan shall not be appropriated even temporarily without prior sanction of the Government to any object other than that for which the loan is raised. There is provision that accounts of loan funds should be maintained separately and will be subject to audit. The above provision of the Act/Rules has been observed more in its breach. The Government has also failed to maintain rigidity in proper administration of loan funds. Professor Gyanchand observed: "The maintenance of control over the borrowing powers of local authorities has its justification in the necessity of providing safeguards against the abuse of public credit which can arise so easily if the public authorities are given complete freedom to have their own loan policy".[42] Slackness on the part of Government has led the local authorities to indebtedness.

Sinking Fund

There are various methods of redemption of loan depending

upon the method adopted for raising the loan. Most of the loans raised by the urban local bodies in Orissa are obtained from the State Government and Life Insurance Corporation of India. Under the provisions of the loan agreement, the principal is repaid in equal annual instalments during the whole period of the loans and interest is paid on the diminishing balance. The instalment for repayment of borrowed money is fixed by dividing the principal amount by the number of years fixed for the repayment of loan. There is provision under section 111 in the Orissa Municipal Act, 1950, for creation of a Sinking Fund to meet the loan liabilities. For the creation of a sinking fund, a certain amount is set apart every year and invested in some form of approved security. Interest accruing from the investment is also invested so that the original amount grows at compound rate of interest. The creation of sinking fund is a convenient method of discharging the debt liability. No sinking fund has been maintained as required under rules and in some local authorities initial funds have been set apart but proper maintenance in shape of reinvestment of the interest thereon has not been ensured. Government's interference in this respect would go a long way in easing the loan burden of the local authorities.

Conclusion

Generally the capital expenditure of urban local bodies is financed by borrowing, mostly from the State Government. Loan assistance provided by the Central Government through the State Government is hardly adequate for the purpose. It has, therefore, been recommended by the Committee on Augmentation of Financial Resources of Urban Local Bodies that "each State should draw up a programme of five years indicating the loan requirements of local authorities within the State and how far they can be met from the State resources. On this basis, allocation in the National and State Plans may be made showing the sources from which the funds for Urban Development will be procured".[43] This view was also supported by the Rural Urban Relationship Committee. The State Municipal Finance Commission, Orissa (1975) while agreeing with the above views deplored that "this has not been done so far. Rather the development works in the urban local bodies for all purposes are limited to the fund available from the State Government".[44] This recommendation, however laudable it may be, may not serve any effective purpose since provision in the State Plan is subject to rigid scrutiny by the Planning Commission and it is doubtful if the development programme of urban local bodies would stand the test and get the approval of the Planning Commission for loan assistance. Many of the State schemes also do not get approval of the Central authority.

The Rural-Urban Relationship Committee further recommended that a Municipal Finance Corporation should be set up to advance loan to the local bodies, which should be run on commercial lines with an authorised capital of Rs. 10 crores subsidised by Government of India, Reserve Bank of India, State Bank of India, Life Insurance Corporation of India and other financing institutions as also the local bodies.[45] The State Municipal Finance Commission, Orissa (1975) also suggested to set up one Urban Development Finance Corporation, Kerala-type, to finance development schemes of urban local bodies, for establishing and subsidising training and research, to provide technical and administrative assistance and guidance and to act as agents of Central and State authorities. The suggestion of both the above Committees is not workable as the working of a corporation with the borrowed funds from different authorities would increase the rate of interest which would cause further hardship. If the Government with sufficient authority and rigid provision of rules are not able to enforce proper administration of loan funds in the urban local bodies, it is not considered safe to entrust the work to a corporation with all the ancillary vices of loose administration and heavy overhead expenditure. Ultimately the urban local bodies would have to bear the cost of maintaining such corporations. This would not attain the expected result.

Of course the Central Borrowing Agency like the Public Work Loan Board for financing the capital expenditures of local authorities in United Kingdom has been acceptable due to the financial discipline of such an authority. Moreover in the United Kingdom, the local authorities have got capital funds, the system of overdraft and even they are allowed to utilise the deposits for capital expenditure. A general reserve fund is created by transfer of surplus from the trading services. In the line of practices in the United Kingdom it is suggested that a Central Reserve Fund as in England should be created by transferring a percentage of income from the remunerative schemes for formation of a base capital for financing productive purposes.

The administration of borrowing by local authorities should be entrusted to the high powered committee suggested earlier for administration of grants-in-aid. The loan application should be considered on the basis of the general financial condition of the local authorities as revealed from the Audit Reports of previous 3 years. The consideration for loan should also include the ability of the local authority to utilise such loan. Detailed plans and estimates of the projects need be finalised before sanction of the loans. There should be a suitable machinery for the effective supervision of the projects executed out of loan funds. Rigidity in repayment of the loan should be enforced. In Orissa, loans available are not scanty, but the will and the ability of the local authorities as well as of the State Government to utilise and administer such a fund are inadequate. In view of the financial weaknesses of the local authorities, the Government should reconsider their policy to augment subsidies in shape of grants-in-aid to finance capital expenditure of non-productive nature.

Moreover, water-supply schemes should no longer be a source of subsistence for the Public Health Department of the State. Considering the length of time consumed in completing such projects, the State Government should not insist on the recovery of loans and interest thereon until the project is completed and yields revenue. In discussing about the local borrowing in the United Kingdom, N.P. Hepworth expressed that "Those services which can be expected to contribute to the revenue or even to pay for themselves are very much in the minority".[46] What is true of the United Kingdom, largely holds good in India and more particularly in Orissa. It is, therefore, suggested that such schemes which are of national importance and involve high cost should as a rule be fully financed by the State and National Government and handed over to the local authorities for upkeep and maintenance. The idea of borrowing cannot be abandoned. As Professor Gyanchand has said, "We have to forge ahead, but in order to get the best results, we must have an order of precedence and a well considered plan of development".[47]

ANNEXURE-IV

List of Incomplete Water Supply Projects in Different Urban Local Bodies

Sl. No.	Name of the Urban Local Body	Amount of estimate	Year of Commencement	Govt. share as Grants/Loan	Urban Local Bodies'share	Amount invested upto march 1979
1	2	3	4	5	6	7
1.	Balasore Municipality	67.05	1963	29.66	37.39 (LIC)	60.49
2.	Berhampur Municipality	60.95	1960	40.63 (2/3rd)	20.32 (Loan)	52.86
3.	Jajpur Municipality	40.00	1962	22.67	8.00 9.33 Govt. loan	40.00
4.	Koraput N.A.C.	32.14	64-65	25.38	7.33 Govt. Loan 6.76 LIC Loan (Not paid)	25.49
5.	Baripada Municipality	66.19	1962	29.52	7.46 Govt. Loan 29.21 LIC	36.99
6.	Bhubaneswar N.A.C.	47.93	1961	23.72	7.74 Govt. Loan 16.47(Urban Local Bodies) share (LIC)	32.84 (Old town water supply scheme)
7.	Khurda N.A.C.	39.86	1971	13.29	26.57 (LIC Loan)	39.79
8.	Nayagarh N.A.C.	12.05	1972	4.02	8.03 (LIC Loan)	12.02
9.	Puri Municipality	76.54	60-61	38.39	12.67 (Govt. Loan) 25.68 (LIC Loan)	73.21
10.	Cuttack Municipality	49.50		16.50	33.00 LIC Loans (Not paid yet)	(Interim Relief Scheme)
11.	Deogarh Municipality	7.35	69-70	No grant	3.27 LIC (69-70)	1.19
12.	Padmapur N.A.C.	13.80	1973	4.60	9.20 Loan	13.80
13.	Rourkela (CT) N.A.C.	135.16	60-61	110.13	45.03 Loan (Govt.)	135.16

(Based on the information furnished in the proceedings of the Review meeting of on-going Urban Water Supply Schemes held on 24.7.78, and 24.8.78 in the Urban Development Department,Government of Orissa and another meeting held on 23.4.79 (Proceedings of the meeting issued in Urban Department Memo No. 32129 dt. 19.10.78 and No. 17555 dt. 25.5.79).

ANNEXURE-V
UNSPENT BALANCE OF LOANS, OUTSTANDING PRINCIPAL AND INTEREST AT THE END OF MARCH 1976.

Sl.No.	Name of the Urban Local Body	Amount of loan unspent at the end of March 1976	Outstanding principal	Outstanding Interest
1	2	3	4	5
1.	Koraput	89,715.00	89,715.00	-
2.	Sunabeda	-	31,000.00	-
3.	Jeypore	2,000.00	8,80,540.04	2,360.00
4.	Cuttack	6,33,029.32	5,13,523.00	7,63,475.70
5.	Jajpur	56,253.16	1,25,027.64	8,918.09
6.	Athagarh	10,000.00	-	-
7.	Joda	74,310.00	63,980.00	2,425.75
8.	Angul	45,006.49	1,38,468.83	2,164.81
9.	Talcher	2,948.18	1,61,680.68	40,683.91
10.	Khariar Road	55,977.00	52,320.00	1.00
11.	Rourkela	1,13,578.71	99,888.21	-
12.	Sonepur	21,429.77	40,843.75	9,049.77
13.	Titilagarh	-	25,319.83	-3,867.18
14.	Phulbani	28,514.40	1,10,648.21	52,955.63
15.	Sambalpur	25,400.00	13,76,159.01	5,05,876.50
16.	Deogarh	1,11,572.25	2,91,990.00	-
17.	Brajarajnagar	-	56,540.00	-
18.	Padmapur	716.00	50,998.75	465.40
19.	Rairangpur	20,000.00	55,264.00	-
20.	Baripada	37,000.00	2,83,669.00	-
21.	Khurda	22,160.58	2,69,159.68	10,367.42
22.	Nayagarh	41,934.01	9,91,757.82	55,462.66
23.	Puri	4,92,342.82	4,92,342.82	90,015.33
24.	Bhubaneswar	1,15,264.33	3,07,306.32	-
25.	Berhampur	17,01,621.00	24,81,297.22	18,921.73
26.	Gopalpur	-	88,695.50	9,968.24
27.	Rambha	20,776.65	69,685.00	15,169.95
28.	Hinjilicut	25,423.81	69,347.12	12,130.81
29.	Soruda	34,355.00	55,982.50	23,949.50
30.	Balasore	2,09,037.41	39,861.62	22,436.52
31.	Jaleswar	-	-	-

(Taken from the Annual Report of Local Fund Audit organisation of Finance Department for the year 1976-77

ANNEXURE-VI

RECEIPTS FROM MUNICIPAL PROPERTY AND ENTERPRISES DURING THE YEAR 1961-62 TO 75-76.

Sl.No.	Name of the Urban local bodies	1961-62		1965-66		1971-72		1975-76	
		Amount	Percentage to total receipt	Amount	Percentage to total receipt	Amount	Percentage to total receipt	Amount	Percentage to total receipt
1	2	3	4	5	6	7	8	9	10
1.	Koraput N.A.C.	5205	6.91	25486	10.13	27608	6.97	54299	7.61
2.	Sunabeda N.A.C.	-	-	-	-	20273	9.94	46967	11.68
3.	Jeypore Municipality	52294	18.82	72189	10.91	40979	12.54	250663	10.20
4.	Cuttack Municipality	51953	1.02	76530	2.33	46603	1.58	1056150	8.93
5.	Jajpur Municipality	1263	1.04	4520	2.58	16504	0.29	27332	3.66
6.	Athagarh N.A.C.	-	-	-	-	-	-	6538	7.27
7.	Joda N.A.C.	-	-	7376	1434	12769	7.04	73645	15.49
8.	Angul N.A.C.	2419	7.14	7410	12.65	15158	2.28	190342	25.51
9.	Talcher N.A.C.	7588	10.74	34515	6.75	63531	20.60	59917	12.42
10.	Khariar Road N.A.C.	-	-	4593	20.51	13605	4.96	12559	3.15
11.	Rourkela(CT) N.A.C.	-	-	45755	15.96	171951	17.42	118526	8.63
12.	Sonepur Municipality	829	1.35	2513	3.48	2207	1.52	5557	2.12
13.	Titilagarh N.A.C.	12300	16.31	51092	12.23	60796	32.81	112216	19.64
14.	Phulbani N.A.C.	-	-	3625	8.22	5893	5.06	16339	7.01
15.	Sambalpur Municipality	96367	11.09	125910	6.52	190913	6.47	322022	5.53
16.	Deogarh Municipality	9310	11.92	17552	16.84	54169	17.88	71489	14.93
17.	Brajarajanagar N.A.C	-	-	-	-	19355	4.24	23293	2.51
18.	Padmapur N.A.C.	-	-	18242	32.40	55728	37.15	65843	34.75
19.	Rairangapur N.A.C.	3301	12.74	10690	4.23	26715	17.18	25089	8.82

Contd.

20.	Baripada Municipality	39238	10.03	86276	19.02	78096	9.98	207371	24.04
21.	Khurda N.A.C.	4579	10.46	2833	2.71	5468	9.50	37250	10.94
22.	Nayagarh N.A.C.	4887	13.28	11891	2.99	23447	4.03	53495	16.15
23.	Puri Municipality	77344	8.20	83505	5.38	87702	2.74	264517	5.32
24.	Bhubaneswar N.A.C.	18831	3.27	34119	3.37	37408	2.01	148492	4.81
25.	Berhampur Municipality	144704	12.53	178081	7.35	406551	6.68	487204	5.72
26.	Gopalpur N.A.C.	2234	6.12	4071	8.03	7976	5.60	16831	8.40
27.	Rambha N.A.C.	-	-	629	4.23	2968	6.20	6817	5.32
28.	Hinjilicut N.A.C.	-	-	32520	52.24	85169	31.92	131598	36.46
29.	Soruda N.A.C.	-	-	7887	18.18	15458	9.65	17386	8.22
30.	Balasore Municipality	20454	4.96	29791	5.55	76944	5.80	100046	4.05
31.	Jaleswar N.A.C	-	-	-		14637	17.53	31134	36.42

NOTES AND REFERENCES

1. Hepworth, N.P : *The Finance of Local Governments*,p.194
2. Gyanchand : *Local Finance in India*, p.173.
3. Hepworth, N.P. : *The Finance of Local Government*, p.195.
4. Thacker, N.H. : *Nagarlok* - Volume -IX October-December, 1977,p.103.
5. Pande, V.K. : *Municipal Finance in Marathwada*.p.221.
6. *Report of the Rural-Urban Relationship Committee*, Volume-I.p.105.
7. Hepworth, N.P.: *The Finance of Local Government*,p.200.
8. Gyanchand : *Local Finance in India*,p.175.
9. *Report of the Committee on Urban Waste*, p.30-31.
10. *Report of the Orissa State Municipal Finance Commission*, 1975.p.75.
11. From the unpublished work of Prof. Devraj of National Institute of Urban Affairs (Resource mobilisation for Urban Areas).
12. *Audit Report No.178* of 76-77 on the accounts of 1975-76 (Para 10).
13. *Audit Report No.7* of 1979-80 on the accounts of Bhubaneswar Municipality for the year 1977-78.
14. Rao V.V. : *A Hundred Years of Municipal Government in Assam*, p.387.
15. Gyanchand : *Report of the Departmental Committee on Local Taxation, 1914*. Quoted at p.185 "Local Finance in India".
16. Hicks, U.K. : *Development from Below*, p.409.
17. *Report of the Rural-Urban Relationship Committee*, 1966,p.103.
18. *Report of the Taxation Enquiry Commission-Volume-VI* Ministry of Finance, Government of India, p.367.
19. *Report of the Rural-Urban Relationship Committee, Volume-I*, p.103.
20. *Report of the Committee on Augmentation of Resources of Urban Local Bodies*.
21. *Report of Grants-in-aid Code Committee for Municipalipties and Municipal Corporation*, Government of Gujarat, 1972 as reproduced in Nagarlok-Volume-V April-June 1973,pp.45-46.
22. *Report of the State Municipal Finance Commission*, Orissa, 1975.p.74.
23. Alderfer, Harold F. : *American Local Government*, p.172.
24. Pande, V.K. : *Municipal Finances in Marathawada*,p.272.
25. Hepworth, N.P. : *The Finance of Local Government*, pp.103-104.
26. Based on an unpublished work of Prof. Dev Raj of National Institute of Urban Affairs. (Collected figures by the town and Country Planning Organisation).
27. *Report of State Municipal Finance Commission,* Orissa, 1975,p-69 (based on Average figures for five years from 1969-70 to 1973-74).
28. *Report of the State Municipal Finance Commission*, Orissa, 1975,pp.72-73.
29. *Report of the State Municipal Finance Commission*, Orissa, 1975,p.73.
30. *Annual Report of Local Fund Audit Organisation*, Finance Department, Orissa for the Year 1977-78. p.13(Para 5).
31. *Report of the Public Accounts Committee 1st Report*, (fifth Assembly), Para11.
32. Mehta, M.R. : *Notes on Municipal Finance, Accounts and Audit*, p.58.
33. Gyanchand : *Local Finances in India*, p.199.
34. Section 3 of the Local Authorities Loans Act, 1914. Act No.IX of 1914 (28th February 1914).
35. Based on the figures collected by the Town and Country Planning Organisation and compiled by the National Institute of Urban Affairs, New delhi. (Unpublished work of Professor Devraj, Director of the Institute.)
36. Hepworth, N.P. : *The Finance of Local Government*,p.129.

37. Dalal, C.B. : *Municipal Finance*,p.35.
38. *Report of the States Municipal Finance Commission*, 1975,p.95.
39. *Report of the State Municipal Finance Commission,Part-II.*
40. Government of Orissa, Urban Development Department in their letter No. 32214 dt. 19.10.79 sanctioned loan of Rs. 1,12,000 to Nayagarh N.A.C. and Rs. 5,08,000 to Khurda N.A.C. in U.D. Dept. Letter No.32204 dated 19.10.79 for repayment of L.I.C. loans, outstanding against these Notified Area Councils.
41. Various loans from State Government and L.I.C. incurred by N.A.C./Municipalities remained unspent to the tune of Rs.5,61,087.16 at the end of March 1976. Further loans were diverted unauthorisedly for meeting routine expenditure paying huge amount of interest from Municipal Fund (pp.13-14,Annual Report of L.F.A. Organisation for 1976-77 & 1977-78, Finance Department, Government of Orissa).
42. Gyanchand : *Local Finance in India*,p.211.
43. *Report of the Committee on Augmentation of Financial Resources of Urban Local Bodies*,p.68.
44. *Report of the State Municipal Finance Commission*, Orissa, 1975,p.79.
45. *Report of the Rural-Urban Relationship Committee*,p.108.
46. Hepworth, N.P. : *The Finance of Local Government*,p.398.
47. Gyanchand : *Local Finance in India*,p.202..

FIVE

LOCAL EXPENDITURE

The pattern and source of income of urban local bodies, discussed in the previous chapters, show that the sources have not been fully harnessed to meet the needs of the local authorities. With slender sources these authorities have been saddled with the responsibility of providing many services and amenities and performing other statutory functions. To reconcile the objectives with limited resources, there must be a careful assessment of these objectives to which resources are devoted and there should be a control mechanism to ensure that those objectives yield the maximum possible benefit. Normally, profit should not be the criterion, but benefit to the community. The object of this Chapter is to present and analyse the growth in local expenditure, the widening gap between desirable standard of expenditure and the current expenditure, the control mechanism available for proper regulation of such expenditure and the need for cost consciousness in making decisions to spend the local funds. In conclusion, an attempt has been made to suggest ways and means for proper utilisation of the funds with the improved management technique.

Its significance

Local expenditure is a part of the public expenditure and is incurred by the local authorities. The principle of public expenditure is equally applicable to local expenditure. "Resources should be so distributed between different uses that the marginal return of satisfaction is the same for all of them".[1] To a large extent, local expenditure is incurred to promote the welfare of the inhabitants of a locality but it would be wrong to contend "that the local expenditure is essentially an outlay for local benefit".[2] Local expenditure is a factor in the economic feature of a country as it renders health and sanitation, provides education, carries business enterprises, stimulates municipal housing, and because of manifold activities, a large spender and consumer of goods. It creates national wealth in the form of streets, roads, buildings and other permanent assets. It contributes to the earning power of people in various ways by provision and development of infrastructure in urban areas which serves as trading and vocational center for rural people.

Classification of Expenditure

The pattern of expenditure depends upon the functions assigned to the urban local bodies. The functions of local authorities in all the States are more or less similar. The State Municipal Finance Commission (Orissa) 1975 has, however, classified the functions of an urban local body as (i) basic obligatory function, (ii) obligatory function, and (iii) discretionary function giving details of activities under each category.[3] The nature of functions the urban local bodies are assigned broadly include sanitation, water supply, medical relief, provision of street lighting, vaccination, registration of births and deaths, maintenance of pounds, ferries and burial grounds, provision of regulation of private markets, slaughter houses, etc. Provision of primary education is also the responsibility of these authorities in some States including Orissa. These activities necessitate maintenance of large number of employees.

The expenditure incurred to discharge these functions may be broadly classified as ordinary and extraordinary expenditure. The current and recurring expenditure is known as ordinary expenditure and is generally met out of the Revenue Account. On the otherhand the extraordinary expenditure is non-recurring in nature and is financed either from Revenue Account or from Capital Account depending upon the nature of expenditure. Expenditures which are unproductive in character are usually met from current revenue and expenditure involving creation of permanent assets which entail heavy investment and yield revenue is financed from Capital Account. The expenditure met from revenue account is known as revenue expenditure and that from capital account is called capital expenditure. The capital expenditure may be incurred from grants or borrowed funds or from the funds created for the purpose.

There is no uniform method of classifying the expenditures in the urban local bodies of different States. Even the classification of expenditure under Revenue and Capital Account is not done in many States. The Committee on Budgetary Reforms in Municipal Administration observed, "out of 63 responding units, 49 are not even maintaining capital accounts separately".[4] The Zakaria Committee in their report have adopted the classification of local expenditure under the following heads:

a. General administration and Collection charges
b. Public Safety and Convenience
c. Public health
d. Education
e. Public works
f. Miscellaneous
g. Repayment of loans and
h. extraordinary; whereas the Rural Urban-Relationship Committee[5] have classified the expenditure of urban local authorities under(1) Establishment (2) Water Supply (3)Sewage including swerage disposal and drainage (4) Street lighting (5) Public health and sanitation (6) Medical Services (7) Engineering Services (8) Education (9) Grants given by local bodies and (10) Miscellaneous revenue Expenditure. The classification of receipts and expenditure is a device to keep proper accounts and to facilitate preparation of budgets. Such variations in adopting different pattern of classification do not vitally affect the pattern of expenditure.

In Orissa, the classification of receipts and expenditure prescribed in the Orissa Municipal Rules, 1953, for preparation of the budget [6] of urban local bodies has been adopted for the classification of expenditure and maintenance of accounts under such heads. Section 117 of the Orissa Municipal Act, 1950 prescribes the purposes for which expenditure may be incurred from the local fund. In this study figures have been collected for 15 years, from 1961-62 to 1975-76, in respect of 31 urban local bodies pertaining to expenditure under these heads and grouped them under the heads of classification shown in Table-V-I to facilitate analysis and discussion.

The particular type of activities grouped under each head of expenditure is as follows:

1. General Administration	Office Establishment, Contingencies, T.A., D.A. and other allowances including pension & gratuity.
2. Collection Establishment	Establishment pertaining to collection of taxes and other charges as above.
3. Public Health	Establishment charges, drainage and sewage works, conservancy, epidemic and vaccination charges, Medical.
4. Water Supply	Water supply Establishment, Works and maintenance and repairs.
5. Public Works	Public conservancy, public safety, roads, tanks, pounds, buildings.
6. Education	Primary and Secondary education, Scholarships, libraries etc.
7. Miscellaneous	Interest on loans, Law charges, stationery and printing, Provident Funds, Unforeseen charges.
8. Extraordinary & Debt	Investment, Repayment of loans, Advances and deposits.

All India Pattern

The pattern of expenditure in Orissa as revealed from the details in Table-V-I is in keeping with the pattern of expenditure of urban local bodies in India. The Town and Country Planning Organisation, New Delhi collected data relating to expenditure pattern of urban local bodies for 1975-76 from all the States in India which were compiled by the Institute of Urban Affairs.[7] The all India pattern of expenditure in urban local bodies vis-a-vis the pattern of expenditure of urban local bodies in Orissa in respect of some important items is given below:

The comparison shows that the percentage of expenditure of urban local authorities in Orissa under Public Health, repayment of loan and education is more than the All India local expenditure. In all other cases, all India percentage of expenditure is greater than that of Orissa. In case of the United Kingdom, the local authorities invest 38 percent of their local expenditure on education and 15.4 percent on housing. In India, local expenditure on housing is negligible and on education is much less than that of the United

Kingdom. However, In India local expenditure on public health is much more than that of the United Kingdom, being only 7 percent.

		All India Percentage of expenditure	Percentage of expenditure in Orissa.
1.	General Administration	9.9	6.08
2.	Collection Establishment	5.7	7.29
3.	Public Health	21.4	28.50
4.	Education	10.7	11.69
5.	Water Supply	5.9	2.81
6.	Miscellaneous	17.4	13.82
7.	Repayment of Loan	5.1	10.18

Growth of Expenditure

The figures in Table-V-1 indicates that the increase in the volume of total expenditure during the 15 years from 1961-62 to 1975-76 is quite significant. The increase in the volume of expenditure during 1975-76 over 1971-72 was 64.02 percent and over 1965-66, 259.31 percent and when compared with the volume of expenditure in 1961-62, the increase in 1975-76 was 673.38 percent. A few instances of increase in expenditure under different heads of account during all these years are cited. The expenditure under 'General Administration' has shown the highest percentage of increase during 1975-76 being 1156.90 percent when compared with the expenditure of 1961-62. Similarly the increase in expenditure under 'Collection Establishment' has recorded a growth of 927.99 percent over 1961-62.

The table further shows that public health constitutes the highest percentage of expenditure in all the years. Next in importance is expenditure on public works. Then comes the repayment of debt. Though there has been variation in percentage in different years, the order of importance is not much changed.

Causes of growth

It is not necessary to analyse the growth of expenditure of individual local bodies since it is not very pertinent to the subject

Table-VI-1: Classification of Expenditures for the Period from 1961-62 to 1975-76

Head of Expenditure	1961-62 Amount of expenditure	1961-62 Percentage to total expenditure	1965-66 Amount	1965-66 Percentage to total expenditure	1971-72 Amount	1971-72 Percentage to total expenditure	1975-76* Amount	1975-76* Percentage to total expenditure
General Administration	244315	3.74	402534	2.83	1294700	4.21	3070792 (1156.90)	6.08
Collection Establishment	357954	5.48	559370	3.93	1439422	4.68	3679738 (927.99)	7.29
Public Health	2268428	34.71	4593227	32.24	8535942	27.74	14386767 (534.22)	28.50
Water Supply	91137	1.40	785126	5.52	2196336	7.14	1413199 (1450.53)	2.81
Public Works	1057285	16.20	3573245	25.08	6753768	21.95	9909758 (837.23)	19.63
Education	803082	12.32	1447537	10.16	3627781	11.79	5898897 (634.53)	11.69
Miscellaneous	736713	11.28	811000	5.69	2675086	8.69	6973251 (846.54)	13.82
Extraordinary & Debt	970248	14.87	2073190	14.55	4249079	13.80	5139653 (429.73)	10.18
Grand Total	6529162	100	14245229	100	30772114	100	5042055 (673.38)	100

The figures in the brackets show the percentage of increase in expenditure in relation to the expenditure of 1961-62.

Growth rate of Expenditure during 1975-76 Over 71-72 is 64.02, Over 65-66 is 254.31, Over 61-62 is 673.38

concerning financial administration. The growth in the volume of total expenditure is analysed with a view to highlighting the problem associated with administering such expenditure. The following factors are responsible for such abnormal growth in local expenditure:

1. The change in the concept of the State from maintenance of law and order to providing welfare activities for the people and decentralisation of functions have increased the activities of the local bodies. These new functions necessitate heavy expenditure.

2. Under the assistance of Five Year Plans there has been a tendency on the part of National and State Governments to extend financial assistance to the local bodies in the shape of grants and loans. Loans have also been advanced by institutions like Life Insurance Corporation of India, HUDCO for financing developmental activities.

3. Growth in industrialisation has led to urbanisation necessitating investment of more funds in building the infrastructure i.e. roads, transport, buildings and markets.

4. The inflow of people to urban areas in quest of employment and better living standards has increased expenditure to meet the growing needs of urbanisation. The urban population in Orissa increased from 11.10 lakhs in 11961 to 16.85 lakhs in 1971.

5. New areas have been included in the urban localities and the number of urban local bodies has increased from 64 in the year 1961 to 91 in 1975-76. This increase has added to the volume of total expenditure.

6. Employment of a large number of people in different local bodies to manage the administration of heavy expenditure has also caused heavy increase in the total expenditure. (The establishment cost has increased by 1150.90 percent.)

7. Above all, the inflationary state of the Indian economy has its impact on the local expenditure giving rise to high rate of increase in wages and salaries, costs of materials and other services. The rise in prices has resulted in preparing inflated budgets.

Standard of Expenditure

The volume of expenditure has risen by 673.38 percent during the last 15 years, but if the rate of increase in the prices is taken into account along with the increase in the numbers of urban local bodies and also the increase in population during the period, the expenditure of the local authorities in real terms does not show any perceptible increase. The services and amenities required to be provided to the local community have not been provided to the extent desired. Apart from the quality of services, the extent of such services is not adequate. It is interesting to quote the findings of the State Municipal Finance Commission (1975) on provision of some of the important services by the urban local bodies in Orissa:

a. The present urban population of the State being 18,73,546 the estimated requirement of latrines is 3,64,108 against which there are only 91,578 latrines (28,902 septic and 62,676 service latrines) which serve a population of 4,71,627. Hence practically 14,01,919 people have no provision of latrines and therefore they are easing at open places.

   The present study reveals that though the total expenditure on 'Public Health' which covers expenditure on latrines is the highest, yet the provision of services is the poorest as pointed out by the Commission (p.-50 of the Report).

b. As regards provision of street lighting, 68.98 percent of the Municipal roads are served with street lights and they serve 3736 K.M. of urban roads out of total urban roads of 5416 K.M. and in some urban areas the streets are provided with kerosene lamps. The Commission observed that against an expenditure of Rs. 23,29,542 during 1973-74, the collection of lighting tax amounted to Rs. 7,04,977 only. Therefore the expenditure is far in excess of the receipts from such services. Yet the position of street lighting is not adequate (p.86 of the Report).

c. 60 urban local bodies took up projects for supply of piped water to the inhabitants of the locality during the plan period out of which 16 projects were completed by the end of 4th Five Year Plan. The per capita water supply provided in the schemes already executed is far less than the standard prescribed for the purpose (p. 95 & 101 of the Report).

As pointed out earlier, water supply schemes involve heavy investment which is met mostly from borrowed funds entailing payment of heavy interest. Most of the loans incurred by the urban local bodies are meant for meeting the expenditure on water-supply projects.

The element of establishment charges is present in almost all the heads of expenditure and such charges constitute more than 50% of the total expenditure, but the return of employment of such a large number of personnel has never been calculated. On the other hand misutilisation and wastage of man-power have been sadly commented by different commissions and committees.

The Committee on Augmentation of Financial Resources of Urban Local Bodies in its report (1963) prescribed the standard of services for the local authorities and estimated the per capita requirement of each service pertaining to different category of urban local bodies. For assessment of standard of each service, the urban local bodies were divided into six categories on the basis of population i.e. special 'A' constituting metropolitan cities with a population of above 20 lakhs, standard 'A' cities with a population of 5 to 20 lakhs, standard 'B' cities with a population of 1 to 5 lakhs, standard 'C'towns with a population of 50,000 and standard 'D' towns with a population of 20,000 to 50,000, standard 'E' towns with a population below 20,000. The cost estimates were made in 1960-61 at the then price level. The per capita expenditure for standard of services prescribed for different categories of cities/towns was as follows.[8]

Special 'A' - Rs. 53.50, 'A' Class - Rs. 39.03, 'B' Class - Rs. 33.40, 'C' Class Rs. 27.62, 'D' Class - Rs. 24.27 and 'E' Class - Rs. 21.07. The Committee went to the extent of preparing the estimates based on the prescribed standard for cities and towns of each State. As regards Orissa, it was estimated that there was a gap of Rs. 1.74 crore between the standard needs and the existing resources.

Without making an exercise to find out the requirement of resources to meet the need for standard services, it may be mentioned here that inspite of unprecedented growth in expenditure, the standard of services prescribed by the Committee has not been attained by the urban local bodies in Orissa. According to the classification made by the committees there are no cities under 'A' special or 'A' ,as no city in Orissa has a population of more than 5 lakhs. The cities and towns existing in this State belong to categories 'B' to 'E'. The expenditure pattern of 31 urban local bodies and the per capita expenditure of these towns/cities have been arrived at to compare the existing pattern of expenditure on services and the desirable standard of expenditure on such services.The Committee worked out the per capita expenditure for different categories of cities/towns in 1960-61. In the meantime the cost of providing such services has increased by 3 times as worked out by Professor Mahesh Bhatt in calculating the desirable standard of services for towns/cities of Gujarat.[9] According to the rate adopted by him on the basis of the standard per capita expenditure prescribed by the Committee, the per capita desirable expenditure for different rates (1975-76) is as follows :- 'B' Class Rs. 100.00, 'C' Class Rs. 82.76 'D' Class Rs. 72.81, 'E' Class Rs. 63.21.

Accordingly, the position showing the per capita expenditure of different categories of urban local bodies in 1975-76 has been projected in Table-V-2. It will be seen there from that among the 3 urban local bodies under Class 'B' two have per capita expenditure of less than Rs. 60 and the one exceeding Rs. 60 has per capita expenditure of Rs. 72.81 (Berhampur Municipality). Between the two 'C' class towns both of them have percapita expenditure exceeding Rs. 60, one has per capita expenditure of Rs. 91.18 (Sambalpur Municipality) and the other has Rs. 73. Thus one Municipality has more than desirable per capita expenditure of Rs. 82.76. Among the 7 'D' class towns, the per capita expenditure of only 2 towns exceeded Rs. 60 (Jeypore Rs. 69.22 and Balasore Rs. 60.67) but both of them fell short of the desirable per capita expenditure. Under category 'E' there are 19 towns out of which only 4 had per capita expenditure exceeding Rs. 60 (Angul Rs. 71.94, Deogarh Rs. 69.96, Nayagarh Rs. 70.32 and Gopalpur Rs. 63.01). However, only three of them had more than the desirable standard of percapita expenditure. As such, all the remaining 16 out of 19 had a per capita expenditure much below the required standard. On the whole out of 31 towns only 4 had the desirable standard of per capita expenditure.

TABLE-V-2 : Per-capita Expenditure Distribution by Class of Towns, 1975-76

Class of town (Population)	Number of Urban Local Bodies							
	Less than Rs. 10.00	Rs. 10-20	Rs. 20-30	Rs. 30-40	Rs. 40-50	Rs. 50-60	Rs. 60.00 & above	Total No.
'B' Class Above 100000	-	-	-	1	-	1	1	3
'C' Class 50000-100000	-	-	-	-	-	-	2	2
'D' Class 20000-50000	-	1	2	1	1	-	2	7
'E' Class Less than 20,000	1	1	4	6	3	-	4	19
Total	1	2	6	8	4	1	9	31

It goes to prove that in spite of large input, the standard of services produced lacks the standard prescribed. The position as discussed shows an utter disappointing trend in meeting the needs of the local community.

Control of Expenditure

The factors responsible for the shortfall on local expenditure may be outlined here. An attempt is made to examine the method of financial control to regulate the expenditure.

While discussing about control of local expenditure, N.P. Hepworth has quoted the Plowden Report giving emphasis on efficiency on control of Public EXpenditure. The Report states: "The preparation of materials on which decisions are taken; the technical efficiency with which large operations of administration are carried out; the cost consciousness of staff at all levels; the provision of special skills and services (scientific, statistical, accountancy, organisation and method etc.) for handling particular problems and the awareness and effectiveness with which they are used, the training and selection of man and woman for posts at each level of responsibility.These are the real substance of management, and it is upon them that the effective control of expenditure and value for money must in the last resort depend".[10]

In the context of above factors, the forms of control over expenditure that are prescribed under statutes to ensure efficient and effective management may now be discussed. Such controls may be broadly analysed as (i) Statutory Control (ii) Control through Committee (iii) Internal Control and (iv) Audit Control.

1. **Statutory Control**

a. There are numerous provisions in the Orissa Municipal Act, 1950 and Orissa Municipal Rules 1953, which regulate expenditure. Section 117 of the Act gives a detailed list of purposes for which the funds of a local authority should be applied. It also prohibits the use of such funds outside the municipal area and for purposes other than that provided in the rules. It is interesting to point out that the provision of Maharashtra Municipal Act,1965 made the person who voted for the expenditure personally liable for misapplication of the municipal fund. Any rate payer can sue him for this misapplication. Under the Law in England "if a rate payer objects to the expenditure of a local authority on the grounds that it is illegal, then he could either raise the issue with the District Auditor and ask him to investigate the allegation or he could apply to the courts seeking an order to restrain the activities of the local authority".[11] Such a provision works as a deterrent measure against the elected council and executive authorities of the urban local bodies. Unfortunately the Orissa Act does not make any such stringent provision for misapplication of municipal funds. The result is obvious. Misutilisation and misapplication of municipal funds are rampant and the audit reports on the accounts of such local authorities speak of numerous instances of the above category.

b. A few instances of misapplication of municipal funds are given below which show that Government grants received for specific purposes were spent for other purposes in meeting the day-to-day expenditure of the local body resulting in diversion of funds for unauthorised purposes.

Sl. No.	Name of the Municipality /N. A. C.	Year of accounts	Amount of grant diverted (in Rs.)
1.	Jajpur Municipality	1975-76	185156
		1971-72	267470
2.	Baripada Municipality	1975-76	45862
3.	Rairangpur N.A.C.	1975-76	13463
4.	Balasore Municipality	1975-76	150368
5.	Deogarh Municipality	1975-76	107402
6.	Sambalpur Municipality	1975-76	55193
7.	Sonepur Municipality	1975-76	100735
		1971-72	57958
8.	Rambha N.A.C.	1975-76	174807
9.	Berhampur Municipality	1975-76	793654
		1971-72	307760
10.	Puri Municipality	1975-76	125917
		1971-72	474035
11.	Phulbani N.A.C.	1975-76	80762

(Taken from Annual Report of the Local Fund Audit Organisation 1976-77 and 1972-73, Finance Department, Government of Orissa).

c. It is not possible to illustrate the large number of cases of diversion of municipal funds brought to light through several audit reports. However a few cases of interesting and important nature of such expenditures which are neither authorised by rule nor by special sanction of Government are cited below:

i. Sambalpur Municipality spent a sum of Rs.1,231 for according civic reception to Khan Abdul Gufar Khan during 1969-70 which was disapproved by Government in Urban Development Department Memo No.21751 dated 25.3.70.

(Annual Report of Local Fund Audit, Finance Department for1968-69.)

ii. An expenditure of Rs.41,371 representing payment towards wages of labourers attached to each councillor in Cuttack Municipality was unauthorised as there was no out turn from the engagement of such labourers.

(Annual Report 1968-69 of Local Fund Audit, Finance Department.)

iii. Disregarding the Government order, Sambalpur Municipality spent Rs. 21,850 towards the salary of a lady doctor.

(Annual Report 1968-69 of Local Fund Audit, Finance Department.)

iv. Cuttack Municipality spent Rs.7,891 towards cost of brass badges supplied to the food vendors for food license. As the income goes to Health Department, the cost should have been borne by the Health Department and not by the Municipality.

(Annual Report 1968-69 of Local Fund Audit, Finance Department.)

v. Bhubaneswar N.A.C. spent Rs.18,865 against the estimated cost of Rs.35,000 for the construction of Kindergarten school in Goutam Nagar which is not permissible under rules. The scheme was subsequently abandoned.

(Audit Report of 1979-80 of Bhubaneswar Notified Area Council.)

vi. In Puri Municipality a sum of Rs.2,72,706 was paid as off-day allowances to its employees during the year 1977-78 in violation of Government order issued in Urban Development Department, letter No. 34955 dated 20.12.75.

(Audit Report No. 156 of 1978-79.)

vii. A sum of Rs.25,000 was withdrawn from Depreciation fund on 31.3.78 in Puri Municipality and was merged in general fund to meet the ordinary expenditure of the Council which amounts to misutilisation of the fund.

(Audit Report No. 156 of 1978-79.)

viii. The Chairman of Berhampur Municipality travelled in the municipal jeep from Berhampur to Delhi from 1.12.72 to 14.12.72 incurring an expenditure of Rs. 888 from the municipal fund without any specific purpose and without any sanction of Government.

(Annual Report of Local Fund Audit Organisation, Finance Department for 1974-75.)

ix. A sum of Rs 73,000 was withdrawn from time to time from the Employees Provident Fund pass book No. 30994 and Rs.325000 from the pass book No. 1234 to meet day to day expenditure of Municipality involving loss of interest and against the canons of financial management.

(Audit Report No. 115 of 1976-77 on Puri Municipality.)

2. Budgetary Control

Budget serves as a powerful instrument to control expenditure. It is the pivot around which the whole financial management of a municipal Government revolves. According to the provision in the Orissa Municipal Act, 1950, no expenditure can be incurred without necessary provision in the budget and no expenditurre in excess of the budget provision is permissible.The authorities in charge of the execution of the budget are also liable to explain for avoidable savings against budgetary provision. Budget is supposed to be the tool of management as it carries the will of the elected council to spend for different purposes. Thus it carries the will and the aspiration of the people at large. Sanction and approval of competent authority is necessary to divert money from one head of account to another. As such it is normally not permissible to transfer funds from one head of account to spend for other purposes. The authority is required to ensure that the expenditure sanctioned in the budget is spent for the purpose for which sanction is accorded.

The study shows that the sanctity of the budget has not been observed by the urban local authorities. The budget estimates have neither been framed properly nor timely. Expenditures have been incurred without budget provision and in some cases budget provision has either exceeded or not fully uitilised. These irregularities have been discussed in the subsequent chapter with detailed illustration. A few instances of ineffectiveness of the budgetary control are cited below:

Name of the Municipality/ N.A.C.	Year of budget	Head of Account	Provision in the budget. (in Rs.)	Actual expenditure icurred (in Rs.)
1. Sambalpur Municipality	75-76	Public Health	618575	349822
-do-	75-76	Water supply	591845	48774
-do-	75-76	Public Works	1116500	664117
2. Nayagarh N.A.C.	75-76	Public Works	264646	110110
-do-	75-76	Public Works	628553	107629
3. Talcher Municipality	75-76	Miscellaneous	65700	105996
4. Khurda N.A.C.	75-76	Public Health	599000	75968
-do-	75-76	Miscellaneous	216800	44216
5. Baripada Municipality	75-76	General Administration	62981	76410
6. Berhampur Municipality	75-76	Water Supply	821110	518869

As can be seen from above, except in cases of miscellaneous and General Administration, the budget provision in other cases was far in excess of actual expenditure. This state of affairs is a recurring one and enquiries reveal that no action has been taken against any local authority for such lapses. The crux of the problem arises from the fact that the local bodies are not subject to any legislative control in respect of their budgetary activities and it has become an internal management device, the deviation from which warrants no action. Their public accountability would, perhaps, improve matters.

3. The expenditure incurred by the local authorities is broadly on (i) establishment (ii) works (iii) purchase of store and stock including stationery.

i. As regards entertainment of establishment the Municipal Council is competent to entertain its employees with the sanction of Government (Section 73 of the Orissa Municipal Act). But in case of emergency, the council may make provision for temporary employment not exceeding six months. But the provisions of this section have been observed more in their breach. The State Municipal Finance Commission observed "Expenditures are to be incurred for duty sanctioned posts. But the study revealed that posts continued in the local bodies like, Cuttack, Talcher, Rourkela and others without obtaining sanction from Government for months and years together".[12] Expenditure incurred on the continuance of these posts is unauthorised and irregular. Therefore there is laxity in exercising control over expenditure on establishment. A few instances are quoted below:

(a) Despite Government Order issued in their letter No. 1974 dated 17.10.74 refusing to continue the temporary posts beyond the sanctioned yardstick, Berhampur Municipality spent Rs. 1,19,332 during the year 1974-75 in making payment towards salary of temporary staff maintained without sanction of competent authority.

(Annual Report of Local Fund Audit Organisation, Finance Department for 1974-75.)

In the same Municipality provident fund contribution of the municipal employees deducted from their pay to the tune of Rs. 2,67,406 was kept in the municipal fund with the result that the provident fund account lost interest of Rs. 6740. Municipal contribution of Rs. 1,21,541 was not deposited into provident fund account losing interest of Rs. 18,564-00.

(Annual Report of Local Fund Audit Organisation, Finance Department, 1976-77.)

(b) In Bhubaneswar Municipality 53 posts were continued for years without sanction of competent authority which resulted in an unauthorised expenditure of Rs. 2,32,242 incurred during 1978-79.

(Audit Report of Bhubaneswar Municipality for 1979-80).

This is in regard to the employment of staff in regular establishment. A large number of staff are also maintained by the local authorities on daily wages basis on nominal muster roll and in work-charge establishment debiting the expenditure on such account to different works and projects. Employment of such daily wage earners is not subject to higher control and is thus maintained without restraint. Their work is required to be measured but is often certified as not susceptible to measurement. Thus huge amounts are spent from year to year on such appointments without adequate return from such expenditure. The State Municipal Finance Commission discussing about such employment of Mulias in Cuttack Municipality observed: "Service of 2 mulias each has been placed at the disposal of each councillor in Council resolution dated 26th December, 1964. This sanction of the Council is extra ordinary as public money is spent without any regular supervision over the work of these Mulias".[13]

In Bhubaneswar Municipality payment of Rs.30,507 was made to conservancy staff through Nominal Muster Roll working in different units without sanction of the Council during 1975-76 and the work done by them was never measured or assessed as required under rules relating to payment of Nominal Muster Rolls (Audit Report No. 71 of 1976-77).

Rule 174 of Orissa Municipal Rules imposes a condition that the Council may incur maximum expenditure on general office establishment not exceeding 5 percent of the normal income and 20 percent of the expenditure on works. The present study reveals that the scales and maxima Iaid down for employment of regular establishment were not adhered to and sanction of competent authority for such establishment was not obtained, a few instances of which are tabulated below.

TABLE-V-3: Expenditure on General Establishment during 1975-76

Sl No.	Name of the Local body	Expenditure on general Establishment (in Rs.)	Normal income of the local body (in Rs.)	Admissible expenditure 5% of the income (in Rs.)	Excess expenditure on Establishment (in Rs.)	Percentage of Excess expenditure
1	2	3	4	5	6	7
1.	Baripada Municipality	62961	550213	27511	35450	128.886
2.	Jeypore Municipality	113686	1490241	74512	39174	52.57
3.	Rambha N.A.C.	30548	40817	2040	28508	1397.45
4.	Bhubaneswar N.A.C.	207239	2078470	103923	103316	99.42
5.	Balasore Municipality	110204	1598090	79904	30300	37.92
6.	Rourkela (C.T) N.A.C.	74530	1144360	57218	17312	30.26
7.	Joda N.A.C.	38755	354430	17721	21034	118.70
8.	Gopalpur N.A.C.	20582	97187	4859	15723	323.59
9.	Cuttack Municipality	704221	8145458	407273	296948	72.91
10.	Berhampur Municipality	593887	6309851	315492	278395	88.24

Similarly the expenditure incurred on 'conservancy' is far in excess of the receipts from the latrine tax and sale of compost taken together. A few instances are given below.

(ii) Detailed procedure has been laid down in the Orissa Municipal Rules, 1953 under Section 330 to 386 for works expenditure. The

Council approves of the works to be taken up during the year and the amount required for the execution of these works is included in the budget. No new work can be commenced until there is sanction of plan and estimate. The estimate of the works which are based on the rates provided in the schedule of rates and approved by the Council. The powers of sanctioning estimates rests with the technical authorities. The Municipal Engineer (if he is of the rank of Assistant Engineer) is competent to sanction estimates not exceeding Rs. 20,000 and if the Engineer belongs to subordinate cadre, he may sanction estimates not exceeding Rs. 10,000. The Inspector of Local Works if he is in the rank of Executive Engineer may sanction estimate not exceeding Rs. 50,000 and in the case of Superintending Engineer up to Rs. 2 lakhs. The Chief Engineer is competent to sanction estimates upto Rs. 10 lakhs and if the amount exceeds Rs. 10 lakhs Government sanction is necessary.

Sl. No.	Name of the urban local body	Expenditure on conservancy (in Rs.)	Receipt from latrine tax and sale of compost (in Rs.)	Excess expenditure (in Rs.)
1.	Phulbani N.A.C.	46,171	5,801	40370
2.	Puri Municipality	11,20,040	1,78,631	941409
3.	Talcher Municipality	1,02,246	11,949	90297
4.	Berhampur Municipality	2,69,115	1,73,526	95589
5.	Cuttack Municipality	21,80,000	4,00,000	1780000
6.	GopalpurN.A.C.	34,158	3,363	30795

Similarly powers for acceptance of tenders for execution of works have been decertraalised basing on the monetary limits. The works executed are to be measured and check-measured before payment. It is interesting to note that Rule 365(2) of Orissa Municipal Rules 1953, empowers the Executive Officer to check- measure any work costing upto rupees ten thousand and in the case of earth work, upto twentyfive thousand where there is no Municipal Engineer. The work bills are subjected to usual routine check before being passed for payment. The power to authorise payment (to record pass order) vests with the Executive Officer of the Municipality. The works may be executed departmentally or entrusted to contractors on the basis of open competetive tenders.

The rules and procedures for execution of works have been outlined briefly which will show that the final authority rests with the Executive Officer who is not technically qualified to handle the works. In the absence of a Municipal Engineer, he is empowered to check-measure the works. The ultimate responsibility for payments rests with him. He is supposed to scrutinise the bills both technically and from the accounting and financial point of view. For this purpose he is assisted by the Accountant of the office who exercises preliminary check after bills are presented for payment.

In most of the urban local bodies, there is no Municipal Engineer. One Engineer is required to attend to the work of 3 to 4 local authorities. Many local authorities have only one Subordinate Engineer and some local authorities avail of the part-time services of Subordinate Engineers of other Departments. The staffing pattern of local authorities is so inadequate that it is hardly possible to observe the formalities prescribed under rules to carry out the execution of works. Several authorities are associated with the sanction of estimate, acceptance of tenders and execution of works. This system delays matters and hinders execution and stands in the way of timely utilisation of budgetary grants. In such a situation, not only the controls prescribed are not exercised but the works executed suffer from technical soundness and abound with financial irregularity and impropriety. The result of such impropriety and irregularities is manifested in consecutive audit reports issued by the Local Fund Audit Organisation of the Finance Department, which is in charge of audit of the accounts of local authority.

Indiscrimate and unauthorised advance payments have been made to contractors for works in progress for materials brought to site but not adjusted on finalisation of works. Such advances outstanding in the accounts of the local authorities of the State at the end of March 1976 amount to Rs. 62.11 lakhs. Similarly advances paid to the municipal employees for obtaining supplies and for departmental execution of works outstanding at the end of March 1976 amount to Rs. 36.25 lakhs.[14] Scrutiny of these advances revealed that some of these amounts were paid prior to 1961-62. According to rule 138 of Orissa Municipal Rules, 1953 no advances are payable unless there is reason to believe that the work for which money is required shall be paid and adjusted within the financial year. Many a financial years have passed and the amounts advanced remain unadjusted. Such advance payment amounts to undue and unauthorised assistance to the contractors and employees and depletes the municipal fund to the extent of amounts outstanding against them.

Execution of works in local authorities is not subjected to rigid controls prescribed due to various reasons, firstly due to inadequacy of technical and qualified staff and secondly due to pressure of the local council, third and the most important factor being sheer disregard for rules and procedure due to the temptation of illicit gains. The employees of local authorities are no exception to the situation prevalent in the country. A.D. Gorwala observes: "The ordinary citizen gets tired of having to wait for an answer and he is apt to ascribe any undue delay to a desire to obtain illicit gain on the part of the official".[15]

Details of irregularities, fraud, overpayments and infructuous expenditure on work accounts have been discussed in the Audit Reports of Local Fund Audit Organisation which have placed under objection an expenditure of Rs. 4,56,927 pertaining to works (as a result of the audit of the accounts conducted during 1976-77). Huge amounts on works accounts are placed under objection in the Audit Reports of Local fund Audit Organisation from year to year on grounds of impropriety and severe irregularities, a few instances of which are given below.[16] It has been pointed out that payments were made at rates higher than that provided in the schedule of rates or accepted tendered rates, lowest tenders were not accepted, extra items were executed without sanction of competant authority, misutilisation of materials, non-recovery of cost of materials from contractors due to inadequate scrutiny of works bills. Payments were made in violation of terms of agreements and the penel provisions of agreement were not enforced leading to infructuous payments. The State Municipal Finance Commission, Orissa (1975) also referred to the above facts in their findings[17].

a. In Puri Municipality the old market building was dismantled and three separate estimates for Rs. 2,00,000, Rs. 53,000 and Rs. 30,000 were approved for construction of a new building by the Municipal Engineer to avoid the sanction of higher authority. The work bill disclosed overpayment of Rs. 14,445 to the contractor due to wrong measurement, totalling mistakes. Dismantled materials worth Rs. 2,212 were neither used in the new construction nor taken to stock. The overpayments and other irregularities were possible due to inadequate scrutiny and due to absence of prescribed checks and control. (Annual Report of Local Fund Audit Organisation, Finance Department for 1974-75.)

b. Cuttack Municipality sustained loss to the extent of Rs. 3500 and Rs. 4526 in repairing the wheel barrow and double wheel barrow respectively due to non-acceptance of lowest tender of Rs. 83 and Rs. 218 against which payments were made @ Rs. 118 and Rs. 231 each. Higher tenders were accepted without assigning any reason. (Annual Report of Local Fund Audit Organisation, Finance Department for 1974-75.)

c. In execution of drain works in Cuttack Municipality the estimates were often revised to give undue benefit to contractors in profitable items of work. In a particular work, against the provision of 45 cum. of cement concrete works, payments were made for 100 cum. The estimate was revised thrice and ultimately the contractor was paid Rs. 31,391 in excess of the revised estimate of Rs. 30,000 unauthorisedly. (Annual Report of Local Fund Audit Organisation, Finance Department for 1968-69.)

d. Due to payments to coolies at rates higher than the approved rates in Sambalpur Municipality there was an overpayment of Rs. 6,693.

Further due to inadequate scrutiny of work bills, there was an overpayment of Rs. 27,193 in different work bills. (Annual Report of 1968-69.)

e. In Berhampur Municipality a total sum of Rs. 27,038 was paid in excess to the contractors due to recovery of the cost of cement at rates lower than the approved rates by adopting vague and irregular stipulation in agreements. (Annual Report of 1976-77).

f. Due to non-recovery of the hire charges of steam road roller at the correct rate and for the actual number of days used, the contractor was given undue financial aid of Rs. 1,975 in a road work in Puri Municipality. (Annual Report of 1975-76).

g. Undue financial aid to the tune of Rs. 38,150 was extended to some of the contractors entrusted with the execution of different works in Puri Municipality ignoring the restrictions laid down in rules (Annual Report of 1975-76).

h. In Rourkela (C.T.) Notified Area Council, the check measurement of one work "construction of Malgodown road" was made by the Municipal Engineers on 17.10.76 even though the measurement was recorded on 20.10.76. The design of the road was changed in course of execution of the work from 1100 ft. x 13 ft. to 1000 ft. x 13 ft., but while making payments, the cost of materials collected for 1100 ft. was paid resulting in an overpayment of Rs. 2,758. The entire execution of the work is not free from suspicion (Annual Report of 1977-78).

i. In Balasore Municipality payments were made to contractors in respect of four construction works towards the cost of M.S. roads used in the works far in excess of the approved specification without change in the design of the construction resulting in a loss of Rs. 15,960 to the council (Audit Report No.60 of 1976-77).

j. (i) In Sambalpur Municipality almost all the works executed on the basis of agreements during 1975-76 were not completed on the scheduled time and no penalty was imposed against any contractor as per the penal provision of the agreement.

(ii) A contractor was entrusted to execute one road work within 2 months on 23.1.71 but the work remained incomplete till March, 1976. The contractor refused to do further work at the rate provided in the agreement due to rise in prices. No penalty was imposed against him and on the other hand, he was paid the cost of the work amounting to Rs. 2,790 (Annual Report of 1975-76).

k. Due to non-acceptance of lowest tender without assigning sufficient reason in the execution of "Distempering and colour washing to Gandhi Smruti Bhawan", the council sustained a loss of Rs. 958 (estimated cost Rs. 12,910) as the 3rd lowest tender was accepted. The 3rd tenderer should have been asked to execute the work at the lowest tendered rate if the lowest tenderer did not deposit the required amount of security deposit (Audit Report No. 68 of 1976-77 on Balasore Municipality).

l. Due to non-acceptance of lowest tender in respect of construction of slum quarters in Baripada Municipality, the Council sustained a loss of Rs. 4813 (amount sanctioned was Rs. 61,284 actual payments made came to Rs. 66,097 to the higher tenders). Even though estimates for Rs. 52,950 were technically and administratively approved an expenditure of Rs. 66,097 was incurred without sanction of the competant authority.

Estimate of the work of Rs. 13,250 in respect of extension of S.C. Vidyapitha was not approved by the Inspector of Local Works, but the execution of the work was completed.

iii. Coming to the expenditure towards cost of store and stock and stationery articles purchased by the local authorities, it is needless to point out that scant regard was paid in observing the prescribed rules and procedures in making such purchases which resulted in diseconomies and it can be said that the best value for money paid was not obtained in these transactions. The State Municipal Finance Commission observed in this regard as follows: "Selection of articles is often made by persons who have a very limited knowledge of different quantities available in the market. Quotations are often invited without proper specification to favour some merchants stocking them. These quantities merely beguile the auditors or inquisitive members into the belief that lowest tenders were accepted and that every thing was above board"[18]. Stocks were neither purchased economically nor as per requirement leading to loss and wastage. Due to want of timely supply of materials to different projects the completion of the projects was delayed causing higher costs to local authorities. On the other hand, piling of store and stock not required for immediate use also involved loss. Numerous cases of the above category have been reported by the

Examiner of Local Accounts in individual audit reports and Annual Reports of the organisation[19]. A few instances of the above category are given below:

1. a. In Balasore Municipality, untested M.S.rods of different sizes were purchased from a private firm (M/s S.L. Gupta) for which a sum of Rs. 68,300 was paid. Purchases were made at higher rates than the rates quoted by Messrs Hindustan Steel Ltd., for tested rods. Untested rods also involved extra expenditure for use in different works. The case record examined disclosed that the Municipal Engineer favoured the firm inspite of higher rate and bad quality of materials. The transaction put the municipal council to a loss of Rs. 5204. The quality and economy were overlooked in this case.

A further study disclosed that there was no urgency in making such purchases from a local supplier at higher rates as the materials purchased in March 1975 for construction of guest house were lying unutilised till March 1976 and the construction work was not commenced till December, 1976.

b. Even though lowest quotation for supply of Rolling Shutters was accepted, by avoiding to fulfil all the requirements of the purchase order, the firm was favoured with an excess payment of Rs. 5224 in a transaction of Rs. 13,869 paid in May 1975. The rate of Rs. 1544 (lowest quotation) was inclusive of cost of fittings, ball bearings, nuts and bolts, but the firm was paid at the above rates without supplying all the fittings including ball bearing, nuts and bolts, etc. and further expenditure was incurred on all such fittings by engaging another contractor.

c. Purchase of 230 pieces of A.C. sheets and 110 pairs of A.C. ridges was made in April 1975 from a private firm at higher rates on payment of Rs. 17,756. The Municipal Engineer showed favour to the firm by making such purchases involving a loss of Rs. 888. The materials were neither required for immediate use nor was economy observed in making such purchases (Audit Report No. 68 of 1976-77).

2. Due to the negligence of a compost mistry there was loss of

compost stock worth Rs. 1125 (Annual Report of Local Fund Audit Organisation for 1977-78).

3. In Sambalpur Municipality, there was a loss of Rs. 559 in purchasing furniture due to the non-acceptance of lowest quotation (Annual Report for 1968-69).

4. In Cuttack Municipality the Head Clerk and the Overseer were issued 40 and 20 bags of cement respectively for their personal use and no cost was recovered from them (Annual Report for 1968-69).

5. In Puri Municipality out of balance stock of 3880 bags of cement on 31.3.76, 88 bags of cement were clodded due to long storing the cost of which comes to Rs. 1638 (Audit Report No. 115 of 1976-77).

Technique of Material Management

It has been indicated earlier that the municipal Governments have to meet the growing needs of development expenditure with limited resources. This is possible by proper application of the modern techniques of management. The cost of service can be reduced by proper management of men and materials employed for the purpose. Material management is one of such techniques which if adopted will go a long way in reducing the cost of materials. "Excess buying and over stocking lead to high carrying charges, a high rate of obsolescence, deterioration and pilferage and an excess of tied up capital. Material shortage on the other hand, may interrupt municipal projects, make machines and men idle, disrupt schedules and cause public resentment"[20]. Delays in completion of works lead to inflation of estimates which upsets the budgetary provision and leads to chaotic financial management. Delay in completion of different works is attributed to non-availability of materials in times of requirement. Such possibilities could be avoided by ensuring regularity in supply. Therefore an effective system of material management should be adopted to ensure that the right materials in right quantity and of the right quality are made available at the right place and at the right time. The following steps are necessary to ensure effective materials management:

a. Goods should be ordered in economic quantities.
b. Materials should be standardised in order to reduce the variety and number of items in the stock.
c. Excessive stocking of non-essential and damageable materials should be prevented.
d. Adequate inspection should be undertaken to reduce loss due to damage, deterioration, obsolesence, waste, theft.
e. Elaborate system to be provided for cost accounting and financial accounting.

As regards management of men, the discussion in the concluding chapter may be seen. In view of the growth in the volume of expenditure, the old practice of entrusting the financial responsibility to a lone clerk in the municipal office in the rank of an Accountant to check all bills according to the financial rules and procedures, giving ultimate responsibility to the Executive Officer to authorise all bills for payment need be changed. The Executive Officer has neither the time nor the training required to check the preliminaries associated with the vast range of payments. There should be diffusion of financial responsibility. The financial rules and procedures should not be the exclusive ingredient of the person working for financial system but such knowledge can be of great use if possessed by persons in charge of spending (in charge of execution of works and purchase of store and stock etc.).

ii. Control through Committees

Under the existing system of Local Government in England, there are several committees in each local Government to control and regulate the activities of several spending departments. These committees mostly supervise the functions of the concerned departments mainly to ensure efficiency and adequacy of the services. The function of the Finance Committee relates to all departments as decision on proposals for expenditure cannot be taken without the consideration of the Finance Committees. "Finance Committee is the common thread running the administration of all the services and is, with few exceptions, an important consideration in all policy matters"[21]. The role of the Finance Committee is to render advice on the financial implications of all proposals before a decision is taken to implement them. This induces financial awareness at the policy making level.

Similar committees function in the local Governments in India. But these committees have not proved their effectiveness in controlling expenditure and regulating services. The Orissa Municipal Act, 1950 provides for the appointment of Committees on (a) Finance, (b) Public Health, Hospitals and Dispensaries (c) Public Works, (d) Education and (e) any other special subjects by the council. The committees approve of all proposals for new works, regulate establishment, appointment and other service matters, approve contracts and agreements, frame regulation and by-laws, approve annual report and accounts. The committees perform such functions to facilitate the working of the council and being smaller bodies transact business more efficiently and without delay. The Committee is capable of exercising clear supervision over the activities of concerned department. Above all, like the English system, the Finance Committee being concerned with the activities of all departments, plays a vital role in controlling expenditure. This Committee is associated with preparation of the budget and approval of accounts and disposal of audit reports. Thus the committees control the financial administration of the local Governments to a great extent. The discussion in earlier chapters and in subsequent chapters show that inspite of the existence of committee system in the urban local bodies, there is much scope to improve the standard of financial administration.

iii. Internal Control
(a) Pre-audit

In addition to exercising pre-check of all claims before payment by the Accountant and the Executive Officer of a local Government, as indicated earlier in this chapter, such checks would be more effective if exercised through a system of pre-audit. Arrangement of pre-audit does not exist in any local Government in this State except in Cuttack and Berhampur Municipalities. The system presupposes checking of all payments according to details of checks prescribed under the Act/Rules which broadly aim at ensuring regularity in payment from the point of view of financial propriety as well as from the point of view of accounting and financial procedure. This point has, however, been dealt elaborately in the chapter relating to audit.

Introduction of the system of pre-audit would go a long way to control irregular and infructuous expenditure and ensure financial regularity saving the local body from loss and wastage of public funds.

(b) Accounting

As a measure of internal financial control, the system of accounting is of vital importance. The Municipal Rules have prescribed maintenance of several accounts registers and prescribed different forms for recording the transaction in the correct manner and under the proper head of accounts. The classification of transaction is determined according to administrative classification of functions and also by the classification of nature of transaction. As the local authority derives its income from the tax payers and spends it, it is of primary importance that the system of accounting should be elaborate to account for such trust funds. It is all the more necessary that the accounts should be maintained from the aspect of sound financial practice and control.

The present study reveals that the maintenance of the most important accounts registers is in a very bad shape. This has been repeatedly commented upon by the Examiner of Local Accounts in his audit reports. In such a context, accounting system as an aid to management does not serve its purpose. Even the basic requirement of maintaining separate accounts for Capital and Revenue Expenditure has not been fulfilled in many urban local bodies in the country including Orissa (pointed out by the Committee on Budgetary Reform, 1974). It has been disclosed that most of the capital works are executed through the state agency. In the case of urban local bodies in Orissa, the capital projects mostly involve water supply schemes which are executed by the Public Health Department of the State Government. Hence the capital and revenue accounts are not required to be maintained by them. But other schemes like drainage and street lighting are works of capital nature which are financed from borrowed funds. There is thus the need for maintaining of capital and revenue account for these projects. The State Municipal Finance Commission, Orissa (1975) also pointed out that the non-maintenance of important account registers has led to chaotic situation in assessment and collection of different taxes.

In addition to non-maintenance of accounts, omission and deficiencies in proper accounting of transactions are numerous. The staff in charge of accounts have neither interest nor the training for their proper maintenance. The lone Executive Officer of the local authority has neither the time nor the knowledge to supervise the accounts. Training in maintenance of accounts creates interest and without training the position of accounts cannot be improved. In the absence of proper accounts of different transactions the decision making authorities do not get the correct picture of the finances of the local authorities which leads to irregular decision making. The council also fails to exercise control over either receipts or expenditures due to improper and non-maintenance of accounts.

Moreover, under the existing system of accounting, the accounts of costs are kept and not returns. Thus the management does not know the result of its spending and, as such, its decision cannot be based on past performances. The citizens are not enlightened enough to balance what they are getting against what they must pay. Nature of social services cannot have quantitative expression. This difficulty has, perhaps, retarded the growth of cost accounting.

iv. Audit Control

The accuracy and correctness of accounts can be ascertained through an independent audit. It not only helps administration in bringing to light the lapses in financial transactions but discloses the financial results of the administration. In such a process all accounts, vouchers and registers relating to both payment and receipts are subjected to audit. Scrutiny of such payment discloses cases of over-payments, irregular payments and also manipulation of accounts. Such scrutiny is conducted in relation to the rules and procedure prescribed for regulating such payment. Audit scrutiny is extended to examining sanctions and orders, grants and appropriations and the sanction of expenditure. In auditing the expenditure, the auditor has to ensure that :

a. expenditure has been incurred by the officer competent to incur it;
b. the expenditure has been sanctioned by the competent authority;

c. it is covered by budget grant;
d. it does not involve any breach of canons of financial propriety.

The detailed checks prescribed for conducting scrutiny of expenditure are too numerous to be mentioned. The audit of the accounts of a local authority is taken up by the external auditors after the close of a financial year. Does such a system of post-audit long after the transaction is over really serve any effective purpose in controlling the expenditure? It points out several cases of serious lapses on the part of the local authorities in their financial administration in the successive audit reports. The system of audit of local Government is as old as the Governments themselves. The volume of audit objections is increasing from year to year. All these points have been discussed in detail in the next chapter with suggestion to improve audit practices as an aid to financial administration of urban local bodies.

Planning the Expenditure

The Committee on the Mnagement of Local Government in England (Chairman, John Maud) observed: "There is a lamentable disparity between the financial responsibility of local authorities and the taxable resources allotted to them. Their development is mostly influenced and rather determined by Government grants available. They have limited control over this expenditure as they depend upon the central assistance"[22]. What was spoken of local Government in England is hundred percent applicable to the local Government in India today. The release of grants by the Government is very uncertain and is not based on any approved principle or policy. As such, the expenditure planning cannot be made unless the funds are assured.

The system as it prevails cannot make expenditure planning a success unless there is control over resources. Yet incurring expenditure without proper planning would very well compare with an unchartered ship in an ocean. "In a developing country if the local Government Sector is outside the orbit of effective planning, its rate of growth may be adversely affected by the perverse fiscal behaviour of the local Government" [23]. It is, therefore, necessary that the local expenditure policy must be co-ordinated with the planning at the

State and central levels. It requires to have a planning unit at the local level and a definite assurance of flow of funds from the higher level of Government to local units.

The first two Five Year Plans did not take note of the requirement of urban local Governments and whatever efforts were made by provision of funds in the Third Five Year Plan for development and planning of local authorities, these proposals 'could make no progress in the absence of any clear policies about the organisation of municipal Governments' [24]. As regards planning in the urban local bodies in Orissa, the position has been sadly commented upon by the State Municipal Finance Commission (1975): "The Planning Commission instructed that all the schemes should form a part of the State plans and thereby integrated with the national plans. This has not been done so far. Rather the development works in the urban local bodies for all purposes are limited to the funds available from the State Government. The amount that can be available to different urban local bodies is not known"[25].

The present study reveals that such a state of affairs has resulted in "no fund, no work". There are several instances in different urban local bodies to show that funds are allotted to different works not as per estimates but as per availability of grants from Government as a result of which the projects are not completed on time and estimates of these projects are often revised requiring higher amounts. When the delay in execution was due to the fault of local authorities, the penal provision of work on time was not enforced causing further loss to the local authority. A few typical cases are cited below :

a. Bhubaneswar Notified Area Council

The road work at 'Tangi Bhoi Sahi' started with an estimated cost of Rs. 5000 but was subsequently revised to Rs. 36,189 in April 1979 as the work was continued beyond stipulated date of completion for want of funds. For similar reasons the estimate of the work, 'Two numbers of school building in Kedarpali for Rs. 15000 was revised to Rs. 38,000 in September, 1979 and for special repair to slum quarters, the estimate was revised from Rs. 20,000 to Rs. 45,000 in May, 1978.

b. Puri Municipality

The estimate of Construction of Town Drain' for Rs. 20,500 was revised to Rs. 26,300 in December, 1978 due to delay in execution. Further the estimate for the work "Filling the ditches in Municipal High School" was revised from Rs. 16,353 to Rs. 31,000 in January, 1979 for the above reason. Estimate of Rs. 27,000 for construction of roads in 'Nata Das Bastee' was revised to Rs. 62,000 in January, 1979 for the reasons discussed earlier. Because of lack of planning even the grants received from Government for various schemes remained unutilised for years (indicated in previous chapter). Not only essential services have been neglected, but delay in execution of projects has put the local authorities to incur heavy expenditure due to rise in prices. Therefore expenditure planning is to be "programmed in such a way that the final outputs are realised with the minimum of inputs - human, material and financial"[26].

The planning of expenditure involves several stages. Firstly the items of different schemes and programme are to be listed taking the requirements of different activities into consideration. Secondly priorities of different programmes are to be determined taking into account the long felt basic needs of the local authority with reference to the objectives of State and national planning, availability of funds for the purpose, being of value to develop economic base of the local authority and revenue generation in nature. Thirdly capital improvement programme has to be planned taking the available technical manpower and funds into consideration stipulating the period of commencement and completion. Finally the balancing must be made between needs and resources.

It has already been discussed that the needs are far above the present standard of expenditure in relation to provision of services and other activities. As indicated earlier one of the constraints is resources. By resources we mean finance, material and manpower. The constraints need no illustration. The planning has not yielded desired result due to lack of these resources. Suitable and skilled manpower is necessary not only to plan but to execute the planning. Supply of material is to be kept steady and finance must be available. This state of ideal condition cannot be created by the local authorities alone unless the State and Central Governments extend their co-operation in this regard. In the words of Professor G. Mukherjee: "The State Government must create the machinery for this and make it available to local bodies but the latter must show active awareness of the significance of planning and preparedness to execute a Plan"[27]. The local authorities are not educated to think in terms of planning and they are yet to develop their own resources to match the needs with state aid. They should be guided to prepare plans with the aid of State Government. The Planning can prove its success only when all the constraints are removed.

Cost Consciousness in Municipal Expenditure

Cost consciousness in expenditure planning may improve the efficiency of local authority's spending. The traditional accounting system does not create awareness of the cost as accounts of returns are not kept. Expenditure involves application of resources on particular object with the expectation of getting benefits from the outlay. All benefits cannot be measured quantitatively. For example provision of street lighting cannot indicate the benefits in quantity, but it provides benefits to the people in general in safeguarding their property, preventing road accidents, enabling free movement of men and materials and many other benefits in making the city look beautiful and so on and so forth. There are three main classes of costs and benefits[28]:

a. direct costs and benefits which can be easily measured in monetary terms - these are the financial costs and benefits directly associated with the project and which traditional forms of analysis would take into account. Examples are the cost of constructing the project under review, the costs of maintenance and income likely to accrue throughout its life;

b. indirect costs and benefits which may be quantified in monetary or statistical terms, though with not the same accuracy as those indicated in (a). These would include costs and benefits accruing to third parties e.g., road users from the development of a new motor-way;

c. intangible costs and benefits which cannot be measured satisfactorily in any way. Examples would include improved amenities, improved hygiene, etc.

Such modern techniques of measuring the costs and benefits of different expenditure investments in urban local bodies are rarely in use in India. This practice has gained currency in the United States of America and is practised in some local authorities in England. Its importance and necessity in the present management system needs no emphasis but this can be applied to such projects having alternate method of achieving the objective. The technicalities involved in adopting the method requires training. The personnel engaged in local body in India do not have adequate training in the traditional account keeping. Their standard of efficiency need be raised to adopt to the changing of the time.

The present study reveals that in the urban local bodies of Orissa, the expenditure on 'Public Health' is the highest. The expenditure involves mostly employment of large number of employees for scavenging and road cleaning. Construction of drainage and sewerage is usually taken up by bigger local authorities. The capital expenditure incurred by the local authorities mostly relates to the construction and maintenance of water works. Most of the urban local authorities have undertaken water-supply schemes at high costs which are mostly financed by borrowing entailing payment of heavy interest. Even though the schemes are executed by the State Public Health authorities, the burden of the expenditure is borne by the local authority. These schemes are aimed at giving benefit to the urban community even though these facilities involve heavy costs increasing the tax burden on the present and future generations.

Measuring of cost and benefits in any investment for expenditure largely depends upon the type of project undertaken. In some projects indirect benefits and costs cannot be quantified, but some are quantifiable and some are not. Even though cost and benefits in projects like water supply schemes taken up by the urban local bodies are quantifiable, it is not intended to undertake such a study as the required statistical data are not readily available since the accounts of such projects are not maintained by the urban local authorities but by the Public Health Department of State Government. The present study, however, reveals that due to lack of cost consciousness in expenditure planning, in water supply schemes the projects are not completed timely which lead to high costs. The estimates of such projects are frequently revised due to rise in prices and other reasons. The burden of such high costs increases the liabilities of urban local authorities in shape of repayment of loans and interest thereon. Abnormal delay in execution has increased the cost of schemes and consequently the benefits that should accrue to the tax payers have been delayed. Such a situation can be avoided if the authorities become cost conscious and avoid delay in the execution of such projects. Thus, cost consciousness is one of the essential criteria in expenditure planning which should work as a guideline for the authorities of urban local Governments.

NOTES AND REFERENCES

1. *Pigou - Quoted* by Dr. K.M. Rastogi in Local Finance - Its theory and working in India. p-37.
2. *Ibid* - p.39.
3. *Report of the State Municipal Finance Commission* (Orissa) 1975. p. 26-28.
4. *Report of the Committee on Budgetory Reforms in Municipal Administration* - Government of India, Ministry of Works & Housing, June 1974. p. 62.
5. *Report of the Rural-Urban Relationship Committee.* (Volume-III) p. 99-110.
6. *The Orissa Municipal Rules - 1953*, Government of Orissa, Urban Development Department (Reprinted 1978) p. 41-44.
7. *From unpublished work of Professor Devraj* - Director, Institute of Urban Affairs. (Resource Mobilisation for Urban Areas).
8. *Report of the Committee on Augmentation of Financial Resources of Urban Local Bodies*, Table-7, p.36.
9. *Nagarlok* - Volume XI - January-March 1979, p. 25.
10. Quoted by Hepworth N.P. in *the Finance of Local Government*. p. 289.
11. Quoted by Hepworth N.P. in *the Finance of Local Government*. p. 36.
12. *Report of the State Municipal Finance Commission,* Orissa (1975), p. 114.
13. *Report of the State Municipal Finance Commission*, Orissa 1975 case study. Part-II Cuttack Municipality, p. 26.
14. *Annual Report of the Local Fund Audit Organisation for 1976-77*, p. 15.
15. Quoted in *Local Finance* by K.M.Rastogi, p. 50
16. *Annual Report of Local Fund Audit Organisation for 1976-77*, p. 17.
17. *Report of the State Municipal Finance Commission*, Orissa (1975), p. 115.
18. *Report of the State Municipal Finance Commission*, Orissa (1975), p. 115.
19. *Annual Report of 1976-77*, Local Fund Audit Organisation, Finance Department, p. 16.
20. *Nagarlok*. Municipal Materials Management Volume-V October-December 1973 by G.K. Aman, p. 30.
21. Hepworth, N.P. : *The Finance of Local Government*, p. 276
22. HMSO, London : *Report of the Committee on the Management of Local Government (Volume-I)*, p. 12.
23. Tripathy, R.N. :*Local Finance in a Developing Economy*, p. XX.
24. *Report of the Rural Urban Relationship Committee*, p.14.
25. *Report of the State Municipal Finance Commission*, (Orissa) 1975, p. 79.

26. *Five Year Municipal Development Plans,* IIPA,p. 4.
27. *Municipal Government in India*, Edited by A. Avasti, P.9.
28. Hepworth, N.P.: *The Finances of Local Government,* p.295.

SIX

STATE SUPERVISION AND FINANCIAL CONTROL

I

Objectives of Control

The urban local bodies have been assigned a place in the Constitution of India as a State Subject. These bodies are created under the Act passed by the State legislature. The State Government gives financial assistance in the shape of grants and loans to local Governments. The local Governments administer certain services and discharge certain functions of national importance. These authorities impose such taxes as are provided in the State Act. The State Government is, therefore, responsible to ensure uniformity in their functioning and standard of services including efficiency in administration.

The system of financial management in urban local bodies is completely different from that of State and Central Governments. Their budget is not passed by the State legislature nor their financial working is reviewed by the legislative organ as in the case of State/Central Government. Their financial transactions are not subject to regular treasury scrutiny. In view of the autonomy granted to the urban local authorities in the financial field, the State Government has been authorised by the Act to exercise supervision and control over the activities of these authorities. This apart, the State Government is to serve a balance between the needs and resources, to raise the level of poorer local authorities, to encourage proper development of local resources and to ensure efficiency in financial administration through the instrument of budgeting, accounting, audit, inspection and reports. The statutes which created the urban authorities provided an elaborate system of control and supervision by the State Government.

The Central Government is of course not divested of any responsibility in this regard. In a developing country like India, due to planned economy, there is a tendency towards centralisation and the development of local bodies has drawn the attention of central authorities and provision has been made in the Five Year Plans for urban development (from the Third Five year Plan onwards). The Government of India has also appointed Committees and Commissions to devise ways and means to improve the working of urban local bodies. Therefore, the central Government plays a role in shaping the policy and programmes of these institutions by providing financial assistance for major schemes like water supply, sanitation and housing etc. The Government of India has also taken up research and training programme for the development of local Governments. To this extent the Central Government exercises control and supervision over the urban local authorities.

Desirability of control and supervision

The desirability of State control over the urban local bodies largely depends upon the extent and degree of such control exercised by the State Government. In this context the caution expressed by Lord Ripon as pointed out by the Rural-Urban Relationship Committee is worth mentioning: "Lord Ripon had insisted that Government control should take the form of friendly advice and guidance and that before taking any strong action against a local body, the Government should exhaust all corrective means".[1] The State-Local Relationship should be considered more as a partnership, firstly because the municipalities are democratic institutions consisting of representatives elected by the local community and secondly because they are autonomous bodies and their autonomy should not be too much interfered with. "Rather the optimal relationship would be a partnership of two active and co-operative members, but with the Central Government definitely the Senior Partner".[2] Speaking about the control, the Taxation Enquiry Commission observed: "The goal of the State effort as well as the purpose of State Control should be the development of local self Governing institutions into efficient instruments of administration capable alike of formulating policies and executing them".[3] There is every apprehension that such controls in the hands of State Government may impair the financial autonomy of urban local bodies if not used properly. These controls should serve as safeguards against the possibilities of maladministration which is inherent in the system of representative Government. Close association of the State Government may rather enable it to appreciate the weaknesses of the urban local Governments in their financial administration and provide necessary guidance to overcome them.

State Control in other countries

In United Kingdom, the local authorities derive their power from the Act of the Parliament "which means that local authorities can do those things which they have been given powers to do by an Act of the Parliament".[4] Parliament have provision in the Act for appointment of committees and treasurers, the making of rate estimates, the system of keeping funds and its accounts including audit as a measure towards financial control. The Central Government Departments also control the activities of local authorities through powers derived from the Parliament. The minister also enjoys the powers to reduce or with-hold grants. The sanction of Government is necessary for borrowing by the local authorities. Government Departments enjoy power of inspection to make the financial control effective.

The powers and functions of local authorities in United States of America are defined by the Act of the State. While each State has its own system of local Government there are many similarities. The local authorities enjoy wider autonomy in spite of the State Control through " advice and information, reports, grants-in-aid, inspection, review and approval, state appointment and removal of local offices and instruction to local agents".[5] Sometimes Central assistance in the shape of grants-in-aid flows to the local Governments without state intervention.

In France the local bodies are organs of the Central Government and even if they have freedom in working, they do not enjoy autonomy as in the United States of America or the United Kingdom. "They have inherent powers. The Minister of the Interior at Paris presses the button, the prefects, sub-prefects and Mayors do the rest. All the wires run to Paris".[6]

Nature and Extent of Control

The state control over urban local bodies in India can be broadly classified as Administrative or Legislative, Judicial and Financial. The Legislature enacts the statutes which prescribe powers and functions for these institutions and it has authority to amend the statutes or make any new provision and to discuss and debate on the working of the local authorities. Similarly, the judiciary deals with these institutions as and when the local authorities go to court of law or their action is challenged on legal grounds by other parties. Courts of law interpret local laws and have power to declare any Local Act as ultra-vires if it is deemed to be in excess of the power conferred on them. The administrative powers are quite elaborate and are provided under the respective sections of the Act and Rules. Some of these powers are indirect and are in shape of giving directions, calling for information and reports and review of local action, but some powers are quite rigorous and are in the shape of amendment of resolutions passed by the elected councils, prior approval of actions, suspension and removal of elected members, supersession and dissolution of local councils.

The discussion here is confined to the financial controls exercised by the State Government over the urban local bodies. These controls are based on the provision made in the respective Acts of the State. The broad provisions of these controls are more or less similar in respect of municipalities and Notified Area Councils even though the municipal corporations enjoy wider freedom in their financial activities. As there is no municipal corporation in Orissa, the discussion is confined to Municipalities and Notified Area Councils only. The financial controls exercised can be broadly divided into two categories - internal control and external control. Some of the controls have been discussed in relation to expenditure in Chapter-V. Here more emphasis is given on external financial control which comprises of (i) control over resources (ii) sanction of competent authority over expenditure, approval of budgets and approval of decisions (iii) audit of the accounts by the auditors appointed by the Government.

Control over Resources

A study of the Acts/Rules of different States with particular reference to Orissa Municipal Act, 1950 and Orissa Municipal Rules, 1953 reveals the following features in relation to control over resources.

The State Government constitutes a local area into Municipality/Notified Area Council by notification in the official gazette (Section 4(3)(4)(b), C(d) of the Orissa Municipal Act 1950). The Government may delimit its jurisdiction and may also alter it. The area of a local authority largely determines its tax base as the income depends to a great extent on the nature of the area comprising the local authority (an industrial area or centre of tourist attraction brings more revenue). The Government has authority to vest any property or exclude any road, bridge or drain from local authority (Sec 122 of the Act). No taxes in the nature of holding, lighting, latrine, drainage and octroi tax including any fees can be levied by the local council without the sanction of the state Government (Section 131 of the Act). The Government has power to abolish such a tax or fee, suspend such imposition and may also fix such lower rate as they deem fit (Section 131-A of the Act). The rate of each such tax may be fixed by the Government. The Government also enjoys the powers to exempt any holding from imposition of such taxes. Appeal against the assessment of any such taxes lies with the District Magistrate or any such officer as may be empowered by the State Government in this behalf (Sec 153 of the Act). The Collector of the District has the authority to recover the arrear of taxes on application by the Executive Officer of the Municipality (Section 169 of the Act).

The assessment of the rental value of buildings for the purpose of property tax is made by the Government appointed Valuation Officer based on the rates prescribed by the Government. Moreover, the State Government sanctions grants-in-aid for different purposes and, without prior approval of the Government no local authority can incur any loan. Thus the statutory provision shows that the State Government has wide powers in regulating the income of an urban local body. Therefore the base and sources of income of an urban local body are largely dependent on the discretion of the State Government. Any authority which controls the income of an institution, to a large extent controls the activities of that organisation. Again the Government has also the prerogative of approving the by laws and regulations prepared by the local authorities.

Other Financial Controls

As regards the sanction of estimates, it has been discussed in the previous chapter that the Government has the power to sanction expenditure in excess of Rs. 500 unless there is provision in the Statute to incur expenditure for such purposes (Sec 117-A of the Act). Above all, the local Government budget needs the approval of the State Government before execution which in turn is competent to make any change in the budget provision (Details of budgetary procedure and power of Government in this regard have been discussed later).

Regarding sanction of estimates by higher authorities not only the Government but many other functionaries in the rank of Inspector of Local Works, Chief Engineer etc., enjoy certain powers. Apart from the powers of sanction, the District Magistrate, Revenue Divisional Commissioner and the Technical authorities in the Department of Health, Education, Engineering including the Director of Municipal Administration and the Examiner of Local Accounts are empowered to inspect, supervise and direct the local authorities.

The State Government enjoys the authority to appoint the Examiner of Local Accounts to audit the accounts of urban local bodies who is vested with the powers to surcharge any elected representative of the local authority including the officials who are found responsible for illegal or irregular expenditure causing loss of local fund (Discussion on audit practices has been made later). The form and the procedure of maintenance of accounts have been prescribed by the Government in the Rules framed by it (The Orissa Municipal

Rules 1953) and executive instructions are issued by the Government in this behalf.

These powers of control vested in the Government may serve as powerful instruments in the removal of members and suspension and dissolution of councils. In fact such drastic measures have been applied very often in case of urban local bodies of the State and several municipal councils have been superseded for some reasons or other. The Cuttack Municipality suffered from such action of the Government and was superseded 20 times after 1946 and was under administrative control of District Magistrate for about 21 years. The Rural-Urban Relationship Committee observed: "The dissolution and supersession of local bodies have been frequently resorted to by the State Government on grounds of maladministration, corruption, gross mismanagement of finances, party faction etc. The committee held the view that dissolution and supersession of local bodies is no satisfactory remedy for the maladies from which they suffer".[7] A local Government is not free from maladministration and malpractices due to inherent defect in the system of local Government in India. There is no independent executive authority. The local elected council carries the responsibility of deliberative and executive authority. It sanctions funds and spends them. The members of the Finance Committee are their own critics. The single Executive Officer in a municipalities spends the funds and controls the same. The system of treasury control is absent. Under the circumstances, it would be desirable if such stringent measures are used as a last resort only after all other measures of correcting the evils fail.

Controls - How far effective:-

The State Government including various functionaries are vested with the powers of supervision and control. It is, therefore, necessary to examine as to whether the system of control is effective, whether the existing machinary is adequate to exercise the required supervision and control and what changes, if any, could be introduced to make it more effective.

In spite of various provisions in the Act/Rules for the financial administration of the urban local bodies, the state of affairs is far from satisfactory. Such a deplorable state of activities in different spheres of finance has been commented upon by several committees and commissions. It has also been indicated in earlier chapters of this study that taxes and fees are not levied according to the prescribed rates. The rates of taxes are intentionally kept low by the local council to gain popularity among the voters. The taxes levied are not collected resulting in accumulation of arrears, the major portion of which gets timebarred. There is no system to regulate the sanction of grants-in-aid for different purposes. Government grants remain unutilised for years. Even though the payment of loan and interest thereon is a first charge on local fund, there are numerous instances of non-payment of loans and interest.

The quantum of expenditure on various services is far below the minimum prescribed standard. "Records relating to the accounts are not maintained according to the prescribed procedure with the result that there is often confusion and mismanagement in the matter of handling municipal funds. Failure to observe rules results in misappropriation of funds, leakage of revenue, municipal dues getting timebarred for recovery".[8] The Report has also pointed out in detail the deficiencies in the financial management of the urban local bodies of the State and observed that municipal administration has become synonymous with mal-administration and corruption inspite of the pervading powers of the State Government over the local bodies and in spite of the agencies employed for regular inspection, supervision and giving direction. The administration in municipality also did not improve even though some of them were superseded and the management of these local bodies was vested in the hands of Government. For instance, Cuttack, Puri and Berhampur Municipalities were under supersession for more than 20, 9 and 8 years respectively from 1946 and yet they did not show any perceptible improvement in their administration.

Maladministration is not confined to urban local bodies in Orissa; it is also prevalent in the urban local bodies of other States as well which have compelled State Governments to take drastic action against such maladministration. Thus it goes beyond doubt that the State control and supervision over the municipalities have not been effective largely due to heavy concentration of powers in the Government, lack of suitable machinery for supervision, lack of coordination among different authorities having power of supervision and control and lastly "due to the faulty structure and other inherent defects of local authorities, such as the absence of a strong and independent executive, undue interference by the elected members in executive matters, inefficient and unqualified municipal personnel, meagre resources of local bodies, losses due to improper assessment and collection of taxes, wasteful expenditure and ineffective and slack audit".[9]

Delegation of Powers

The earlier discussion indicates that due to concentration of too many powers in the Government the control and supervision have not been effective. The remoteness of the authority from the urban local bodies results in delay in obtaining sanction, retards the growth of civic responsibility and kills initiative in enforcing different provisions of the Act/Rules. Not only the urban local bodies have increased in number but also in sizes giving rise to multiple problems in raising resources and spending them and in ensuring proper financial discipline in maintenance of accounts and records. Moreover the performances of these local authorities are rarely supervised and no recourse is generally taken to correct them. The present system as pointed out earlier entails upon Government and other functionaries to exercise control over day-to-day administration of the urban local authorities in sanctioning expenditure above a prescribed limit, sanctioning budget and deviation therefrom, sanctioning estimate of works (beyond certain limit) and even sanctioning establishment.

The pattern of administration of local Government is mostly based on the system of administration of State and Central Government. The increase in the volume of activities of State/Central Government has also resulted in the increase in the activities of local Government. In the Government system of financial administration, the problem of centralisation of financial responsibility was considered and it was found that too much concentration of such powers made the working difficult. A.D. Gorwala observed: "What is really needed in financial matters is control and not interference. What would seem to be happening is exasperating interference in small matters leading to a great deal of waste of time, energy and frustration on the part of the administrative departments, that is, the greater part of the Government. This must be avoided".[10] The problem of delegation of powers in respect of financial administration of Government engaged the attention of the Administrative Reforms Commission of India (appointed in 1966) and they recommended for delegation of powers in various matters relating to financial system. The system of delegation of powers as needed for the State/Central Government is also necessary for local Government.

It is needless to emphasise that delegation of power from higher level of administration to lower levels with a system of check would not only increase the financial efficiency at the lower level but would enable the higher authority to control and supervise effectively. "Apart from meeting the operational requirements, delegation of powers would enable the top management to devote its most valuable scarce resources - time - to the most important managerial responsibilities such as planning, policy-making, co-ordination, review and control while allowing the operating and intermediate levels enough elbow room for accomplishing specific tasks of operations and supervision entrusted to them".[11] Important responsibilities like policy formation and structure of the organisation including planning, review, evaluation and discipline should rest with the highest authority. It would, therefore, be expedient if the powers of supervision and control vested in the Government are suitably delegated to lower authorities with a system of check to ensure effectiveness of such delegation.

The Committee on Rural-Urban Relationship recommended that "the controls can be reduced in number and rationalised by working out model by-laws, regulation and budgetary reforms"[12]. The matter is quite delicate and complex as it involves transfer of powers from the higher level to intermediary level of authorities, the details of which could be worked out by a Committee of experts. A few suggestions for the delegation of power from the Government are indicated below:

a. A minimum and maximum limit of each tax (rules varying according to class of urban local bodies) could be prescribed relieving Government from the power to approve change in the rate of tax.

b. The minimum rate of collection should be prescribed for each category of local body and the rate of grants-in-aid should be linked with the percentage of collection.

c. Payments of grants-in-aid and borrowing should be regulated by the decision of a high power committee and not by Government.

d. The budget estimate of each local body and the revised budget need not be approved by the Government. The power should be delegated to Regional Inspector/Deputy Director.

e. Power of sanction of expenditure beyond a prescribed limit should lie with the Deputy Director, if not covered by budgetary provision.

f. There should be enhanced delegation in respect of sanction of estimates of works, check-measurement etc.

The process of delegation may shower increasing responsibility on the local authorities. Therefore the quality of personnel, the Committee system, concurrent check of receipts and pre-audit of payments should be ensured to make the delegation effective.

Machinery for control and supervision

There are many functionaries of the State Government who are associated with control and supervision of the urban local bodies, which directly or indirectly concerns the finances of local authorities. Most of such functionaries function in the state level. The nearest authorities charged with the responsibility of supervision and control are the District Collectors and Revenue Divisional Commissioners. They are not assisted by a well equipped machinery to perform their duties in relation to local Government. They themselves being very much burdened in their multifarious duties have very little time to get into the problems of local bodies and as such are indifferent and keep aloof from the real problems. Therefore they cannot be termed as suitable agencies for the purpose of supervision and control. It is rather apprehended that the association of the District Collector with the administration of local authorities may hinder the progress than improve the position.

In most of the States of India, the administration of urban local authorities is the responsibility of a Department under the State Government. It was however recommended by the Rural-Urban Relationship Committee (1966) that " a well organised directorate at the state level with an effective regional inspecting staff should go a long way towards improving the system of direction, supervision and control of local authorities in the solution of their current and future problems and advocate their cause with the relevent Departments. The Director and inspector should function as friends and guides of local bodies, a body of inspector for sanctioning the work of local authorities and keeping the State Government in touch with their special needs would also serve as a source of information for the state and local officials".[13] The Committee while prescribing the duties of the Director emphasised that in the matter of finance, the director will advise the Government on fiscal polices affecting local authorities, suggest methods for improving the source of local revenue; suggest and advise the tax administration including formulation of rules and regulation in this regard; foster the establishment and maintenances of standards in budgeting, accounting and other aspects of financial administration and ensure adequate finances for local bodies through grants and loans etc.

The long list of functions assigned to the Directorate cannot be discharged efficiently and effectively unless the Director is provided with a suitable and well equipped machinery at his disposal and more particularly at the field level. As observed by Professor Finer, "contact through inspectors has the outstanding merit of flexibility and manifold adaptability. The effectiveness of the mechanism of state inspection depends upon the maintenance of an efficient body of inspectors possessing positive powers, taking action against defaulting authorities" [14]. Of course much depends upon the agility and ability of the Inspectors. There are Directorates in Kerala, Rajasthan, Maharashtra, Gujarat, Andhra Pradesh and Punjab to look after the administration of urban local authorities but they have no field organisation. In West Bengal and Bihar, there are Inspectors appointed by the State Government to inspect the local bodies. There are Inspectors in each District headquarters in Tamil Nadu. These Inspectors are closely associated with the administration of urban local bodies for which the efficiency of urban local authorities in Tamil Nadu is superior in many respects (The average collection of municipal taxes in Tamil Nadu is over 90 percent).

The Administration Enquiry Committee, Orissa (1972) recommended for the establishment of a Directorate with a Director of the status of a Head of the Department to ensure uniformity in municipal administration in Orissa with effective supervision and guidance. Accordingly a post of Director was created in this State with the burden of secretarial status. He has no separate office and there has been no change in the pattern of administration as exercised before. He is a part of the State Department having no specially qualified staff to handle the problems peculiar to local administration. The State Municipal Finance Commission, Orissa (1975) observed that "instead of guiding and helping the local bodies at all stages and responding to their difficulties, the Government cultivates an attitude of aloofness and indifference till political and other considerations prompt them to take positive action" [15]

The creation of a Directorate without requisite field agencies will not improve matters unless the Director is assisted by Regional Inspectors/Deputy Directors in discharging his responsibilities. These Inspectors/Deputy Directors should be delegated with certain powers of control as suggested earlier with trained staff at their disposal, so that they will remain in close touch with the local administration for effective supervision and guidance in their day to day administration. Apart from the creation of Regional Inspectors, there should be regular exchange of ideas through inspection and by organising seminars on specific problems.

The Examiner of Local Accounts who is entrusted with the audit of the accounts of local authorities should be closely associated with such seminars and should be assigned with the duties of inspection relating to financial matters and his reports should be taken into account in policy formulation and decision making concerning the finances of urban local bodies. In the Regional level, his representatives should be associated with such functions. Above all, the Government should evince more interest in the financial activities of local authorities and make periodical assessment of their performance in the financial field with a view to improving the tone of financial administration.

II

Local Budgeting

The main instruments of financial control in urban local bodies relate to budgetary procedure, accounting methods and audit practices. The State Government exercises control over the financial administration of local authorities through these instruments and the local authorities themselves utilise these instruments as a device of internal control. Each of these instruments is discussed separately to see how effective these instruments are and what reforms could be made in these fields.

Characteristics of the budget

The budgetary system regulates the financial affairs of a Government, be it national, States or local. It is through the budget that the executive authority forecasts and plans up its revenue and expenditure for the ensuing year. It is the budget that enables the deliberative wing of the Government to exercise its control over different branches of the administration. It is a plan or programme framed on the basis of past experience and is prepared in financial terms. The budget is not a proposal only but a scheme of action; it is a comprehensive plan of action. It brings together the requirements of revenue and expenditure and all facts relating to the financial condition of the Government. It is an annual plan. The system of budget provides for an orderly financial administration of the Government. It provides for a continuous chain of action at different levels of administration - execution of the schemes, maintenance of accounts, audit and finally the report.

Objectives of the budget

"Budget is a term derived from the old English word bougett, the sack or pouch from which the Chancellor of the Exchequer extracted his papers in presenting to Parliament the Government's financial performance for the ensuing fiscal year".[16] In the context of a local Government the budget carries more or less the same objective as of a State or Central Government excepting that the budget of a local Government is passed by the municipal council and is finally approved by the State Government, whereas the budgets of Government are approved by the Legislature. Thus accountability to the legislature through the budgetary devices which the budget envisages is wanting in the case of local Government. The budget serves as a tool of management. Financial classification of the expenditure in the budget gives a clear picture of the activities of the local Government. It projects the performance in different fields of activities. It serves as a means of co-ordination among different branches of the administration. It facilitates analysis and evaluation of performances. A.H. Marshall while analysing the function of a local budget expressed.

The budget is the handmaid of policy making, both short term and long term, and one of the means by which it is implemented. It brings the various activities of the authority into focus, it helps the council to take a forward look, it enables them to keep policy under review, and provides a means of avoiding either neglect or lop-sided development of the services.

The budget is a plan of action.

The budget is the medium for ensuring that the monies of the local authorities are ultimately laid out in the way the local authority has decided.

A budget does more than ensure that money is spent in the way the local authority has decided by providing suitable yardstick it helps to secure efficient and economical administration".[17]

Thus the budget sets an ideal for the spending departments to restrict their expenditure within the budgetary provision and the earning departments to raise their revenue to the budgetary goals.

Budgetary Procedure

There is no uniformity in the format of the budget in the urban local bodies of the country. In some States the heads of accounts and the form of the budget have been prescribed in the statute governing the working of the local authorities. In some States there are different patterns for different local bodies. In the case of budgets of

State and Central Government, the classification of the budget and heads of accounts have been prescribed by the Comptroller and Auditor General of India, but there is no such central authority in respect of local Government. The Government of India appointed a Committee on budgetary reforms in Municipal Administration under Chairmanship of Professor G. Mukherjee, Director Indian Institute of Public Administration (vide Government of India Order No. F.5-33/70 UCD dated 24.8.72) with a view to suggesting budgetary system, method and procedure. The Committee in their report (June 1974) observed: "uniformity in classification and common head of account which are claimed to be some of the virtues in the accounting and budgetary structure of Government, are thus wanting in case of local bodies".[18] There is, however, uniformity regard to the financial year which begins from 1st April of the year and ends on 31st March of the next year. In some local bodies the budget is sanctioned by the council after scrutiny by the Finance Committee and extracts of such budgets are sent to Government for their information as in case of Municipalities of Tamil Nadu and West Bengal. In case of budgets of indebted municipalities, the sanction of the budget rests with the Government which are in vogue in Bihar and Madhya Pradesh. The budgets of urban local bodies of Punjab, Assam and Orissa are approved by the State Government having authority to alter the budgetary provision.

Budgetary Procedure in Orissa

In this context it is worthwhile to bring to light the practices prevalent in the urban local bodies of Orissa. The details of procedure for preparation of the budget including the heads of accounts under which the budget is prepared had been prescribed in the Orissa Municipal Act, 1950 and Orissa Municipal Rules, 1953. The salient features of such provision are indicated below:

1. The budget estimate of the general fund account shall be prepared in English in form No. I by the Executive Officer in consultation with the Chairman (Rule 74).
2. The budget of the primary education fund shall be prepared in consultation with the District Inspector of Schools and Chairman in form No. II (Rule 75).

3. The budget shall be prepared and presented to the council on or before 1st February of the preceding budget year and copy of the budget estimate passed by the council shall be submitted to Government through the District Magistrate and Board of Revenue relating to General Fund and the Education budget through the Director of Public Instruction on or before 10th March (Rule 76).

4. The budget shall provide for minimum closing balance and make adequate provision for such services imposed by the Act (See 105(2)(a)(b) of the Act).

5. There is provision in the Act that the budget should be published for inspection of the public and their suggestion would be taken into consideration before it is passed by the council (See 106 of the Act).

6. The State Government has the authority to examine the budget in respect of the statutory requirements and may make such alterations as it considers necessary. The Government enjoys the powers to prescribe minimum expenditure to be incurred on certain services. In fact rules 173 and 174 prescribe that maximum of 5 percent of the total income can be spent on establishment.

7. Government approval is also necessary for any variation and alteration to be made in the sanctioned budget estimates.

The relevant provision in the Act proves that the State Government enjoys absolute authority in sanctioning the budget estimate of municipal Government in Orissa. The Government may use this as an instrument for effecting control of the financial administration of the local authorities.

Budget in practice

In the present study, an attempt has been made to study the practices in preparing, sanctioning and executing the budget of 31 Municipalities/Notified Area Councils of the State for the years 1961-62, 1965-66, 1971-72 and 1975-76 and budgets of other years in general. In most of the Municipalities/Notified Area Councils the budgets of earlier periods, even for the years 1961-62 and 1965-66, were not available for examination. It is queer that the copy of the sanctioned budget estimates of bigger local authorities including Cuttack, Puri and Bhubaneswar were neither available in the local offices nor even with the Government. This shows that no importance was attached by either the local authorities or by the State Government in preserving such a vital document which serves the purpose of evaluation and study.

Even though data have been collected in respect of these urban local bodies for the available years under the detailed head of account relating to sanctioned budgetary provision and actuals pertaining to both Receipts and Expenditure, it is not considered proper to present all the details including the date of submission and approval of the budget by the Government in a tabular form for all the institutions as it may lead to confusion and may not serve the purpose of analysis.

Under the statutory provision, the budget is required to be approved by the State Government before the commencement of the financial year since no expenditure can be incurred without sanction of the budget. But the study reveals that no budget of a Municipality/Notified Area Council was approved before 31st March due to delay in transaction by the local authority and the District Magistrate. There was also undue delay in approving the budget at the Government level. There have been instances where approval of the Government was not available for verification for certain years. Thus the sanctity of the budget that no expenditure can be incurred without budgetary sanction was lost.

No amount of scrutiny as is required to be performed at the Government level seems to have been exercised. The budget contains the information on actuals of nine months of the current year under both receipt and expenditure which provide the basis for framing the estimates for the ensuing year on actual experience of the previous years. The comparison of the performance of the previous years including the performance of the nine months of the current year would enable a realistic provision in the budget for the coming year. But such comparison does not seem to have been made either by the local authorities or by the Government. Lack of such scrutiny resulted in inflated provision under both receipts and expenditures of almost all local authorities for all the years indicated in the Annexure.

The wide variations in budgetary provisions and actual performances are so numerous that it hardly requires any discussion. Such variations were equally conspicuous and were beyond any proportion under detailed head of receipts and expenditure which have been reflected in the totals. It is interesting to note that Bhubaneswar Notified Area Council provided in the budget estimate of 1975-76 Rs. 205 lakhs under receipt and Rs. 199.61 lakhs under expenditure, but the actual receipt was Rs. 30.85 lakhs and expenditure was Rs. 38.47 lakhs. In Rambha Notified Area Council for 1975-76, against budget provision of Rs. 24.18 lakhs under receipt and Rs. 24.13 lakhs under expenditure the actual receipts and expenditure were Rs. 1.28 lakhs and Rs. 1.38 lakhs respectively. Angul Notified Area Council provided in the budget of 1975-76 receipts to the extent of Rs. 19.13 lakhs and expenditure to the extent of Rs. 20.21 lakhs but actuals under receipt and expenditure were Rs. 6 lakhs and Rs. 6.51 lakhs respectively. Similar wide variations were noticed in respect of budget estimates and actuals of Sonepur Municipality, Padamapur Notified Area Council, Rairangpur Notified Area Council, Khurda Notified Area Council, Nayagarh Notified Area Council & Jaleswar Notified Area Council. Such instances of wide gap between budgetary estimates and actual performances in respect of other years are common features as indicated in the Annexure.

The cases of such wide variations are due to over estimation of their anticipated receipts from their own sources and from Government in shape of grants-in-aid and loans. The Government grants and loans do not flow as per their expectation nor their tax efforts really bring in the desired revenues. In Brajarajnagar Notified Area Council the provision of Rs. 13.70 lakhs in the budget estimates for 1971-72 for water supply schemes upset both the receipt and expenditure both due to non-receipt of loans under the scheme. Cases of the above category are too many to be discussed here which may be seen from Annexure-XVIII.

It transpires from the cases cited that the local authorities really depend upon the discretion of State Government for financing different schemes. Due to non-receipt of grants and loans their budgetary provisions are upset dislocating their programme of activities. On the other hand, the local authorities do not harness the local resources to meet the budgetary requirements. The local council neither reviews the performance periodically to compare the achievements and shortfalls in relation to budgetary provision nor the State Government even assesses the performances of local authorities either at the time of sanctioning the budget or at a later stage.

The Government should use its powers while examining the budgets to make for provision of actual amount of grants and loans which the Government can provide to an individual local authority during the year and accordingly the budget should be corrected to make it more realistic. Moreover, the Government has never considered the ability of the local bodies to spend such huge budget provision or to earn such a huge income which is far in excess of the actuals of the previous years unless adequate arrangements are made for the purpose. This aspect has been overlooked completely as inflated amounts have been approved in the budget which are beyond the abilities of the local authorities either to earn or to spend.

Therefore, the main objectives of the budget do not seem to be fulfilled in the case of urban local bodies of the State. It neither serves as an instrument of control by the State Government nor as a tool of internal management. It only reflects the imaginary figures which are not workable. Similarly the budget, in practice, does not fulfil the hopes and aspirations of the local community. In order to make the budgetary provisions effective, the State Government should delegate its power of approval to subordinate authorities in the rank of Regional Inspector/Deputy Director who should exercise some real scrutiny to sanction a realistic budget on the basis of past experience with the aid of technical staff who could review the past performance and sanction provision on the basis of funds available.

The State Government should formulate a procedure for regulating grants and loans, and declare the quantum of assistance prior to framing of the budget so that such wide variations could be avoided. Municipal budgets would be more meaningful if the budgetary provision relating to capital expenditure financed through borrowing is shown separately. There should be rigid enforcement for achieving the target of income from own sources. The provision of funds for expenditure should be ability-oriented and provisions in the budget should be related to availability of men, materials and fulfilment of other formalities. There should be a Committee in the Government or the legislative level to review the performances of the urban local bodies in relation to their budgets. The traditional budgetary practices have failed to yield the desired result. It may, therefore, be necessary to examine if the modern technique of performance budgeting will really serve the purpose.

Performance Budgeting

The present system of budgeting in local Government is intended to serve the purpose of accountability of the executive to the council and above all to the Government and within the organisation of the spending departments, to the controlling authorities. Due to the proximity of the local citizens to the Government, they watch the quality and quantity of services rendered in terms of their money's worth. But the present system of budget does not correlate the outlays with the physical targets. The common man cannot know from the budget as to how much is intended to be done and at what cost and by which date. Such difficulties could be obviated by the introduction of a system of performance budgeting which is "a technique of presenting public expenditure in terms of function, programme, activities and projects, and correlating the physical and financial aspects of the individual items comprising the budget".[19]

The system of performance budgeting in local Government in the United States of America is very much in vogue. Attempts have, however, been made to develop the system in England. There is a problem of devising suitable measures of performance. The Administrative Reforms Commission appointed by the Government of India recommended the introduction of performance budgeting in the department of Government which is in direct charge of development programme, as such a budget would fix physical targets to be achieved within a time schedule. Many departments of the Central Government including some State Governments have adopted this modern system of budgeting. Discussing about the reforms on

Municipal Financial Administration, Professor A. Dutta observed: "Unfortunately similar efforts are not being made for the municipal budgets where such conversion is relatively easier, due to the more meaningful classification of municipal facility and the nature of municipal activities as such".[20] The Municipal Government in India performs many activities to provide public utilities and social services under the constraint of resources. The present system of budgeting does not specify targets to be achieved with the expenditure incurred. If their goals and objectives are spelt out, there could be proper planning of programmes for which resources could be allocated.

The Committee on Budgetary Reform in Municipal Government appointed by the Government of India examined at length the feasibility of introducing the system of performance budgeting in local Government and pointed out that the performance budgeting involves a clear definition of the goals and objectives, a long term perspective for budgeting, identification and quantification of physical outputs of expenditure, programmes and their measurement, a system of accounting which provides information on the cost of various services related to output and a system of continuous review of the implementation of the programme and their evaluation. The Committee finally recommended that the system may be introduced especially in Municipalities of population of one lakh or more. If "intensive efforts are made by State Government to introduce the system successfully in one or two carefully selected municipalities, the example of such success is bound to encourage the other municipalities to adopt the system quickly".[21]

There are certain genuine difficulties which stand in the way of introducing performance budgeting in local Governments. The State Government has not been able to adopt the system completely due to lack of knowledge on the subject. Present system of accounts does not provide information on cost of services and other activities. Particularly for the Municipal Government, there is uncertain flow of funds from its own resources and the Government makes the task more difficult as it sanctions expenditure when funds are available. In such a situation, taking financial input with the accomplishment would be difficult. There is no system of planning at the local level. There has been inordinate delay in execution of capital works as such works are mostly executed through the Government agency over which municipal authorities have little control. Budgetary decisions are not based on cost consciousness which may relegate the purpose of performance budgeting.

In spite of these difficulties, efforts made by the Government to introduce the system of performance budgeting in local Government with suitable training and guidance may arrest the irregular trend of budget practices in the local authorities. The new system may also serve as a check on the uncertain flow of funds from the Government as the system cannot operate without assured funds and proper planning. The performance budget when introduced will serve as a real tool of management, planning and programming by assigning clear and definite responsibilities to different functionaries. The system required evaluation and appraisal of performance which will improve the standard of financial management of the urban local bodies by making the operating officials and agencies accountable to the reviewing and administrative authorities.

Accounting Procedure

It has been discussed elsewhere that the present system of accounts does not serve the purpose of aid to management in its decision making nor as a device for internal control. The present system does not envisage maintenance of accounts of returns. Separate accounts in respect of capital and revenue are not maintained. In view of the suggestion given above to introduce the system of performance budgeting in local Government, it is necessary to examine as to how far the present system of accounts will be useful for the purpose.

The present study discloses that even proper accounts are not kept and accounts are manipulated to balance the receipts with expenditure at the end of the year either by putting off certain claims for payment next year or reducing the magnitude of deposits to hide the serious financial situation. Such practices convert a deficit accounting to surplus accounting and present a misleading picture of the financial position of the Government. As per the statutary requirements, the local bodies are required to maintain a minimum closing balance. It seems, such fictitious accounting is made with a view to exhibiting the minimum closing balance. The accounts should, therefore, be accurate, reliable and kept up-to-date to facilitate control of finance. It has been invariably complained in audit that account records are not maintained up-to-date and sometimes do not give correct position of finances. This was also commented by the State Municipal Finance Commission (1975).

The Municipal authorities sometimes take up trading activities as indicated in Chapter-IV. The trading activities envisage the maintenance of profit and loss accounts and balance sheets on the pattern of commercial accounts. But no separate accounts in respect of such transactions have been maintained in the local authorities in Orissa as a result of which it has not been possible to ascertain the economic viability of such schemes. In the absence of systematic accounts, it is not possible to determine the cost of such goods and services. While speaking about the municipal accounts, Professor A. Dutta of Indian Institute of Public Administration observed that as the municipal services are either free-financed or financed through the levy of specific taxes, " it is necessary in this situation to have detailed accounting of not only of their operating cost but also marginal cost. Unfortunately, the various municicpal accounts codes or manuals do not go into the details of the the calculation at all".22.

The forms and classifications of accounts conform to the budgetary requirements. The accounts, thus, form the basis on which budgetary provisions are made. Performance budgeting presupposes budget classification in terms of functions, programmes, activities and projects with a similar classification in accounts. Accounts need be function, programme and activity oriented and account must speak the language as of the performance budget. As an aid to management the accounts classification must be corelated to the activities of the organisation.

The classification of accounts as at present satisfies the twin requirements of accountability and financial control. The classification in accounts indicates the nature of expenditure and not the purpose. For example, construction of 'hospital building' is classified under 'Public Works' but not under 'Medical Relief'. The present system lacks management approach and does not facilitate monitoring and evaluation of expenditure on programmes and activities.

The Government of India has already introduced a revised accounting structure for the purpose of performance budgeting and management control. The Committee on Budgetary Reforms in Municipal Administration recommended that "the State Government can prescribe the broad financial classification by major and minor heads to be adopted by all the municipal bodies in the State keeping in view, inter-alia, the need for obtaining comparative costs of municipal services".[23] In view of the changed pattern in Government accounting, it would be desirable to gradually introduce the new system in municipal Government with adequate training and by augmenting the staffing pattern to cope with the increased work load.

III

Audit

Audit means verification of accounts, documents, vouchers and subsidiary records relating to any Government or business house with a view to helping the administration by bringing to light cases of irregularities in administering the finances of the institutions and presenting the financial results in a simple form. An independent audit plays an important role in effecting Parliamentary control over the finances of State and Central Governments by ensuring that the funds voted by the legislature are utilised by the executive Government for the approved purposes with due regard to economy and efficiency. In the case of local authorities, audit is an instrument of State control. The fact that the local authorities derive their income by taxing the local community and the State Government provides substantial financial assistance to these authorities in the shape of grants and shared taxes, makes it all the more important that the State Government should provide for an independent audit of the accounts of local authorities. The system of check available to Government transactions is continuous, starting from the presentation of claims in the treasury to completion of audit by the Comptroller and Auditor General. There is no such continuous system of check in respect of local accounts which makes the annual audit all the more important.

In India, the responsibility of audit of local accounts was entrusted to the Accountant Generals of the provinces prior to independence. Subsequently the audit of local accounts came under the State control. In almost all States excepting in West Bengal and Bihar, the audit of the accounts of local authorities is entrusted to the Examiner of Local Fund Audit appointed by the State Government. The Examiner is an officer of the State Government and conducts audit of the local accounts either under the provisions of the Local Fund Audit Act or under statute of the local authority with administrative instructions with the auditors and other officers appointed for the purpose. In most States the agency of audit of local accounts is controlled by the Finance Department except in West Bengal and Bihar where the Examiner of Local Accounts is under the control of the Accountant General.

The provision in the Local Fund Act and the procedures of audit in different States are more or less the same with minor variation as to details of procedure. In Maharashtra, the head of the Local Fund Audit Organisation is designated as Chief Auditor, in Madhya Pradesh and Andhra Pradesh he is known as Director, in Karnataka he is called Controller of Audit and Accounts whereas in most other states, he is designated as Examiner of Local Accounts.

In Punjab, Haryana, Andhra Pradesh, Rajasthan, Maharashtra and Gujarat, a certain percentage of accounts of the local bodies (say 3 - 4 months in a year) are subjected to audit check whereas in Orissa, Tamil Nadu, Kerala, Karnataka and many other states audit embraces cent percent transaction. In Punjab and Haryana, there is a system of Resident Audit in respect of the accounts of bigger municipalities whereas in all other States there is a system of post-audit. However, in Orissa, a system of concurrent audit of the accounts of Cuttack Municipality has been introduced since 1975-76.

As regards surcharge, no surcharge action lies against officials in Tamil Nadu, whereas in Orissa all functionaries of the local body including officials and elected members are liable to be surcharged. In Maharashtra, Karnataka, Haryana, Madhya Pradesh, the power of surcharge is not enjoyed by the Chief Auditor/Director of Local Fund Audit. In most States the appellate power against surcharge vests with the Minister in charge of urban local authorities and in States like Karnataka and Rajasthan, the power of appeal lies with civil court and Government.

Position in Orissa

The Orissa Municipal Act, 1950(Sec. 113) provides that provisions of the Orissa Local Fund Audit Act, 1948 shall apply in regard to audit of the funds under the control and management of the municipal council or many of its committees. Accordingly the audit of the accounts of all Municipal /Notified Area Councils is conducted under the provision of the Local Fund Audit Act and rules framed thereunder with administrative instructions issued from time to time. The Local Fund Audit Act provides for the appointment of Examiner of Local Accounts and other subordinates to carry out the provisions of the Act for the purpose of audit of local authorities. The Examiner is an officer of high status and with a view to securing his independence from undue influence and ensuring impartiality in his function, he has been kept under the administrative control of the Finance Department.

The Examiner of Local Accounts is empowered to summon records and persons for the purpose of such audit (Sec. 6 of the Act). He, with the help of his subordinates, while auditing the accounts of local authorities ascertains whether moneys shown in the accounts as having been disbursed were legally available for and applicable to the services or purposes to which they have been applied or charged and whether the expenditure conforms to the authority which governs it. He examines the propriety of the executive action and looks beyond the formality of the expenditure or its wisdom, loss, extravagant or nugatory expenditure. He is thus charged with the responsibility to challenge any improper exercise of discretion and comment on the propriety of expenditure. The result of audit is incorporated in the audit report and the report is issued to the local authorities for furnishing compliance within 3 months from the date of receipt of the audit report. He has the authority to charge/surcharge any person responsible for any loss or for any expenditure contrary to law and for the amount of any sum which ought to have been but not brought to accounts.[24]

Power of Surcharge

Thus the Examiner of Local Accounts has been placed in a position having the power to pronounce his judgement on the financial affairs of the local authorities and take recourse to stringent measures like surcharge for recovery of the loss or deficiency from persons responsible. His position is somewhat analogous to the District Auditor of Local Authorities in England. The duties conferred on the District Auditor in the English Local Government Act, 1933 are as follows which are more or less similar to the provisions of Orissa Local Fund Audit Act, 1948:

"It shall be the duty of the auditor at every audit held by him

a to disallow every item of account which is contrary to law,
b to surcharge the amount of any expenditure disallowed upon person responsible for incurring or authorising the expenditure,
c to surcharge any sum which has not been duly brought into account upon the persons by whom that sum might have been brought into account,
d to surcharge the account of any loss or deficiency upon any person by whose negligence or misconduct the loss or deficiency has been incurred,
e to certify the amount due from any persons upon whom he has made surcharge ".[25]

It has been complained that the power of surcharge vested in the Examiner is not in keeping with the autonomy of the democratically elected local council in as much as it challenges the wisdom of the council. In this context, speaking about the District Auditor, Professor Robson states:" The powers which the law now places in the hands of the auditors is so extensive that it may well be asked whether they are fitted by training or position to exercise it in a satisfactory manner; and in particular why their reasons should be entitled to take precedence over the reasons possessed by the Councillors and electorate".[26] The views held by Professor Robson may not be wholly incorrect but the weakness shown by the local authorities of this State in their financial affairs as revealed in earlier discussions, needs certain corrective and coercive measures in strengthening local audit to av aken financial conciousness of the local authorities.

Effectiveness of audit

Audit is considered as an instrument of State control over the finances of local authorities. It is also intended to ensure financial discipline in the local administration. It is also expected to serve as an aid to management.It may be necessary to examine to what extent the purpose of audit has been fulfilled. The State Government does not seem to have taken audit findings with seriousness and there has been complete neglect on the part of the local authorities to comply with the audit objections. It is curious to note that audit objections are mounting up from year to year and at the end of March 1976 as many as 1054 audit reports containing 31,215 paragraphs with money value of Rs.4.61 crores were outstanding for settlement.[27] There are 91 urban local bodies in the State and one audit report is issued against each during a year. As such the number of pending audit reports implies that audit reports of more than 11 years in respect of all the local bodies are pending for compliance.

It is found that Audit Reports from the year 1951-52 are pending for final settlement in respect of many municipalities. No adequate action has also been taken by the Government against the delinquents even though several cases of misappropriation, loss of cash and store including embezzlement have been reported to Government through individual audit reports and through special reports. The printed Annual Report of the Examiner depicting such cases had not roused the Administrative Department to action. Thus audit mechanism has not been used by the State Government to control the financial administration of the local authorities.The magnitude and the comparative increase of audit objections and audit observations depicted below go to prove that the financial discipline of these authorities has not improved:

Year of Annual Report of the Local Fund Audit Organisation, Finance Department	Observation/Findings
1962-63	"As noticed in previous years most of the local bodies have failed to furnish their

	replies to audit report within the stipulated period of 3 months.The same old policy of indifference and negligence in the disposal of audit reports still continued".
1966-67	Total number of 194 audit reports with 3543 paragraphs with money value of Rs.24.61 lakhs pending for compliance at the end of March, 1966.
1972-73	661 audit reports consisting of 23304 paragraphs with money value of Rs.270 lakhs pending for compliance.
1975-76	987 audit reports consisting of 30775 paragraphs with money value of Rs. 448 lakhs pending for compliance.

Causes of failure of audit

Does it mean that the audit has failed to achieve its purpose ? - Three agencies are connected with this problem-the State Government, the local authorities, the audit organisation. As regards the State Government, it is well established that Government has not taken the financial condition of the local authorities as revealed in the respective audit reports while considering the question of sanction of grants and loans as revealed from the earlier discussion. The Government has not evolved any system or mechanism to enforce the audit suggestion or in settling the audit objection.There is no forum either at the level of the State Government or in the legislature to review the audit findings as exist in some States like Tamil Nadu and Maharashtra.

In Tamil Nadu, particular care is taken at the Government level to settle the audit objections through a high power Triangular Committee and there is a fixed time limit that all audit objections should be settled within a year. In Maharashtra a legislative committee reviews the findings of audit on the local authorities as reported by the Chief Auditor.It is curious to note that instead of devising such a method for settlement of audit objection, it was observed by the

State Municipal Finance Commission, 1975 (of which the Director of Municipal Administration was the member-secretary) that the Local Fund Audit Organisation under Finance Department has failed in discharging its duties and the Commission recommended that "to make audit more effective and useful, the Director of Municipal Administration should perform the duties and function of the Examiner of Local Accounts in respect of Urban Local Bodies".[28] Such recommendations are against the very principles of audit that audit should be independent of administration.

As to the indifference of local authorities to audit findings, it was observed by the Committee on Budgetary Reforms (1974) "how can, the very councillors whose activities are the subject matter of audit criticism, be expected to take action in pursuance of those audit objections?".[29] It was also further observed by the Committee that the councillors felt that the attitude of audit was negative and the present system of audit resulted in curbing initiative and created frictions in executive and deliberative wing. Audit findings disclose cases of misappropriation, irregular use of municipal funds, loss and wastage. No official and elected representative can escape liabilities on any pretext unless the audit objections are finally settled. In such a context the inaction on the part of municipal, council could be averted if a time limit is prescribed by the State Government for settlement of audit objection through the Triangular Committee consisting of representatives of Government, Audit Organisation and Urban Local Body as is in vogue in Tamil Nadu.

The Examiner of Local Accounts has also a share in the blame. The audit conducted by him is of conventional type.It merely finds financial irregularities of common nature. The audit reports do not depict the picture of performance. The financial results of the institution shown in the audit report do not help the administration. It lacks the elements of administrative realism.The audit is conducted long after the transactions are over and there is undue delay in issuing the audit reports. Action on such dilatory reports becomes difficult. No timely follow-up action is taken on the findings of audit in the shape of surcharge action.

The present study reveals that surcharge action at the Examiner's level is taken leisurely. Action on the audit report of 1965-66 onwards for initiation of surcharge was taken during the year 1975-76. This is proved from the figures shown in the Annual Report of Local Fund Audit Organisation, Finance Department for 1975-76. Only 823 surcharge cases involving Rs.6.77 lakhs were started upto March 1975 and during the year 1975-76, 1582 cases involving Rs.15.44 lakhs were initiated. The audit organisation under the State Government has been functioning since 1954. Thus the total number of cases initiated from 1954-55 to 1974-75 were almost doubled during the year 1975-76. Only 170 cases with money value of Rs.62,172 were dropped or certified till the end of March, 1976 leaving 2235 cases with money value of Rs.21.60 lakhs.[30]

Dilatory action on the part of audit makes the power of surcharge ineffective when this power has not been used to bring the desired result. It is desirable to replace the system with some other effective method. The Committee on the Management of Local Government in England while considering the reforms in the local Government in England strongly recommended that the District Auditor's power of surcharge should be abolished.[31]

Performance Audit

The weakness in the audit practices has caused a concern in different quarters and it has been debated if the conventional system of audit should be replaced by the modern method of performance audit. It has been suggested earlier that performance budgeting should be introduced in urban local bodies which envisages review of performances at various levels of operation. This task can be performed by an external audit by changing its present role of regularity audit. The Administrative Reforms Commission recommended that the Comptroller and Auditor General should undertake propriety-cum-efficiency audit to cover all developmental activities of Government. In such a context, the function of audit in respect of local authorities should be performance oriented which means appraisal of performance of an organisation. The system of audit implies the existence of a performance standard and performance objectives - criteria against which the auditor can measure accomplishments. The central idea behind this is cost analysis in all dimensions. But no performance audit can be effective unless the management introduces a system of regular flow of information to auditors.

Conclusion

This aspect including many other problems of audit was discussed in the 4th All India Seminar on Accounts and Audit of local bodies held at Aurangabad (Maharashtra) in September, 1979.[32] The seminar made the following observations:

a. It was agreed that the conventional role of audit should be gradually replaced by efficiency-cum-performance audit practices. But the executive should lay down the standards, norms and targets for the schemes and audit should take into consideration these standards and conduct comparison and evaluation on the said basis.

b. In this context it was considered if audit should take up 'social audit'of different projects as recommended by Ashok Meheta Committee on Panchayati Raj Institutions. It was agreed that efficiency-cum-performance audit would go a long way in achieving the objective of social audit. It was also pointed out by some participants that social audit should be the job of social scientist as the auditors are not equipped either by knowledge or by training to undertake the job.

c. To meet the new challenge and to undertake the new responsibility, the auditors must be provided with adequate training and there should be exchange of audit personnel among different States to acquire knowledge and experiences of audit practices in vogue in such States.

d. Audit Reports should be issued expeditiously. Prompt follow up action should be taken.

e. Multiplicity in audit of the accounts should be avoided and the Examiner of Local Fund Audit should be the only agency of audit of the accounts of local authority.

In addition to the measures recommended above, it is also suggested that the system of post-audit should be replaced by concurrent audit. In respect of bigger Municipalities (A' Class -having population of one lakh or more, where audit takes more than 200 days to complete audit of one year's accounts) there should be a system of Resident audit as in Punjab. A system of Concurrent audit/Resident audit will reduce the bulk of the audit report and regularise the transactions on the spot immediately. Audit reports should be issued within a prescribed time limit. Audit objections should be settled within a year duly reviewed by the Triangular Committee consisting of representatives of Government, audit and local authority on due compliance furnished by the local body.

Another important measure to improve the effectiveness of audit and to ensure accountability of the local authorities is to evolve a system of review of the performance of the local authorities by the State Legislature. Under a parliamentary system of democracy the legislature sanctions funds for the Executive and the legislature reviews the utilisation of such funds through the Audit Report and the Finance Accounts placed by the Accountant General on the result of audit conducted by him. The local bodies receive substantial aid from the Government in shape of grant-in-aid and raise funds by taxation from the local people. As such, the Legislature should have the privilege to review the manner in which the local authorities spend such funds. The study Team on Audit and Accounts of Panchayati Raj bodies (1965) considered this aspect and recommended that a consolidated Finance Account and Audit Review on the Panchayati Raj institutions on the result of audit conducted by the Examiner of Local Fund Audit may be presented to the State Legislature.[34] This recommendation was subsequently endorsed by the Administrative Reforms Commission (1968).

The Public Accounts Committee of the State Legislature (Orissa) while discussing on this aspect felt that similar review of the performance of urban local bodies should be made and demanded that the Examiner's Audit Report and Consolidated Finance Accounts should also include the result of audit of urban local bodies.[35] It is encouraging to note that after a great deal of deliberation it has been decided by the State Government that the Examiner of Local Fund Audit should present consolidated Finance Accounts and Audit Report on the working of Panchayati Raj bodies and urban local bodies from the year 1979-80. There should be another standing committee of the State Legislature as in the case of Maharashtra to consider the report of the Examiner on the urban local bodies. This system of legislative review of the financial affairs of urban local bodies through the audit report will activise the audit organisation and awaken the local authorities and the Government from indifference to public accountability.

NOTES AND REFERENCES

1. *Report of the Rural-Urban Relationship Committee, Volume-1.* P. 117
2. Hicks, U.K.: *Development from Below.* p. 437.
3. *Taxation Enquiry Commission Report, 1954 (Volume-III)* p.374.
4. Hepworth, N.P.: *The Finance of Local Government*, p.265.
5. Boudhyans, P.S.: *Local Self Government in U.S.A.* p.10
6. Nigam, S.R.: *Local Government (England, France, U.S.A. USSR & India)*, p.87
7. *Report of Rural-Urban Relationship Committee* (1966), p.118
8. *Report of the State Municipal Finance Commission,* Orissa 1975, p.112.
9. *Report of the Rural-Urban Relationship Committee.* p.119.
10. Gorwala, A.D. *Report on Public Administration.* pp.43-44 Quoted at p.37-Finance Control and Delegation.
11. *Financial Control and Delegation,*p.7.
12. *Report of the Rural-Urban Relationship Committee*, p.117
13. *Report of the Rural-Urban Relationship Committee.* p.120.
14. Avasti, A.: *Municipal Administration in India,* p.37.
15. *Report of the State Municipal Finance Commission,* Orissa, 1975, p.123.
16. Lall, G.S.: *Financial Administration in India,* p.80
17. Marshall, A.H.: *Financial Administration in Local Government,* p.259.
18. *Report of the Committee on Budgetary Reform in Municipal Administration,* p.39.
19. Thavraj, M.G.K. & K.L. Handa : *Financial Control and Delegation,* p.106.
20. Dutta, A.: Reforms in Municipal Financial Administration *Nagarlok* (IIPA) October-December 1970, p.36
21. *Report of the Committee on Budgetary Reforms in Municipal Administration,* p.79.
22. Dutta, A. : Reform of Municipal Administration, *Nagarlok,* October-December 1973 (IIPA, New Delhi,) p.33
23. *Report of the Committee on Budgetary Reform in Municipal Administration* (G.I.1974) pp.77-78.
24. *Orissa Local Fund Audit Act,* 1948 (Sec.9).
25. Robson, A.William : *The Development of Local Government,* p.349.
26. Ibid, p.356.
27. *Annual report of the Local Fund Audit Organisation 1976-77,* Finance Department, Government of Orissa, p.29.
28. *The Report of the State Municipal Finance Commission,* Orissa, 1975, p.120.
29. *Report of the Committee on Budgetary Reforms in Municipal Administration,* G.I. (1974), p.103
30. *Annual Report of the Local Fund Audit Organisation for* 1975-76, Finance Department, p.29
31. *Report of the Committee on Management of Local Government,* HMSO, London (1967)p-82.
32. Proceedings of the 4th All India Conference on Audit and Accounts of Local Bodies (forwarded by Chief Auditor of Maharashtra to the Examiners of All States in his letter No.393 dated 26.10.79).

33. Paper presented by G.N.Dash in the Seminar of Audit & Accounts of Local Bodies at Aurangabad (September, 1979).
34. *Report of the Study Team on the audit and accounts of Panchayati Raj bodies* (1965) Government of India, Ministry of C.D.& Co-operation, p.35 (Para 8.9).
35. *Second Report (Fifth Assembly) 1971-72*, Orissa Legislative Assembly, Para-15A.

SEVEN

DECISION MAKING IN FINANCIAL ADMINISTRATION

In Chapter-II, the development of local administration in India has been traced. It is Mayo's resolution of 1870 which laid the foundation of decentralisation of functions with a view to raising resources at the local level to meet the functions transferred to the local Government. More prominence was given to local Self Government by Lord Ripon's resolution of 1882 which was an instrument of popular and political education and association of local knowledge with local interest. Local Self Government means making decisions by the local community with local knowledge and for local interest through their elected representatives. As such, decentralisation of organisation facilitates decision-making at the local level where it is necessary to take greater number of decisions at the lower level. Decisions made at the lower level are important as they affect the very functioning of the organisation.

The objectives of the Urban Local Government are to function as an instrument of local democracy and to develop and operate public utilities to provide municipal services and public conveniences. To serve these objectives, these authorities have been vested with powers to discharge certain regulatory functions and to raise resources by levy and assessment of taxes, to manage and maintain public properties. Due to rapid growth of urbanisation, they are required to plan for the development of infrastructure and maintain public utilities and municipal enterprises. Thus the urban local Government is a peculiar combination of a Government organisation and business management. As a Government the municipal administration exercises powers of taxation, issue of licenses, framing of bye-laws, regulation and enforcement of rules. On the other hand, it works as a business enterprise in providing civic services and in maintaining public utilities. Its taxation powers are closely related to provision of services. Thus the very nature of functions assigned to it requires to take decision in many matters of public interest which vitally affect the growth and development of local community.

Decision making by Municipal authorities

Throughout India the powers and functions of the Municipal authorities are regulated under Acts/Rules framed for the purpose by the respective State Governments. Even though the provisions of the Acts/Rules are not same, they are more or less similar. The pattern of local administration is mostly uniform. There is certain variation according to the nature of local body depending on whether it is a Notified Area Council, a Municipality or a Corporation. In Municipal Corporation the powers enjoyed by Committees and the Chief Executive Officer who is mostly known as the Commissioner, are more than the powers given to Municipalities or Notified Area Councils. The powers given to different authorities in an urban local Government may however be examined so as to ascertain their scope in decision making. This aspect may be examined with reference to the provisions contained in Orissa Municipal Act 1950 and Orissa Municipal Rules, 1953.

Scope for decision-making

In earlier chapters, the relevant provisions of the Acts/Rules partaining to the powers of the Municipal Council, Committees and the Executive Officer vis-a-vis the State Government have been indicated. In the Municipal Government many decisions are made and remade by different authorities. The Act makes an elaborate provision for the municipal councils to take decision on many matters but all such decisions are subject to approval by the Government. Yet the Municipal Council decisions are expressed in the shape of resolutions. The Chairman and the Executive Officer also enjoy enormous powers in decision making. A few salient features which provide an opportunity for decision-making in the financial affairs are discussed here.

By the Municipal Council

The Municipal Council is vested with a host of powers and functions and as such the Council is competent to take decision on such matters. A few such powers and functions are as follows:

1. The Municipal Council from time to time determines the officers and servants required to be employed by it with due approval of the Government and fixes or alters the number, grade, designation, salaries etc. and inflicts any punishment or takes action to dismiss any servant (Sections 73 to 76 of the Orissa Municipal Act, 1950).

2. The Council sanctions the budget estimates (Section 107 of the Orissa Municipal Act 1950).

3. It sanctions expenditure from the Municipal Fund for purposes specified in the Act, (Section 117(2) of Orissa Municipal Act 1950).

4. All properties are vested in the Municipal Council and are kept under the direction, management and control of the Council (Section 121 of Orissa Municipal Act, 150).

5. The Council imposes taxes and fees and determines the rate at which such taxes and fees are to be imposed (Section 131 of Orissa Municipal Act, 1950).

6. The Council provides water-supply, provides and maintains sufficient system of drainage and causes the public roads to be sufficiently lighted and makes roads and bridges and maintains them from the municipal funds (Sections 176 & 234 of Orissa Municipal Act, 1950).

By the Executive Officer

The Executive Officer of a Municipality/Notified Area Council is the key person of the organisation. In addition to carrying out the resolution of the municipal council, he also exercises certain executive powers as conferred on him by the Act.In view of the executive powers given to him, he has the authority to take decision on many matters of routine nature as well as on matters of importance. He has also a role in giving aid and advice to the Council in its decision making process. Following are some of the provisions of the Act which empower the Executive Officer to exercise full power in making decisions.

The Executive Officer is the custodian of the Municipal Fund. He has the power to receive, recover and credit to the Municipal fund any sum due or tendered to the Municipal Council (Section 97(a) of Orissa Municipal Act, 1950). He has the authority to spend the Municipal Fund in the manner prescribed under the Act. He is empowered to alter or amend the assessment list of different holdings at any time (Section 147 of Orissa Municipal Act, 1950). He has full authority to take measures for recovery of any tax or fees. He may apply to the Collector of the District to recover any tax arrear of land revenue (Section 160). He may sue persons on behalf of the council for recovery of Municipal dues. He has thus wide powers to shape the financial activities of the Municipality.

By the Chairman

The Chairman of the Municipal Council plays a significant role in the decision-making process of Municipal authorities. He is the presiding officer of the Council and punishments are issued under his authority. By virtue of his influence and position he wields prestige and power in taking decisions. Much depends upon the calibre, integrity and knowledge of the Chairman as council's decision can be shaped according to his ability. Much also depends on his capacity to obtain correct information from the officials to arrive at right decisions at the right time for the right objective. He should have clear vision of the objective and the guidelines framed for achieving the same. The present study shows that except in a few urban local bodies where the Chairman can exercise control over the decision making process(a few instances are cited below), in majority of cases, the decisions are influenced by the Councillors or by the employees of the Municipality or by pressure groups or party in power as discussed later.

a. In spite of the general pattern of entrusting water-supply schemes to P.H.D., the Chairman of Deogarh Municipality insisted upon the Government not to place the funds at the disposal of P.H.D. for the execution of the water-supply scheme of his municipality; on the other hand the municipality took up the execution of the scheme through the municipal agency (during 1969-70) to avoid payment of establishment charges to State P.H.D. at the rate of $17\frac{1}{2}$ percent from the municipal fund.

b. The Chairman of Puri Municipality suspended two tax collectors (during March '80) for misappropriating the octroi collection immediately after detection of such cases (others do not take such prompt action for fear of losing popularity).

Similarly the Chairman took immediate action to pass orders (on 21.8.80) pending approval by the municipal council to recover the hire charges of road roller as per the schedule of rate of 1979 as recovery at old rates caused substantial loss to the municipal fund and provided undue financial benefit to the contractors.

c. The Chairman of Jeypore Municipality insisted on State Government for revaluation of holdings in the municipal area as it was suspected that the valuation made by the State Valuation Organisation was defective. The revaluation was made at the instance of Government (during 1976-77) which increased the property tax of the Municipality.

By the Committees

Committees in a Municipality are constituted with a view to facilitate the working of Municipal Council. The Committees enjoy such powers as are delegated to them by the Council, but they are mostly recommending authorities and their suggestions are ratified by the council. It has been pointed out earlier that Committees do not function effectively due to lack of expertise on the subject. The working of Works Committee reveals that it approves estimates of different works and revises them frequently due to delay in execution which the municipal council approves. The Committees influence the council to that extent. But it is often noticed that the Committees do not work in the manner in which they are supposed to work. Their recommendations are not free from bias.

For example in Bhubaneswar Municipality the role of Works Committee where the Chairman of the municipality was President of the Committee was found to be discriminatory. In its meeting dated 8.5.78,the committee allotted funds to different wards for execution of new works, to complete the incomplete works and for lighting purposes not on the basis of the requirements for each ward. The councillors were asked to prepare a list of works within the amount allotted. An amount of Rs. 60,000 each was allotted to ward Nos. 3 & 4 and Rs. 50,000 each to ward Nos. 1, 2, 5 and 6 - 13 and Rs. 30,000 each to ward Nos.15 - 23 for new works. Again, Rs. 45,000 each was allotted to ward Nos. 1 - 13 for completion of old works and no funds were available for wards Nos. 14-23. Further scrutiny of the list of works approved by the council in their meeting dated 29.6.78 revealed that the (improvements suggested) works listed were concentrated in the locality of the councillor's residence areas in neglect of other areas.

Similarly distribution of funds for 1979-80 was made by the works committee in its meeting dated 10.4.79 which was approved by the council on 11.4.79. An amount of Rs.85,000 was allotted to ward Nos.1 to 13 and no amount was allotted to ward Nos.14 to 23. It was found that wards 14 -23 were represented by nominated members.

The very basis of distribution of funds to each ward without proper plan and estimate is against the approved principles of allotment of funds. Such allotment leads to misuse of funds and makes it necessary to revise the estimate from time to time till the completion of work. Some works do not yield the desired result as they are not completed on time.

There has also been discrimination in allotment of funds between wards represented by elected members and wards represented by nominated members. Equi-distribution of funds to satisfy each elected councillor is not appropriate as the specific requirement of the area is not taken into consideration. Moreover, such a system hinders the co-ordinated approach of development of the whole municipal area. In such a context, the decision-making process of the committee appears sectarian and is against the idea of planned development of the town. The municipal council and the chairman are influenced by the committee and the recommendations of the committee are approved by the Council.

As indicated earlier, the Municipal authorities suffer from several constraints in the process of their decision making. The decision making process of different agencies in the local Government is influenced by the tax payers, pressure groups and sometimes by the Government and bureaucrats and such influence on decision-making process adversely affects the financial interests of the urban local bodies. Lack of proper information from the municipal officials also results in faulty decisions. A few instances of the above category are discussed here.

Decision-making influenced by pressure groups and Tax Payers

1. Puri Municipal Council in its resolution No.11 dated 31.1.78 decided to exempt some variety of handicraft goods from payment of octroi tax. Such goods are appliques, (ornamental work made of one kind of material) silver filgree works, brass and bell-metal articles, horn works, palm leaf engraving works, toys and cans and bamboo works. The town being a place of pilgrimage many people from outside the State visit Puri and such articles are brought in huge quantities inside the town for sale and are consequently liable for levy of octroi. By exempting these articles from levy of octroi tax, the council lost heavy amount of octroi tax. Such decision of the council was detrimental to its own interest and beneficial to the traders of these articles.

2. Further, the rate of octroi tax on different goods was fixed in 1971 on the basis of quantity and not on the basis of value of articles. Even though the price of different goods has risen very high yet the rate of tax has not been increased. On the other hand, Puri Municipal Council in its resolution dated 18.5.79 reduced the rate of octroi tax on potato bags from Rs.1 per bag to Rs.0-80 p. giving undue benefit to potato traders. Such decision put the council to heavy loss as approximately 4 lakh bags are brought to town for sale, consumption or use. Such decision of the Council was influenced by the pressure groups.

3. The most important function of the council is to raise revenue by levying taxes and fees. Discussion in Chapter-III indicates that taxes were not only levied at a very low rate, but also some of the rich municipalities did not levy many taxes and there are numerous instances of irregular and illegal remissions and write offs (a few cases of which are cited below[21]). Decision-making on this score was obviously influenced by the local tax payers since the council did not want to lose popularity. Such decisions adversely affected the greater interest of the municipality.

4. While discussing the pattern of expenditure in Chapter-V, several instances have been given to prove that the municipal funds have not been utilised properly. There have been several cases of misapplication and misutilisation of municipal funds due to decisions taken by the Executive Officer of the Municipality/Notified Area Council. As such his decision on such matters has adversely affected the interest of the Municipality. Moreover the Executive Officer is empowered to reassess or alter the assessment or assess new holdings for taxation but he did not do so from time to time even though in many cases he was reported about the completion of buildings. The present study disclosed that though a number of buildings were constructed long before, they were not assessed for payment of taxes and consequently the urban local bodies lost substantial portion of their revenues due to the inaction of the Executive Officers. Details of such cases have been indicated in Chapter-III. It transpires that in many cases the Executive Officers were reluctant to take decision for assessment and in some cases the information required for assessment was not available to them. It can not be ruled out that the local councillors also played their role in influencing the Executive Officer and Municipal Officials not to reassess the buildings belonging to the local tax payers.

An instance as to how the Executive Officer of a Municipality shifted the responsibility to take decisions in assessing a number of holdings under his jurisdiction may be cited:

In Cuttack Municipality during the period from September 1974 to December 1976, permission was given for 541 new constructions. It was reported that 205 buildings were completed. The Executive Officer instead of assessing these buildings under section 147 of

Orissa Municipal Act 1950 for taxation reported these cases to the Central Valuation Organisation in his letter No. 4285 dated 19.10.76 for assessment. The valuation officer called for certain information with regard to these cases during November,1976. Since then (till the date of inspection) neither any information was furnished to the Valuation Officer nor was the assessment taken up by the Executive Officer. The Revenue Divisional Commissioner assessed that the Municipality lost about Rupees two lakhs per year till the assessment was made due to non-assessment of these buildings.[2]

5. The Executive Officers of many urban local Governments did not take timely action, nor did they take decisions to report to the Collectors for recovery of arrear taxes nor sues' the defaulters in Court of law which put the Municipal Government to a loss of Rs. 54.22 lakhs as the taxes became time barred. Even their decisions were not adequate in recovering the municipal taxes and fees as a result of which the arrears mounted to Rs. 199.41 lakhs at the end of 31.3.76.[3] Such inaction on the part of the Executive Officer is presumed to be due to the influence of pressure groups to evade assessment and recovery causing loss to the municipality.

b. Decision-making influenced by Government and decision made by the council are sometimes challenged and made inoperative by the Government.

i. Bhubaneswar Municipality in its council resolution No.1 of 16.1.78 decided to borrow Rs. 16 lakhs from L.I.C. to finance the water supply scheme in the old town. The loan carries interest @ $8\frac{1}{2}$ percent and can be repaid by 2003 A.D., when the amount of principal and interest together would come to Rs.35.97 lakhs. The work is executed by the State P.H.D. and the revenue accrued from the scheme would go to State exchequer. When the water supply scheme for the entire Bhubaneswar town is financed by the State Government and the revenue therefrom is credited to the Government Fund, the council's decision to borrow from L.I.C. at such high cost is unwise. The Government should have been pressed to undertake this scheme from its own resources. It has been ascertained that the State Government was unwilling to undertake the scheme from its own fund and influenced the municipal council to take up the work from borrowed funds.

ii. During the year 1975-76 many municipal councils in the country took decisions to demolish the unauthorised constructions to keep the cities and towns clean and beautiful. These operations were so vigorous in many cities that they attracted the attention of the Central Government to set up a commission to probe into such cases. In Orissa, many Municipalities/Notified Area Councils undertook such operations and in the process many shops, dwelling houses and other constructions of permanent and temporary nature were demolished. In Berhampur Municipality alone 729 numbers of wooden cabins and 865 numbers of sheds, extensions and other constructions were demolished. In consequence a number of cases were filed in the courts against Berhampur, Puri and Cuttack Municipalities. On the whole 95 cases were brought before the Saha Commission out of which 26 cases pertain to Cuttack Municipality and 12 cases to Puri Municipality. The Municipal Councils also spent huge sums to contest these cases and ultimately most of these constructions were restored.

The decisions of the Municipal Council were based on the instruction of the Government to keep the cities and towns clean. In the process of such operation, most of the poor people who are essential members of an urban community and who contribute to the resources of the municipal Governments through their labour and other economic activities lost their dwelling houses, shops and other constructions. These poor people add to the comforts of the richer sections of the society though they live in miseries and are known as slum dwellers. They are the skilled and unskilled workers engaged in several construction works in the town. Some of them are also peons, and others low-paid employees working in Government offices, factories, shops and small establishments. Many of them come from rural areas in quest of employment and work in towns as porters, rickshaw pullers, cobblers, fitters, mechanics, tailors, painters, hawkers, fruit sellers, workers in wayside restaurants, washermen, barbers and blacksmiths. Most of them are not subject to municipal taxation, yet they contribute substantially to the growth of urban economy and enrich the tax base of the urban areas.

A city or town can-not afford to do away with the services of these people as without them the city life may be paralysed. But the decision-makers in the municipal councils deprived these poor men of their prized possession without making any alternative arrangements for them. In fact the houses constructed for rehabilitating the slum dwellers have been allotted to others at low rates.

The Municipal Councils enjoy inherent power to remove encroachments on municipal lands. But such powers are used sparingly as the interests of the affected persons are well guarded by the elected councillors. In the above cases large-scale operations were made to remove encroachments making many urban dwellers homeless. Many also lost their trade and professions as no alternative arrangements were made for them. This was at the instance of the State Government.

iii. It is interesting to find that the councillors in opposition hinder the process of decision making and at times take the help of other agencies to prevent execution of the decision taken by the Municipal Council in majority. Government also does not hesitate in cancelling the council's decision even when such decisions are well-meaning. A case of the above category which has been adjudged by the Honourable High Court of Orissa is mentioned here.[4]

At a meeting of the council of Cuttack Municipality held on the 2nd April 1979, the Chairman was authorised to sanction expenditure upto a maximum of Rs.50,000 at a time for the smooth working of the various works of the Municipality. This resolution was passed by a majority vote. But the Government issued notice to the Chairman to show cause as to why the resolution should not be cancelled and, the cause being shown, the Government cancelled the council's resolution in their orders No.20671 dated 23.6.79 under the provisions of Sub-Section(2) of Section 398 of Orissa Municipal Act, 1950. A writ was filed by one Councillor in the High Court of Orissa against such Government orders. Some Councillors of the opposition party also became party to the case and supported the stand taken by the Government. The Government submitted that they had powers to cancel such resolutions of the council.

The High Court in its judgment observed that "The power of the State government can be exercised only when there is a statutory excess and Government do (Sic.) not have power at all to exercise when the statutory bodies act within their jurisdiction except as appellate powers. The jurisdiction vested in the Government under Section 398 of the Act is confined to instances of action in excess of powers. If Government exercise (Sic.) such jurisdiction where they do not have any, it would indeed be contrary to the legislative intention and purpose".[5] Accordingly the Government order dated 23.6.79 was quashed by the Honourable High Court. But its result was obvious. The Government used the last weapon in their armoury and dissolved the elected council and the Municipality was superseded and administration of the Municipality was taken over by Government.

c. Cases have been brought to light where decisions made by the Municipal Councils have been challenged in the court of law. Such decisions were made without adequate legal advice resulting in faulty laws. Consequently decisions made under such circumstances were reversed by the court of law which resulted in loss to the municipal fund. A few instances are cited here:

i. In a case pertaining to levy of octroi in Cuttack Municipality, the High Court of Orissa reversed the Municipal decision to compute Octroi on the cost of 'bidi' procured by Star Tobacco House from Gujarat to Cuttack Municipal area. Octroi tax was assessed on the value of 'bidi' taking the excise duty charged on the cost of bidi. The High Court held that the value of bidi should not be computed taking the excise duty into account. As a result, heavy amounts were refunded to the company.[6] Such decisions of the council were not obviously backed by legal requirements and the bye-laws framed under the Act did not provide the method of computation of Octroi tax in such cases.

ii. Puri Municipal Council used to levy octroi tax since 1972 @ 3% on marine fish and prawn brought from Chilka side to Puri town and fish and prawns caught from the sea at Puri town. The municipal council decided to raise the rate of Octroi Tax to 6% in 1976. One ITC company carrying on business of exporting prawns to foreign countries procured through commission agents filed a writ petition in the Orissa High Court against the decision of Puri Municipality to levy Octroi Tax on fish and prawns. The petitioner contended that the prawns were neither procured nor processed, consumed, used or otherwise disposed of either within the limits of Puri Municipality or anywhere else in India. Municipality charged Octroi on purchases made by the firm from the fishermen and at the exit point.

The petitioner challenged that the provision of Section 131(II) (k ii) of Orissa Municipal Act was ultra-vires and irregular and collection of Octroi at the exit point was not envisaged in the bye-laws. The Municipality submitted that the fish and prawn brought from the sea to the Municipal limits were for sale and the bye-laws for levy of Octroi and the rates were approved by the Council and the Government and were not ultra-vires. The High Court decided that the imposition of octroi on the petitioner at the Atharnalla Check-post was not valid. The bye-laws of the Municipality were to be limited only to the power of the Municipal Act which had been enacted under the power conferred by the relevant entries in the Constitution.[7]

Sometimes, the Municipal Councils take decision without jurisdiction. In the aforesaid case the council exceeded its limits with the object of raising its revenues through octroi tax. Ultimately it lost the case and lost the revenue from the octroi and incurred expenditure to fight the case in the Court of law. Such happenings could have been averted had proper legal advice obtained before taking such controversial decisions.

d. Decision-making is sometimes influenced by the municipal officials by not furnishing correct information and at times by not carrying out the decision of the council:

i. As regards determining the staff strength of the council, it is found that many municipal councils have taken decisions to retain employees beyond the approved strength in spite of refusal of the Government to maintain such staff. Details of such cases have been pointed out earlier. Action of the council in taking such decisions has resulted in unauthorised expenditure. Such employees who are retained without Government approval are local people and the council hesitates to oust them from employment because of the closeness of such employees with the municipal councils. It is also observed that because of the laxity of the council, due to influence of Municipal employees, some of the delinquent officials go without punishment in spite of misappropriation and embezzlement of municipal funds etc. committed by them.[8]

ii. Budget making in a Municipal Council involves a series of decisions - decision to raise revenue on various items and decision to spend on various objects. Such decisions are supposed to be based on the information furnished on every item of the budget. It has been shown in detail in Chapter-VI how budget estimates were unrealistic and the decisions taken in processing the budget and approving the same were not based on facts. Periodic reports and management information system (accounting and physical data processing) which are a prerequisite to decision-making process were very much wanting in almost all the urban local bodies. Thus the anticipated revenue fell far below the expectation and in many cases the amounts decided to be spent were left unspent. As such there was no control over receipts or expenditure. These are results of faulty decisions due to lack of proper information system and partly due to limitation on the power of the Council in decision making as it has no control over its own purse due to uncertain flow of grants and loans from the Government.

iii. The municipal council in its resolution on 30.10.76 sanctioned the estimate for 'Repair to town U.P. School at Bhubaneswar" for Rs. 15,000 for roofing by G.C.I. sheets, but the officials in-charge of execution called for tenders for R.C.C. roof without prior approval of the council. At a later stage the council was compelled to accord sanction to the revised estimate of Rs.36,300 in its resolution dated 5.12.77 as the work was taken up with R.C.C. roof due to pressure of officials.

iv. Talcher Municipal Council decided to convert the building constructed for octroi check-gate to a rest shed in the year 1972. The local body had been maintaining the rest shed and paying electric energy charges without any rent. A compost mistry was in occupation of the building and no rent was realised from him. On the other hand the electric energy charges were paid by the council. The council's decision was not worked out due to the influence of municipal officials.

Conclusion

In the existing structure of the municipal Government the

municipal council is both deliberative and executive body. The delegation of power to the Executive Officer and Chairman is limited. Several provisions in the Act/Rules of the local Government prescribing checks and balances create conflict between the elected representatives and the appointed executives which hinders decision-making at respective levels. On the other hand "the municipal councillor, with his local roots and loyalties, is quickly driven to assume the role of an advocate of private interests of his consitituency, seeking relaxation in rules and bye-laws, reduction in assessment, cancellation or postponement of orders of demolition or renewal of encroachments, appointments, postings and transfer of staff, awarding of contracts and the type".[9] All these influences affect the working of officials and the Council.

Similarly the intervention of the State Government even in the day to day working of the Municipality and subjecting all their decisions to be approved by the State Government is quite significant. In addition, the influence exercised by public through the opposition members of the council and Government works as deterrent to the local Government. Even mass agitations have been organised to prevent the decision of councils to impose octroi or to revise tax-rate.[10] Further, the untrained and unwilling officials do not provide the requisite information to the council for proper assessment of a situation. In such a context, the process of decision making in the Municipal Government is not only distorted, but decision on many vital and important matters is delayed adversely affecting financial affairs of the local Government.

Earlier discussion on the subject shows that the attitude of the Government has a frustrating effect on the municipal council's decision making. The Government uses a coercive stick instead of a corrective one. The collective wisdom of the council in decision-making is sometimes challenged by the bureaucratic attitude of the Government. In some cases the ruling parties at the State level do not hesitate to topple the council in case different parties run the municipal administration. On the other hand some municipal councils do not obey the direction of the Government even when such orders are issued in the interest of the Municipal Government.[11] The councils are afraid of losing their popularity. Moreover the councillors are aware that their decisions whether right or wrong are not subject to legislative scrutiny. Legislatures have every right to know as to how the tax payer's money is being spent by the municipal authorities.

At present there is no legislative organ to review the working of the urban local Government.

The decision-making of the Municipal Government will improve and become effective only when their decisions are subjected to review by a legislative committee through a periodic report on their financial activities to be submitted either by the Department or by the Examiner of the Local Accounts who has the full knowledge on the financial working of the urban local bodies through the mechanism of audit. Moreover the Municipal Councils will have a lurking fear when they will be conscious that their decisions are to be reviewed by a higher elective organ and not by a bureaucratic Government. The role of the Government which serves as deterrent to municipal decisions should be reduced to the minimal as the fragile framework of Municipal Government cannot combat the powerful instruments of the Government. Such a measure will in no way curb the power of municipal Government in decision-making, rather will make their decision meaningful and reduce the coercive attitude of the State Government.

Above all, the councillors should be trained and taught the mechanism of Self Government as knowledge of Government can improve the process of decision-making. The Council should be assigned the deliberative functions and the power of control and supervision over the Executive. The Executive Officer and other functionaries should be vested with the power of executive authority. Moreover, there should be proper mechanism for supply of correct information and data to facilitate correct decision-making. The officials (technical, financial and administrative) should be equipped with adequate training and knowledge to render timely and correct advice to the Council. Many of the Council's decisions are ineffective and erroneous as they are not based on sound financial principles and legal requirements. In bigger urban local bodies there should be a regular Finance Officer with legal knowledge to advise on financial affairs and for smaller local authorities such advice should be rendered by the Regional Deputy Directors as suggested in an earlier chapter. The lacuna in the existing Act/Rules should be removed to enable the local authorities to take correct decision on different matters.

NOTE AND REFERENCES

1. Avasti and Maheshwari:- Public Administration. p. 180
2. According to Section 171 of Orissa Municipality Act, 1950 no amount of taxes or fees can be written off by the Municipal Council exceeding Rs. 500 without sanction of the government. But remission exceeding Rs. 500 has been reported in respect of following urban local bodies during the year 1975-76.
   Nayagarh N.A.C.- Rs.7499, Jaypore Municipality Rs.31,683, Koraput N.A.C. Rs. 2069, Suruda N.A.C. Rs.1369 (Source- Annual Report of Local Fund Audit Organisation, Finance Department for 1975-76).
3. Inspection Report of Sri T.U.Vijayasekharan, I.A.S.,Revenue Divisional Commisssioner, Central Division on Cuttack Municipality, inspected on 15.12.77.
4. Annual Report of the L.F.A. Organisation, 1976-77, pp.15-16.
5. Ashirbad Behera Vs. State of Orissa and Others *ILR Cuttack Series, 1979 Volume-II*, July & August pp.77-107.
6. *ILR-Cuttack Series-1979-Volume-II*, p.107.
7. Orissa High Court Case No.739 to 742 of 1975.
8. Orissa High Court- Case No.801 of 1977
   ITC Ltd. and Others Vs.Puri Municipality.
9. In Jajpur, Cuttack and Jaypore Municipalities the collecting staff misappropriated by embezzement Rs.4892.91 Rs.20701.21 and Rs. 4819.90 respectively, but no departmental action was taken against the delinquent employees. (Annual Report of Local Fund Audit Organisation, Finance Department for the year 1977-78.)
10. *Nagarlok*-October-December 1973, IIPA, New Delhi, p.7.
11. Such agitations were organised when Octroi was introduced in Jajpur municipality and Bhubaneswar N.A.C. in 1975-1976 and revision of taxes was proposed in Cuttack Municipality in 1979.
    Similarly water rate imposed on the users of municipal market building in Sunabeda N.A.C. was withdrawn from 15.8.72 on the demand of the market dwellers (Part-II of the Report of the State Municipal Finance Commission, Orissa, 1975).
12. In spite of repeated instructions from Government, the Council of Sambalpur Municipality refused to impose holding taxes for years together (till 1976). Report of the State Municipal Finance Commission, p.38.

SELECTED BIBLIOGRAPHY

BOOKS

Apparao, T. *Municipal Corporation in South India.* Andhra University, Waltair, 1974.

Apparao, T. *Municipal Government in Vishakhapatnam.* Dr. T.A. Rao, Vishakhapatnam, 1954.

Agarwalla, L.N. *Municipal Administration in India.* Dr. A. Avasthi, Agra, 1972.

Argul, R. Municipal *Government in India.* Agarwalla Press Allahabad, 1960.

Avasthi & Maheswari *Public Administration.* L.N. Agarwalla, Agra, 1976.

Alderfer, F. *The American Local Government & Administration.* The Penesylvania State University, U.S.A.

Bhattacharya, Mohit. *Management of Local Government in India.* Uppal Book House, New Delhi, 1976.

Bharadwaj, R.K. *The Municipal Administration in India.* Sterling Publisher, Delhi 1970.

Bardoloi, U.N. *Local Finance in Assam.* Gouhati University.

Chanda, Asok. *Federalism in India*. George Allen & Unwin, London, 1965.

Chandulal, S. *Municipal Finance.* All India Institute of Local Self Government, Bombay, 1957.

Datta, Abhijit. *Urban Government Finance and Development.* The World Press Private Ltd. Calcutta, 1970.

Finer, Herman London. *English Local Government.* Methuin &

Company London, 1946.

Gyanchand. *Local Finance in India.* Kitabistan, Allahabad, 1947.

Government of Orissa. *Fifth five year plan of Orissa.* Director of Printing & Stationeries, Cuttack, 1972.

Hicks, Ursula.K *Development from Below.* Oxford University Press, London, 1961.

Hepworth, N.P. *The Finance & Local Government.* George Allen & Unwin Ltd. London, 1970.

Indian Institute of Public Administration. *Five Year Municipal Development Plans (Proceedings of Seminar)* Indian Institute of Public Administration, New Delhi, 1971.

-do- *State Machinery for Municipal Supervision (Proceedings of the Seminar).* -do- 1971.

Indian Institute of Social Welfare and Business Management. *Municipal Gazeteer West-Bengal-Vol.1* Indian Institute of Social Walfare & Business Management, Calcutta, 1978.

Lall, G.S. *Financial Administration in India.* H.P.J. Kapoor. Delhi,1969.

Maheswari, S.R. *Local Government in India.* Orient Longman Ltd, New Delhi, 1976.

Marshall, A.H. *Financial Administration in Local Government.* George Allen & Unwin Ltd. London, 1967.

Munro, W.B. *Municipal Government and Administration.* The Macmillan Company, New York, 1926.

May, R.J. *Federalism & Fiscal Adjustment.* Oxford University Press, 1969.

Mehata, M.R. *Notes on Municipal Finance, Accounts & Audit.* All India Institute of Local Self Government, Bombay, 1973.

Naidu,Y. Ramaswamy *Local Finance in Andhra Pradesh.* Sri Venksteswar Arts College, Tirupati, Andhra Pradesh.

Nigam, S.R. *Local Government, England, France, U,.S.A. U.S.S.R., India.* S. Chand & Co. Pvt. Ltd. New Delhi, 1975.

Pande, V.K. *Municipal Finance in Marathwada.* Marathwada University, Aurangabad, 1977.

Robson, William A. *The Development of Local Government.* George Allen & Unwin Ltd. London, 1948.

Rastogi, K.M. *Local Finance - It's theory & working in India.* Kailash Pustak Sadan, Bhopal, 1979.

Royal Institute of Public Administration. *New Sources of Local Revenue.* George Allen and Unwin Ltd. London, 1956.

Sinha, K.K. *Local Taxation in a Developing Economy*. Vora & Co. Publishers Pvt. Ltd. Bombay-2, 1968.

Sarkar, B.K. *A comparative Study of National & Local Finance*. 29-B-Bakulbagan Road, Bhowanipur, Calcutta, 1939.

Sharma, M.P. *Local Government & Finance*. Kitabmahal Allahabad, 1954.

Sharma, S.K. & V.N. Chowla. *Municipal Administration in India*. International Book Co. Jullundur, 1975.

Tripathy, R.N. *Local Finance in a Developing Economy*. Planning Commission, Government of India, New Delhi, 1967.

Tinker, Hugh *The foundation of Local Self Government in India, Pakisthan & Burma*. University of London, 1954.

Thavraj, M.J.K. & K.L. Handa *Citizen and the treasuries*. Indian Institute of Public Administration, New Delhi, 1973.

Thavraj M.J.K. & K.L. Handa, *Financial Control & Delegation*. Indian Institute of Public Administration, New Delhi 1973.

Venkata Rangaiya M. & M.Pattabhiram. *Local Government in India*. Allied Publishers, Calcutta,1969.

Venkata Rao. V. *A Hundred Years of Local-Self Government in Assam*. Vani Prakashan Mandir, Gouhati, 1965

Venkataraman, K. *Local Finance in Perspective*. Asia Publishing House, Bombay, 1965.

World Bank, Washington, *The Distributive effects of Local Government Finance in Columbia*. World Bank, Washington, 1976.

World Bank, Washington. *The Incidence of Urban Property Taxation in Developing Countries*. World bank, Washington, 1977.

REPORTS.

Report of the State Municipal Finance Commission, Orissa 1975 - Government of Orissa, Part-I & II.

Report of the Task Force on Planning & Development of Small & Medium Towns & Cities, Volume-I, Ministry of Works & Housing, New Delhi, Government of India - 1977.

Report of Committee on Budgetary Reforms in Municipal Administration, Government of India, Ministry of Works and Housing, New Delhi-1974.

Report of the Study Team on Audit & Accounts of Panchayatiraj Bodies - Ministry of Community Development and Co-operation, Government of India - 1965.

Report of the Rural-Urban Relationship Committee. Volumes-I to III. Government of India, Ministry of Health & Family Planning - 1966.

Report of the Committee on Panchayatiraj Institutions. Government of India, Ministry of Agriculture & Irrigation, New Delhi - 1978.

Report of Public Accounts Committee (1974-75) First Report (Sixth Assembly) Government of Orissa, 1975.

Report of the Committee of Ministers Constituted by the Central Council of Local Self Government - November-1963. On Augmentation of Financial Resources of Urban Local Bodies.

Report of the Orissa Local Body (Urban) Administration Enquiry Committee, Orissa. Government of Orissa - 1963.

Report of the Taxation Enquiry Commission (1953-54) Volume-III. Ministry of Finance, Government of India, 1955.

Orissa Taxation Enquiry Committee Report, Government of Orissa, Finance Department, 1961.

The Annual Reports of Local Fund Audit Organisation of Finance Department for the years 1960-61 to 1977-78, Government of Orissa, Finance Department.

The Audit Reports on the accounts of 31 Urban Local Bodies under study for the year 1975-76. Local Fund Audit Organisation, Finance Department, Government of Orissa.

Report of the Municipal Rationalisation Committee, Gujarat State, Government of Gujarat, 1961.

Report of the Indirect Taxation Enquiry Committee Part-I, October, 1977.Ministry of Finance, Government of India.

Report of the Committee on the Management of Local Government, Volume-I (John Maud, Chairman) Published by H M S G London.

Report of the Local Finance Enquiry Committee - 1951. Government of India.

Report of the Municipal Finance Commission - Government of Karnataka - 1975.

Report of the Municipal Finance Commission, Maharashtra. Bombay Urban Development Department, 1974.

Report of the Committee on Urban Wastes - Part-I. Government of India, Ministry of Works & Housing, New Delhi - 1975.

Draft Five Year Plan 1978-83, Government of India, Planning Commission, New Delhi, 1976.

ACTS/RULES AND MANUALS.

Regulation I of 1905. The Mayurbhanj Municipal Regulation, Mayurbhanj State, Baripada - 1905.

The Tamil Nadu Local Fund Audit Manual. Volume-II Part_I. Government of Tamil Nadu, 1977.

The Madras District Municipalities Act, 1920. Government of Madras, Law (Legislative) Department - 1930.

The Orissa Panchayatiraj Manual - Part-I. Government of Orissa - 1962.

The Bihar & Orissa Municipal Act - 1922. Government of Bihar and Orissa - 1931.

The Orissa Municipal Act, 1950. (LSG) Department, Government of Orissa - 1972.

The Orissa Municipal Rules - 1953. Health (Law) Department, Government of Orissa - 1969.

The Local Authorities Loans Rules - 1915. Government of India.

The Local Authorities Loans Act - 1914, Government of India.

The Orissa Local Authorities Loan Rules - 1975, Government of Orissa.

The Orissa Local Fund Service Rules - 1975. Government of Orissa.

The Orissa Local Fund Audit Act - 1948. Government of Orissa.

The Orissa Local Fund Audit Rules - 1951, Government of Orissa.

Nayagarh Town Municipal Rules - 1945.

Nayagarh State Gazette - October, 31, 1945, Vol.VII-No.7.

JOURNALS AND PERIODICALS

Journal of the National Academy of Administration, April-June 1971, Volume-VVI. No.2, New Delhi.

Civic Affairs (26th Annual Number) June '78, August'78 Suresh Meher - Allahabad.

The Indian Law Report - 1979 (Volume-II). Government of Orissa, Cuttack.

Urban Research - January 1978 to June 1978. Bulletin of National Institute of Urban Affairs, New Delhi.

Souvenir - On the occassion of the Fourth General Body Meeting of the State Municipal Councils Union, Government of Orissa, Urban Development Department - 1976.

Urban Research - National institute of Urban Affairs, New Delhi,

July 1979.

Nagarlok - Urban Affairs Quarterly. Indian Institute of Public Administration, New Delhi.
Vol - II - July - September '70 No. 3
Vol - II - October-December'70 No.4
Vol - III- April-June '71 No.2
Vol - V - October-December '73 No.4
Vol - V - April-June'73 No.2
Vol - Vi - April-June'74 No.2
Vol - VII - July-September '75 No.3
Vol - VIII- October-December '76 No.4
Vol - IX - January-March '77 No. 4
Vol - IX - October-December '77 No. 4
Vol - X - October-December '78 No.4
Vol - X - January-March '78 No.1
Vol - X - July-September '78 No. 3
Vol - X - April-June '78 No.2
Vol - XI - January-March '79 No. 1
Vol - XI - April-June '79 No 2
Vol - XI - October-December '79 No.4

The Indian Journal of Public Administration, Indian Institute of Public Administration, July-September 1978 - Vol.XXIV - No.3, New Delhi.

The Cuttack Weekly Report, Vol-XIV - March '77. Published by A.N. Samanta, Cuttack.

Government of Orissa - State Level Conference of Urban Local Bodies - February 1966, L.S.G. Department, Bhubaneswar.

INDEX